Kitty Holland is a staff reporter with *The Irish Times* newspaper in Dublin. On November 14, 2012, she broke the story of the death of Savita Halappanavar on 28 October in Galway University Hospital. Kitty has been covering social and human rights issues since 1998. She lives in Dublin with her two children.

www.**transworldbooks**.co.uk

www.transworldireland.ie

SAVITA

The Tragedy that Shook a Nation

Kitty Holland

TRANSWORLD IRELAND

TRANSWORLD IRELAND
an imprint of The Random House Group Limited
20 Vauxhall Bridge Road, London SW1V 2SA
www.transworldbooks.co.uk

First published in 2013 by Transworld Ireland,
a division of Transworld Publishers

A CIP catalogue record for this book
is available from the British Library.

ISBN 9781848271838

This book is a work of non-fiction based on the author's research and journalism.
The author has stated to the publishers that, except in such minor respects not affecting the
substantial accuracy of the work, the contents of this book are true.

Addresses for Random House Group Ltd companies outside the UK
can be found at: www.randomhouse.co.uk
The Random House Group Ltd Reg. No. 954009

The Random House Group Limited supports the Forest Stewardship Council® (FSC®),
the leading international forest-certification organisation. Our books carrying the FSC label
are printed on FSC®-certified paper. FSC is the only forest-certification scheme
supported by the leading environmental organisations, including Greenpeace.
Our paper procurement policy can be found at www.randomhouse.co.uk/environment

Typeset in 12.25/15pt Ehrhardt by Falcon Oast Graphic Art Ltd.
Printed and bound in Great Britain by
CPI Group (UK) Ltd, Croydon, CR0 4YY

2 4 6 8 10 9 7 5 3 1

For Mary Holland

Foreword

Ireland has always been a nation of storytellers – and as Irish people we have an innate love of stories. Through the centuries, there have been many stories of great tragedy – often-treasured myths and legends. However, there are some contemporary stories of such tragedy that we wish they never had to be told; and one of these is the story of the death of Savita Halappanavar. These are stories that *must* be told, and which we as a society must take ownership of, and learn from, to try and ensure that they are never repeated.

We are indebted to Kitty Holland for her brave and determined journalism, which initially brought this story to national attention, and for authoring this account of a modern day tragedy, which should never have happened.

The book opens with an insightful description of Savita's geographical and cultural background. We learn that she and her family belonged to the Lingayat religion – a religion founded on tolerance and total rejection of inequality between humans. An important symbol of the religion is the ishtalinga, an oval-shaped emblem, which is worn on the body hanging by a cord around the neck. The Lingayat wear the ishtalinga throughout life – and one is tied to a newborn a few days after birth so that 'the child will attain enlightenment as part of their journey through a life of dignity, honesty and meaning where they may be great, not by virtue of their birth, but through the way they live their life'.

All of the anecdotal evidence available tells us that Savita did indeed live a life of great dignity but, unfortunately, her death did not have honesty or meaning. And it is on Savita's death and its aftermath that Kitty Holland focuses – in the process addressing the complexities of the Judicial, Church, Parliamentary and citizen action and inaction in Ireland. The religious, societal and cultural differences between Ireland and India are explored – and it is explained how they became entwined in Savita's story.

Following her death, Savita's husband Praveen became a powerful representative for her; he always showed enormous dignity yet was resolute in forcing us to accept and address some unpalatable truths. After seven days of evidence, an eleven-member jury at Savita's inquest returned a verdict of medical misadventure in relation to her death. It endorsed nine recommendations put by the coroner Dr Ciaran McLoughlin – including one that the Medical Council should lay out in its guidelines exactly when a doctor can and should intervene to save a mother's life. At this point Savita's death took on a great meaning for the lives of future mothers in Ireland.

We must learn and apply the lessons. And we must never forget the tragic loss suffered by Savita's husband, Praveen Halappanavar, her parents Andanappa and Akhmedevi Yalagi and their families.

Mary Robinson, September 2013

SAVITA

1

Savita Andanappa Yalagi was born in the town of Bagalkot in Karnataka province, south-west India, on 29 September 1981. She was the youngest child and only daughter of Andanappa and his wife Akhmedevi Yalagi.

Bagalkot is where her father Andanappa is from and is also the most important holy place of the Lingayat religion, to which the Yalagis belong. A religion founded on tolerance and the total rejection of inequality between humans, Lingayatism is an offshoot of Hinduism. It was founded in the twelfth century by philosopher Lord Basavanna who lived and preached in northern Karnataka.

Followers of Lingayatism believe in a direct relationship between the individual and Lord Shiva and that the intervention of a priestly class is therefore unnecessary. (There is an obvious rough parallel with the line of difference between Protestants and Catholics in Christianity.)

The term 'Lingayat' comes from the Kannada (the indigenous and still the main language of the Karnataka region) word *Lingavanthain*, meaning 'one who wears ishtalinga'. The ishtalinga is an oval-shaped emblem symbolizing Parasiva, or the aspect of Lord Shiva which is beyond human comprehension – absolute reality. The ishtalinga is worn on the body; it hangs by a cord around the neck. Savita wore the ishtalinga all her life and worshipped Lord Shiva daily, her father told me.

Anyone can become Lingayat through the ceremony of Ishtalinga Deeksha. Children are consecrated to the religion in a ceremony known as Ishtalinga Dharane, performed when a pregnancy reaches around seven months. The mother will wear the coming child's ishtalinga entwined with her own. After birth, the baby is adorned with her or his own ishtalinga in a ritual known as Lingadharane.

In the Lingadharane, as in Lingayat ritual and literature generally, it is spelt out that differentiation between individuals as they grow into adulthood must be based only on the knowledge and wisdom they acquire. This helps explain the very high premium which Lingayatists put on the education of both girls and boys.

One piece of sacred writing lists the caste gradations preached by the Hindu Brahmins and goes on: 'In this society Guru Basaveshwara came as light of hope and . . . started equality in all humans by providing education . . . When education reached the downtrodden people they started writing [down] their spiritual experiences: a drummer, woodcutter, cobbler, barber, potmaker and so all became great writers as they explained their spirituality.'

Gandhi told the Indian National Congress in 1924: 'It has not been possible for me to practise all the precepts of Basaveshwara which he taught 800 years ago and which he also practised . . . Eradication of untouchability and dignity of labour were among his core precepts. One does not find even shades of casteism in him. Had he lived during our times, he would have been a saint worthy of worship.'

The Lingayat community make up about 17 per cent of the state's 65 million people. They would be classified as Hindu in census counts, with Hindus making up 83 per cent of the Karnataka's people.

Modern Lingayatism is regarded as progressive and reformist and the Lingayat community are enormously influential in politics and socially across southern India.

Savita was immersed in Lingayat values throughout her life in India, and then in Ireland. The Yalagis thus taught their children to be the best they could be as individuals and within their community.

Savita was their third child and much adored. 'She was always funny, always smiling and always the little ruler,' recalls her mother. 'We knew she would be a ruler of the house the moment she was born.' She was the precious little sister of her brothers, Santosh and Sanjeev, and they were hugely protective of her. 'They would do anything she asked.'

Andanappa's work as an electrical engineer with the Karnataka Electricity Board took him away frequently, travelling around the state. While the boys were out at school, Savita was always with 'Mumma' and her first love was dancing. 'She taught herself, from the television,' Akhmedevi says. 'She would come and show me her new steps while I was working in the kitchen. Always she was practising and dressing up. She was a good dancer from very young.'

In 1990 Andanappa's work took him to a position in Belgaum, about 140 kilometres from Bagalkot and so the family moved. Belgaum was a rapidly expanding city with a population of around 500,000 people (it is now about 800,000), with students and workers coming from across India and beyond.

The city is about 130 miles inland from Goa. A journey by taxi brought this writer to Belgaum on a three-hour journey over hilly, bumpy roads. Belgaum itself is full of activity, hectic and loud, with motorists beeping at motorcyclists to get out of the way, automated rickshaw drivers doing the same and some reacting, others not. In the rainy season of late June 2013, roads and verges are full of puddles, and buildings appear grubby and worn after the rain. Women hold their saris over their ankles to keep them clean. Everyone seems to be going somewhere, doing something; there is no sign of the abject poverty found elsewhere in India – very little begging and certainly no beggars who appear to have mutilated themselves or to have been mutilated in an effort to attract more generous donations.

There did not seem to be ostentatious wealth, either. Everyone looked well enough dressed, but that was all, though some of the women were magnificent in their saris. Also striking was the absence of Western branded stores, even in the busy shopping street Khade Bazaar.

When nine-year-old Savita moved here it was already a centre for a number of industries, including textile production, machinery and tool production and it is also a national centre for education. Almost everywhere one looks in Belgaum there is a sign for an institute or college, a training centre or university. As well as eight engineering colleges, five medical and several dental colleges, there are numerous degree colleges, nine polytechnics and three law colleges. This, and the relatively pleasant climate, attracts students from all over India and beyond. According to Dr Alka Kale, principal professor at the Institute of Dental Sciences at the KLE (Karnataka Lingayat Education) university where Savita studied, many non-resident Indians send their children back to India and specifically to Belgaum for their university education.

It was in the leafy, quiet area of Sri Nagar that Mr Yalagi decided to build the family home in 1990. Across the road from a pretty park he constructed a single-storey 'villa', behind garden walls and with three steps up to a porch at the front door. Orchids, lotuses and sandalwood trees grow in the garden area. 'Every day while I was building, she would come down after school and would stand here,' he says, looking around the open-plan living/dining room, 'and she decided on the colours,' he says, pointing to the pale yellow walls. 'She would tell me what to do and where to put things. She would say, "This is my house."

Even when Praveen came to see her, she would tell him, "You know, Praveen, this is my house,"' he smiles. 'It was always "her house". Funny.'

She attended the prestigious Vanita Vidyalaya secondary school in the town, a coeducational school, where she was a high achiever and popular. 'She was first in her class every time,' says her mother. 'She loved sciences and wanted to be a dentist very young. She was a class monitor. She knew what she wanted to do and she worked hard. Very determined and strong.'

And she wanted to be a dentist.

Aged 19, she first attended the Maratha Mandal Dental College in Belgaum in 2000, but after flooding in 2002 the college had to close for a year and Savita moved to the KLE college to complete her training. Dr Kale remembers a young, very friendly woman who worked hard and helped her fellow students.

The KLE Society was founded in 1916 by the Lingayat community. Its mission was to bring education to the largely under-educated region of northern Karnataka, and to make it available to all. KLE was formally recognized as a university by the Indian Ministry of Human Resource Development in April 2006.

The KLE university, in the Nehru Nagar district of Belgaum, is a large campus offering undergraduate, postgraduate and post-doctoral programmes in medicine, Ayurvedic (traditional Indian) medicine, nursing, dentistry, public health medicine, physio-therapy and pharmacy.

The university has a diverse student body and in its mission statement says: 'The students in the campus are from different countries and different cultures and all the efforts are taken for smooth induction of the students into the campus and for that purpose student orientation programmes, [and] language classes for enabling the students to interact with local patients are regularly conducted.'

Savita was also involved in the college's dramatic, literary and dance societies. 'She was a very good dancer and that is something she was really interested in,' says Dr Kale. 'She was very well liked by all the teachers here and she did well in her exams.' After graduating with a degree in dental science, Savita did a year's internship with a dentist in Belgaum who, Andanappa recalls, referred to Savita as 'like my own daughter'; she continued to work with him until 2007.

Had she not met and married Praveen, she would have had no difficulty in finding long-term work in Belgaum, says Dr Kale. 'With the girls, they marry and they accompany their husbands so that is why she went to Ireland. If she had not there would be no problem. She would have worked easily in Belgaum.'

They met on a matrimonial website, Shaadi.com. Praveen Halappanavar, also from Karnataka state, had been in Ireland for two years, living in Galway in the west of the country working as an engineer for the medical implements company Boston Scientific.

Praveen's family came from Haveri, a city of about 1.5 million about 175 kilometres south of Belgaum. 'I knew his family for many years and I knew Praveen was a good man so we were happy to give them our blessing,' says Andanappa. He talks of how Savita and Praveen were on Skype every day between Ireland and Belgaum and how she would talk about him all the time. 'All the time she was talking about Praveen,' recalls Mr Yalagi. 'Praveen, Praveen every day.' For his part, Praveen admitted that he was 'kind of amazed that someone like Savita was interested in me. She took my breath away.'

It was during a meeting in April 2008 that Praveen and Savita decided to get married, and the wedding was organized there and then. Mr Yalagi booked the banqueting hall in the premises of the Indian Institute of Engineers in Belgaum and over 500 guests were invited. Savita decided on every detail, though she was worried about the heat. It was summertime in India and in April – on average the second-hottest month of the year after May –

temperatures can reach 39 degrees Celsius. Praveen recalls Savita worrying that her make-up would get messed up in the heat.

'We got married in summer and she wanted to get married in winter. It was very warm and she was concerned because she was wearing a 10-metre sari. It was very heavy with all the ornaments and she was complaining.'

The wedding photographs show a dazzlingly beautiful bride and a smitten groom. She wore a long, vibrant red, gold and bejewelled wedding sari and he was almost regal in a traditional, long cream jodhpuri shirt with Nehru collar over cream trousers and gold embroidered slippers. Her hands and forehead, in true Lingayat tradition, were painted elaborately with henna. Among the pictures are images of Savita feeding Praveen sweet rice, part of the matrimonial ritual, and throwing her head back laughing as she does so.

'She was so happy that day,' smiles her father. Though clearly the plan was that Savita would join Praveen in Galway once her visa came through, Mr Yalagi and his wife hoped the couple might return to India eventually. 'I said "Let her go. Let her try for a year." If she didn't like Ireland, Praveen said, they would come back. We encouraged her to go. We always supported her to be who she wanted to be.'

During the few months it took for the visa to come through, Savita spent her remaining time in India with friends and family. In late April she took a trip to Mumbai with her best friend, Smita.

Savita arrived in Galway in July 2008. Praveen had been sharing an apartment with two other men, in the Ballybrit area, in the eastern outskirts of the city. He moved out and rented an apartment across the road in preparation for his wife's arrival. Praveen's friends in Galway have spoken of how shy and reserved he was before Savita came. He didn't socialize, but when Savita arrived she threw herself into the social scene, pulling Praveen along with her. Soon the couple were at events every weekend, taking part in dancing competitions and organizing events for the Indian community in the city.

'I soon came to understand what her family told me about her,' said Praveen in an interview with Indian journalist Aimee Ginsberg in November 2012. 'Savita was not only the leader of our house but of her circle of friends, as well. No one ever questioned this. It was not a matter of ego, either. She just led, and people naturally accepted that. She always said exactly what she was thinking,' he adds: 'people liked that about her.'

Soon, as their circle of friends grew and the couple wanted to invite people over, they decided they needed a house and moved to An Luasan, an estate also in the Ballybrit area.

Bright and vivacious, Savita was called 'the girl with the diamond smile', and not just because she had a tiny diamond in one of her teeth. Her personality shone. Children used to ask her where she got the diamond and she would laugh, saying, 'Oh you'll have to go to India to get one.'

She soon had Praveen dancing with her in performances at numerous events for the Indian community – at Indian Independence Day celebrations in 2009; at the Indian festival of lights, Diwali (the most important religious festival in the Hindu calendar) in November 2009, and again the next year. At the 2010 Diwali in Galway Savita won the prize for best dancer of the night. She choreographed several dance routines for each event, in some of which she danced herself.

After the 2010 Diwali the organizing committee asked her to get involved, and also to teach children in the local community, which she took to with gusto. She had the children dancing in events for Special Olympics as well as in the St Patrick's Day parade in 2011.

'Children loved her and she choreographed their dance routines for cultural events,' says friend Devi Chalikonda.

Savita also loved to travel and every April, for their wedding anniversary, she and Praveen would visit Europe. 'On our first wedding anniversary we went to Paris. Every year on our anniversary we went to a different country,' Praveen said. 'We went to Venice, Rome and Santorini in Greece.'

Throughout this period in her life, he said, she visited dental clinics 'to observe in preparation for her exams. She wanted to see how things were done here.'

Determined to practise her dentistry in Ireland, Savita applied to sit the Irish Dental Council exams. Dentists with qualifications obtained outside the EEA must pass the Council's exams to get a licence to practise in Ireland. Savita had sat Part 1 of the exams in the spring of 2012, which had tested her knowledge of general and oral anatomy; physiology, biochemistry and pharmacology, pathology and microbiology. Part 1 also included a practical examination of Savita's skills in such areas as fillings and preparing crowns. She passed Part 1 and moved on to Part 2, held in the Irish Dental College at Lincoln Place, Dublin, in June 2012.

She and Praveen spent a week in Dublin while she did the exams. Part 2, held over three days, is a far more hands-on examination. There were nine candidates that June, said David O'Flynn, registrar with the Council. They were examined in a clinical setting in their knowledge of general medicine/general surgery, restorative dentistry, preventive dentistry, paediatric dentistry, therapeutics, anaesthesiology, radiology, and law and ethics.

The exams, according to the Council's website, are 'searching and test, to a standard not less than that required of an Irish graduate, the knowledge and skill required for the delivery of primary dental care to patients'.

Though he would see many candidates over the years, O'Flynn remembers Savita clearly. 'There's a lot of interaction with the candidates over those three days so you do get to know the candidates quite a bit. So we would have got to know what type of person Savita was. Savita was highly likeable. She was very helpful to the other candidates, just a very pleasant individual. I met her husband too, I seem to remember, and they were just a really nice couple.'

Savita passed her exams and registered on 11 July 2012. She was then granted a licence to practise as a dentist in Ireland. Says O'Flynn: 'I know she would have made a really lovely dentist to visit.'

That month she was delighted when she did a pregnancy test at home and it was positive. She called her best friend in Ireland, Mrdula Vaseali, to ask what to do and Mrdula told her to register with a GP. Savita hadn't needed to before, being in excellent health. She was vegetarian, did not smoke or drink and did yoga every day.

She registered with the primary healthcare centre in Doughiska, a residential area adjacent to Roscam, where she and Praveen had moved the previous year.

Savita was seen at the GP service in Doughiska in October 2012 and was referred for her first appointment at Galway University Hospital, with Dr Katherine Astbury on 11 October. Dr Astbury performed an ultrasound scan to pinpoint how far along Savita was in the pregnancy.

'Dr Astbury confirmed that Savita was 17 weeks pregnant and she told us Savita was doing well,' Praveen said in his statement to the Gardai following her death. 'She gave us the date the baby was due as 30 March 2013. Savita shed tears of happiness when she saw the baby on the monitor.'

Her parents had arrived to visit in August. Because she had become pregnant, Savita decided she would not set about practising as a dentist until she was ready, after the baby's birth. While Praveen went to work, Savita took her parents to 'all the important sites' around Galway, said her father. He was particularly taken with Irish supermarkets and he loved going to the supermarket on his own, to look at the vegetables and fruit displays. Though Savita and her mother cooked Indian food in the house, Savita took her parents to some hotel restaurants, where Mr Yalagi was underwhelmed by the food. 'Some is OK,' he grimaced, then smiled.

He and his wife, Akhmedevi, liked the Irish people a lot. 'I liked talking to the people. Everyone was so open and friendly.'

With her parents Savita viewed houses around Roscam, as she and Praveen planned to buy a house before the baby was born. 'Some very fine houses,' says Mr Yalagi. It meant, he and his wife realized, that she was not planning on returning to India to live in the near future, which saddened them. 'But she was so happy. She loved Ireland and the peace there. She was happy and so we gave them our blessing. She was making a life in Ireland and she was home every year for one month.'

They were very excited about Savita's pregnancy too. Life in Ireland seemed to be as good as they could have dreamt of for their daughter. For her parents' last few days in Ireland, Savita arranged a going-away party and baby shower at her home on Saturday evening, 20 October.

Savita planned that they would then all go to Dublin the next day, to see the capital city for a few days. On Tuesday the 23rd she and Praveen would take her parents to the airport for their flight home.

First, however, she had a baby shower to plan.

2

Saturday 20 October

Savita is so happy. She and her mother are preparing for the Garbhalinga Dharane – the traditional Lingayat baby shower – which they will hold this evening at Praveen and Savita's home in Roscam. Though the tradition in Karnataka is that the Garbhalinga Dharane is held in the eighth month of a woman's first pregnancy just as the woman is about to embark on mother-hood, Savita has decided to hold hers this evening as her parents are going back to Belgaum on Tuesday.

The Garbhalinga Dharane is quite different to Western baby showers, which centre on giving gifts for the baby. It is a hugely important ritual in the Lingayat community. As noted in the last chapter, the Lingayat wear the ishtalinga (the linga is the image of God) on the body throughout life, to eradicate untouchability, establish the equality of all human beings and as a means to attain spiritual enlightenment. During Garbhalinga Dharane the baby's ishtalinga is blessed and tied on a cord around the mother's belly until the birth. It will be tied to the newborn a few days after birth, so that the child will attain enlightenment as part of their journey through a life of dignity, honesty and meaning where they may be great, not by virtue of their birth, but through the way they live their life.

'Savita and her mother organized the shower and Savita's mother prepared food Savita liked,' recalls Praveen. 'They dressed up in new clothes and said prayers and there were some friends around too. Savita was on top of the world. We were so excited, all talking about the baby.'

That night she can't sleep. Her back, which has been giving her lower-area pain for the past nine months, is worse than usual and the pain is radiating around her pelvis. She is up and down to the toilet all night and the pain becomes unbearable. At about 9 a.m. Praveen calls St Monica's ward, the maternity ward, at Galway University Hospital.

'I spoke to a midwife and explained what was happening and she said to come on in. So we told her parents we were going to the hospital because of Savita's lower back pain. When we got there they asked us to go into a waiting room,' says Praveen. A midwife takes Savita's temperature. It's 36.8 degrees Celsius, her heart rate is 82 beats per minute and her blood pressure is 113/73. All seems well. A urine analysis shows no sign of infection.

'Savita told the midwife that there was some fluid as well every time she went to the bathroom. She kept having to change her undergarments,' says Praveen. 'The midwife nurse came out to me as well because I was panicking also. She was very nice. She held my hand and told me it would be OK. She said Savita is fine, nothing to worry about, she has a history of back pain and she is seeing a physio. The midwife nurse got on to the on-duty doctor who was an African female doctor and she spoke with Savita.' The foetal heart can be heard, which reassures them both. She is given some medication for pain and told she can go home. 'She was relieved when they said the baby was OK. When we got home we were having some breakfast when Savita went to the washroom. She immediately came out of the toilet and she was in tears. She said, "Something is wrong." She felt something hard coming. She was in tears, in shock.' They tell

13

her parents she has an appointment at the hospital and leave to go back.

The same midwife sees them and forms the impression that Savita is miscarrying. She calls the senior house officer in obstetrics, Dr Olufoyeke Olatunbosun, who is on call that weekend. Savita is 'tearful and anxious' and Dr Olatunbosun examines her internally. Savita's foetal membranes are bulging and the senior obstetrics registrar on duty, Dr Andrew Gaolebale, is called. He too carries out an internal examination and finds the membranes bulging almost to the entrance of the vagina. A miscarriage is almost inevitable.

Praveen, who has been waiting outside the examination room, is called in. 'Savita was crying loudly. I think they had already told her. The male doctor said, "You need to be brave because of what I am going to tell you." He said: "There is cervical dilation. The cervix is open. The baby won't survive."'

Dr Gaolebale, recalls Praveen, tells them it will be over in a matter of hours. Dr Gaolebale tells Dr Olatunbosun to take blood for a full blood count, to establish a baseline in case Savita loses blood during the miscarriage. Dr Olatunbosun sends the blood to the lab, but no one follows it up or records in Savita's notes the fact that blood has been taken. There is no sign of an infection and the plan is to admit Savita and await events. 'Both of us were shattered,' says Praveen. 'We didn't know what to do. I was consoling her and telling her everything was all right. She said, "It's not all right. Why did this happen to me?" Then she held my hand and said, "Sorry," that she wanted to be a good wife.

'Then the registrar [Dr Gaolebale] came in alone. He asked me did we have any questions. I asked him how long it would be. I asked him specifically. Basically we wanted to go home, she was in shock. We thought if we could spend some time with the family it would be all right. She was in terrible mental pain. He said it will be four or five hours,' says Praveen.

14

(Dr Gaolebale will dispute at the inquest that he told them it would be over in a few hours. He will tell the Health Service Executive [HSE] inquiry into Savita's death, chaired by Professor Sir Sabaratnam Arulkumaran and published in June 2013, he had felt 'it would probably be a matter of hours before miscarriage'.)

Savita is taken to a bed, in a room of her own, in a wheelchair. 'Once the midwife put Savita on the bed she held her hand and said she was very sorry,' says Praveen. Praveen stays with her.

5 p.m. vital signs* : temperature 36.5 degrees; pulse 90 bpm; blood pressure 115/75
10 p.m. vital signs: temperature 36.6 degrees; pulse 89 bpm; blood pressure 100/60

Monday 22 October

At 12.30 a.m. that Sunday night/Monday morning Savita's waters break. Savita vomits a significant amount and nurses note she has had spontaneous rupture of the membranes. More senior medical staff are not informed. Savita is now worried about what to tell her parents. She says it will be hard for her father to take because he had a bypass eight years before. The couple decide not to tell her parents until they get back to India.

---

*Savita's vital signs will be critical indicators of her deterioration. According to the Green-top Guide No. 64a, from the Royal College of Obstetricians and Gynaecologists (RCOG), published April 2012, *Bacterial Sepsis in Pregnancy*: 'Sepsis may be defined as infection plus systemic manifestations of infection.' Clinical signs suggestive of sepsis, it says, include one or more of the following: pyrexia, or a temperature over 38 degrees Centigrade; hypothermia, a temperature below 36 degrees Centigrade; tachycardia, which is a heart rate above 90 beats per minute; tachypnoea, which is rapid breathing – more than 20 breaths per minute; hypoxia, which is lack of oxygen to the body's major organs; hypotension, which is low blood pressure, lower than 90 over 60; oliguria, which is reduced urine output; impaired consciousness; and failure to respond to treatment. The presence of any of these indicators in Savita's case will be indicated with bold text.

'She was concerned especially about her father.' The midwife caring for her notes that Savita is very anxious, about her parents and about the impending miscarriage.

6.05 a.m. vital signs: temperature 37 degrees; **pulse 94 bpm**; blood pressure 108/65. It is five and a half hours since her membranes ruptured.

At 6.30 a.m. she is told she is fasting from now on, but not told why. At 8.25 a.m. she is seen by her consultant, Dr Katherine Astbury, and her team. Dr Astbury recalls discussing the risk of infection with Savita now that the membranes had ruptured. 'I sent her for an abdominal ultrasound scan to confirm the presence of a foetal heartbeat and I discussed the rationale for this in terms of the risk of sepsis with ruptured membranes and therefore the need to avoid her sitting on the ward undelivered.' She prescribes an antibiotic, erythromycin, as a prophylactic against possible infection. After the scan confirms the foetal heartbeat presence, says Praveen, they both ask Dr Astbury about a termination of the pregnancy as Savita is very anxious to get home to her parents in Roscam before they leave for India the next day. 'She wanted to get back to tell them she had lost the baby before they got home and started telling friends at home she is going to be a mum. She was very determined.' He says Dr Astbury said initially it was not possible at this point but when Savita kept pushing her on it, Dr Astbury said she would go and check with someone else, but did not return. Dr Astbury will dispute, at the inquest, that this conversation about a termination took place at the Monday ward round. Her description of the conversation to the HSE inquiry will suggest that a conversation about a termination may have taken place on Monday.

8.30 a.m. vital signs: temperature 36.6; **pulse 92 bpm**; blood pressure 102/59. Eight hours since the membranes ruptured.

That afternoon Savita's parents come to see her. Determined not to worry them Savita sticks to her story that everything is fine. She is, says Praveen, in a lot of pain. 'Her dad was very impressed with the hospital. In India government hospitals are very shabby. Savita was all prepared, she had washed her face and she was sitting up in bed. I was very impressed with her. She was so bold. She had just eaten lunch. Her dad was walking around the ward and her mother was just focused on her. So, they discussed who to give presents to and after 15 minutes Savita had enough and she signalled at me to take them. Then there was a discussion about how they would get to the airport. They were willing to take the bus but Savita wanted me to take them. A friend of ours had offered to take them because he knew the real story but Savita wasn't having any of that either.'

He takes the Yalagis back to Roscam and returns to Savita.

3.25 p.m. vital signs: temperature 36.8 degrees; **pulse 98 bpm**; blood pressure 98/58. Fifteen hours since membranes ruptured.

6 p.m. vital signs: temperature 37.1 degrees; **pulse 102 bpm**; blood pressure 98/62. Seventeen and a half hours since membranes ruptured.

9.40 p.m. vital signs: temperature 37 degrees; **pulse 102 bpm**; blood pressure 110/62. Twenty-one hours since membranes ruptured.

At about 10 p.m. she is administered her first dose of antibiotics, ordered that morning.

Tuesday 23 October

Praveen leaves at about 4 a.m. to pick up the Yalagis and take them to the airport. 'Before we left the house there Savita texted me again a big text with instructions about what to bring. When I showed Savita's text to her mum there were tears in her eyes. She was so concerned about Savita and she said she was so lucky to have a daughter like her.'

6 a.m. vital signs: temperature 37 degrees; pulse 84 bpm; blood pressure 95/52. Twenty-nine and a half hours since membranes ruptured.

At 8.20 a.m. Dr Astbury and her team come to review Savita. Savita is very upset and asks her if she could be given some medication to expedite delivery of the foetus. 'I recall informing Ms Halappanavar that the legal position in Ireland did not permit me to terminate the pregnancy at that time,' she will tell the inquest. This discussion about a termination is not recorded in the medical notes.

8.35 a.m. vital signs: temperature 36.4 degrees; **pulse 92 bpm**; blood pressure 100/64. Thirty-two hours since membranes ruptured.

While on the road to Dublin Praveen gets a call from a friend, Sunil Vaseali, to say he is dropping his wife, Savita's best friend, Mrdula, to the hospital to keep Savita company. She arrives about 9.30 a.m. At 11.30 a.m. third-year student midwife Elaine Finucane checks on Savita. She is sitting up in bed talking to her friend, Mrdula. Savita doesn't want to eat any lunch and student Finucane tells her if she doesn't she won't have strength for the next pregnancy. 'She was in good form, chatting. We had a joke about hospital dinners. I returned and she had eaten her dinner and Savita asked could she have a bath and she wanted to go for a walk,' recalls Finucane.

About noon, senior midwife Ann Maria Burke comes to listen to the foetal heart and Mrdula steps out. She hears Savita crying and comes back into the room. They both ask midwife Burke whether, given that the baby will die, Savita could have a medical termination. Midwife Burke feels pity for Savita, who is pleading and saying it would not be a problem in India, and she tries to explain why the approach to termination in Ireland is different to that in India. She says: 'It's a Catholic thing. We don't do it here.' Savita asks for a bath but is advised against it. She does have a walk on the ward with Mrdula, though.

2.45 p.m. vital signs: temperature 37 degrees; **pulse 100 bpm**; blood pressure 108/74. Thirty-eight hours and fifteen minutes since membranes ruptured.

Praveen arrives back mid-afternoon and takes Mrdula home. On the way they discuss Savita's situation and the fact that she cannot have a termination of pregnancy. Praveen had told Mrdula's husband the day before that the hospital told them a termination wasn't possible while there was a foetal heartbeat, so he is not surprised when Mrdula tells him about the conversation with midwife Burke.

Rush-hour traffic is heavy on the way back to the hospital and it is about 6.30 p.m. by the time he gets there. Savita seems 'much better mentally', recalls Praveen and he suggests she take a bath as she hasn't had one since Saturday. He goes to ask a midwife about this and then has some dinner with Savita in the room. While they eat, they talk about the day and Savita says how good it was of Mrdula to come and spend the day with her. She sends Mrdula a text to say 'thank you'. Mrdula phones her back and says, 'Come back home. Don't be sending texts. Just come back home. We will have fun.' It is the last time she speaks to her friend.

7 p.m. vital signs: temperature 36.6 degrees; **pulse 114 bpm**; blood pressure 108/66. Forty-two and a half hours since membranes ruptured.

Student Elaine Finucane takes these recordings at 7 p.m. and rechecks the pulse: it is again **114 bpm**. She reports this to midwife Burke. Midwife Burke will tell the inquest she called the on-duty senior health officer (SHO), Dr Ikechukwu Uzockwu, to advise him of the raised pulse. Dr Uzockwu will say he did not get this call. This call is not documented in the report of the HSE investigation.

8 p.m. vital signs: temperature 36.8 degrees; **pulse 108 bpm**; blood pressure 106/68. Forty-three and a half hours since membranes ruptured.

9 p.m. vital signs: temperature 36.9 degrees; **pulse 106 bpm**; blood pressure 105/60. Forty-four and a half hours since membranes ruptured.

Savita is feeling weak and tells the midwife Cathy Gallagher; but she is eating and drinking normally. Some time between 9 and 10 p.m. midwife Gallagher calls Dr Uzockwu and asks him to come and see Savita because of her feeling weak but makes no mention of her raised temperature and pulse. Dr Uzockwu has a heavy caseload this evening and says he will come to the ward as soon as he can.

Wednesday 24 October

Dr Uzockwu comes to the ward at about 1 a.m., in response to the call from midwife Gallagher earlier. Savita is asleep, however, and midwife Gallagher tells Dr Uzockwu that she seems to have settled. Praveen is also asleep on a camp bed beside her bed and the doctor decides not to disturb them.

At 4.15 a.m., midwife Miriam Dunleavy responds to the call-bell from Savita's room where both Praveen and Savita are awake. They are cold and ask for blankets. When she returns, midwife Dunleavy notices Savita is shivering so much that her teeth are chattering. 'I recorded her temperature, which was 37.7 degrees. She was alert . . . no complaints of pain. I administered one gram of paracetamol.'

Fifty-one hours and forty-five minutes since membranes ruptured.

Savita's temperature has increased since 9 p.m. when it was 36.9 degrees and she is shivering intensely. She is experiencing a rigor, a sign of sepsis, but midwife Dunleavy does not check her pulse. 'There were no signs she was septic to me,' she will tell the HSE inquiry. '[Savita] appeared to settle after being given the second blanket.' Savita is also complaining about uneasy breathing and she vomits up some water, a possible indication of early toxic shock, according to the RCOG Green-top Guide *Bacterial Sepsis in Pregnancy*.

At 5 a.m. midwife Dunleavy rechecks Savita's temperature: it has come down a little, to 37.5 degrees. Fifty-two and a half hours since membranes ruptured.

At 6.30 a.m. midwife Gallagher notices Savita is feeling weak and has general body aches and she records her vital signs:

temperature 39.6 degrees; pulse 160 bpm; blood pressure 94/55.
It is fifty-four hours since membranes ruptured.

Midwife Gallagher immediately calls Dr Uzockwu, who is on the ward with another patient, and also calls midwife Dunleavy. He arrives at 6.40 a.m. and cold compresses are applied to try and bring down Savita's temperature. Supported breathing is also started via an oxygen mask. Dr Uzockwu notes a significant amount of a foul-smelling vaginal discharge and takes a high vaginal swab. He forms the impression that Savita is suffering from 'at least chorioamnionitis' but probably sepsis, he will tell the HSE inquiry, and inserts a note of this in Savita's notes.

Chorioamnionitis is an infection of both the chorion and the amnion, which are membranes around the foetus, and also of the amniotic fluid. It can lead to infections in both the foetus and mother and delivery of the foetus is essential along with antibiotic treatment. It is potentially fatal for both mother and foetus.

Dr Uzockwu takes bloods and sends them to the lab for a full blood count as well as blood cultures to measure renal and liver function, and orders a serum lactate test. A lactate test is important as rising lactate levels indicate possible sepsis. When body tissues are being inadequately supplied with oxygen excess lactic acid accumulates, giving rise to increased lactate. The bloods taken from Savita are not marked 'urgent' and the serum lactate sample is sent to the wrong place in an incorrect bottle. It should have been tested on the ward, a process that would have taken five minutes, but Dr Uzockwu did not know this at the time. The lab receives the samples at 8.07 a.m. The crucial lactate sample is discarded. The lab does not tell Dr Uzockwu it has discarded the sample.

Dr Uzockwu also orders that Savita be started on intravenous paracetamol, intravenous antibiotic coamoxiclav (Augmentin) and intravenous fluid therapy.

Dr Uzockwu carries out an electrocardiograph test to examine Savita's heart activity and she is found to have a **heart rate of 168 bpm**.

At 7.20 a.m. Savita is noted as having vomited a small amount of bile and she is given the anti-nausea drug Stemetil.

7.20 a.m. vital signs: no temperature recorded; **pulse 164 bpm**; blood pressure 100/60. Respiratory rate 20 per minute. Almost fifty-five hours since membranes ruptured.

7.30 a.m. vital signs: temperature 37.9 degrees; **pulse 154 bpm**; blood pressure 98/54. Fifty-five hours since membranes ruptured.

Praveen recalls: 'The doctor looked very concerned. The midwives were very busy with Savita. At around 7 a.m. I went looking for the doctor who took the blood samples because I was anxious to know what the results were. I found him at the midwives' station. I asked him, "Is there any concern?" He said "No, there is nothing at the minute [he] can tell me." Then he left.' He returns to Savita's room to find her with an oxygen mask and at least one drip. Savita asks for some water and vomits it back up.

7.50 a.m. vital signs: temperature 37.9 degrees; **pulse 140 bpm**; blood pressure 100/55.

At 7.50 a.m. Dr Uzockwu has a conversation in the corridor with Dr Astbury's specialist registrar, Dr Ann Helps. He tells her about the foul-smelling discharge and his clinical impression that Savita has chorioamnionitis and sepsis. Dr Helps wonders if Savita should be started on a different antibiotic regime. Dr Uzockwu returns to Savita and she asks him about the results of the electrocardiograph test.

'She was talking to me. She asked me about the ECG, seemed to have some medical knowledge, she was aware. I explained my management and my findings and stayed with her until the team came.'

At 8 a.m., following the midwife nursing shift change, midwife manager Patricia Gilligan comes straight to see Savita. She believes Savita is a 'septic abortion', having heard about her deterioration overnight. She is very concerned about her. She does not talk with Dr Astbury but will tell the inquest she felt Dr Astbury would 'see what I was doing' on her ward round.

At 8.25 Dr Astbury and her team come to review Savita. Dr Helps is carrying Savita's medical notes and Dr Astbury does not read them. Dr Helps does not read Dr Uzockwu's insert in the notes and does not tell Dr Astbury of Dr Uzockwu's finding of a foul-smelling discharge. Dr Astbury also forms the impression that Savita may have chorioamnionitis and commences a second antibiotic, metronidazole. Another high vaginal swab is sent to the lab with a urine sample, to rule out a urinary tract infection. It is noted that blood test results are also awaited. A plan is made to await test results. Praveen is advised by Dr Astbury and

Dr Helps that if she does not improve termination may be necessary, regardless of foetal heartbeat. This second acknowledged discussion about a termination is not recorded in the medical notes.

8.25 a.m. vital signs: temperature 37.9 degrees; pulse following intravenous paracetamol at 6.45 a.m. is **144 bpm**; **blood pressure 98/54**. Fifty-six hours since membranes ruptured.

At 8.29 a.m. Savita's blood samples are received at the lab. Results showing she has a dangerously low white cell count of 1.7 (normal for a pregnant woman would be between 6 and 15) and an elevated C-reactive protein of 38.9, indicating sepsis, are accessed at ward level at 8.50 a.m. It is not clear whether Dr Astbury is still on the ward. She is not told about the blood results.

At about 9 a.m. midwife Gilligan has Savita moved from Room 9 near the ward exit to Room 2 near the nurses' station, to keep a closer eye on her. There is also piped oxygen in this room. A care assistant clears the room of excess furniture in case 'equipment [is] needed later' and midwife Gilligan assigns a staff midwife to her.

Savita's blood pressure is falling.

At 10 a.m. it is **88/50**
At 10.30 it is **84/50**

At 11.25 a.m. Dr Astbury accesses Savita's blood test results: they indicate her low white cell count and elevated C-reactive protein. She does not come to review her. Fifty-nine hours since membranes ruptured.

At noon Savita's blood pressure is **74/44**.

At 1 p.m. it is **72/40**. Her pulse is **156 bpm** and Savita has chest pain and is finding it more difficult to breathe. Savita's life is now in peril.

At 1.10 p.m. midwife manager Gilligan is informed of the relentless fall in Savita's blood pressure. She immediately contacts Dr Astbury, who arrives on the ward 'promptly'. Dr Astbury collects a scanning machine on her way to the ward and arrives at 1.20 p.m. to find Savita sweaty, her breathing laboured, she has severe muscle aches and low **blood pressure, 81/40. Her pulse is 150 bpm**. Dr Astbury sees that Savita is now 'very unwell'. An internal examination finds her cervix 2 cm dilated with visible ragged membranes. Dr Astbury diagnoses septic shock and calls the microbiology department. It is the first time microbiology is consulted and Dr Astbury is advised to commence Savita on Tazocin and gentamicin antibiotics, and continue on metronidazole. A central line is to be inserted in Savita's neck to assess fluid needs, administer drugs and stabilize blood pressure.

Dr Astbury leaves to see a senior colleague, Dr Geraldine Gaffney, consultant obstetrician and gynaecologist and clinical director for women and children, to discuss her opinion that Savita should be delivered regardless of the foetal heart as her life is now threatened. It is the first time she has sought advice from a more senior colleague on Savita's situation. Dr Gaffney agrees Savita should be delivered and offers to write this up in Savita's notes. Dr Astbury says she will check if the foetal heart is present before asking her to write a note. She returns to the ward with an ultrasound scanner to check again for the foetal heart. A scan finds the foetus has died.

Dr Astbury contacts the High Dependency and Intensive Care consultant anaesthetist Dr John Bates to discuss Savita's transfer. Dr Bates sends Dr Aidan Magee, senior house officer in ICU, to assess Savita. He arrives on the ward at 2.30 p.m. Savita is in septic shock with a **temperature of 39.03 degrees, a pulse of 150 bpm and blood pressure 60/30**. It is sixty-two hours since her membranes ruptured.

Dr Magee stays with her, monitoring her blood pressure, while the theatre list is being interrupted for Savita.

'I explained to her husband who was waiting in the corridor what we were planning,' recalls Dr Magee. At 3.15 p.m. Savita is brought into theatre. It is an appropriate action to transfer Savita to a theatre for the insertion of lines and to commence therapies to stabilize her low blood pressure, the HSE report will comment.

While in theatre she spontaneously delivers a female foetus, a daughter she and Praveen name as Prasa. Praveen sees her but Savita does not want to.

It is almost nine hours since Dr Uzockwu diagnosed sepsis, almost 31 hours since Savita's first acknowledged request for a termination, almost 53 hours since the disputed Monday request and 63 hours since her membranes ruptured. It will be commented at her inquest, by the coroner and several medical experts, that her risk of death is now about 60 per cent.

Dr Astbury asks Praveen to sign some forms. 'Then she said Savita is fine, that they are taking her to the High Dependency Unit for a few hours to keep a close monitor of her,' recalls Praveen. 'I asked if I could accompany Savita. She said for me to stay in the room and Savita would be back in a few hours. I went back to the room.'

At 4.45 p.m. Savita is transferred to HDU. On admission she has a temperature of 37.4 degrees, **a pulse of 153 bpm**, blood pressure of 143/99, a high lactate of 6.8 (normal is 1.5), a white cell count of 1.4, all in keeping with severe infection. She is drowsy and on oxygen support. Her outlook at this stage is 'pretty poor', according to the on-call consultant anaesthetist in ICU/HDU, Dr Brian Kinirons.

Praveen is still waiting at St Monica's ward as he has been told to, but asks to go to HDU. A nurse comes out of HDU to take him to see Savita. She tells Praveen she is sorry, and that Savita is a beautiful girl, before giving him a plastic apron and a chair to sit with his wife. Savita is in septic shock but manages to have a brief conversation with him. 'Basically as soon as she saw me she asked if her parents had reached home safely and I said "Yes" and showed her the text from her brother,' he recalls. 'She was fine then. That's it. That was 7 p.m.' It is his last conversation with her. Praveen goes home for a few hours to get something to eat and take a shower. He believes Savita will be OK now. He is relieved the baby has been delivered and the ordeal of the miscarriage is over.

It is an extremely busy night between the HD and IC units, and in the accident and emergency department, where a number of critical patients are arriving. A scan is performed on Savita to ensure there are no retained products of conception in her womb. None is found.

During the course of Wednesday evening her condition deteriorates. Dr Kinirons adds further haemodynamic resuscitations and fluids. Over the course of the evening he gets a number of calls from HDU about several other patients and Savita is discussed in all of them. She is reviewed at 9 p.m. and again at 11 p.m. Her haemoglobin has dropped during the day and during the night her platelet count falls. She seems more distressed and her condition worsens.

Thursday 25 October

At 1 a.m. Savita is given her first dose of vancomycin, an antibiotic: 900 mg intravenously. She continues to deteriorate and at 3 a.m. a decision is made to transfer her to ICU, where she is intubated. Praveen is called at home and in shock he rushes back to the hospital. He goes to ICU and has to phone in from the corridor outside. A nurse tells him they are very busy and asks him to wait for fifteen minutes. He waits outside all night.

At 7.30 a.m. the same nurse, according to Praveen, sees him and asks him whether a doctor has spoken to him. He says none has and she apologizes, telling him it was a very busy night. She calls someone inside the unit and tells them, 'Praveen is waiting outside.' She apologizes again and tells Praveen she will pray for

Savita. He is called in about an hour later and is told Savita's oxygen requirement has reduced a little and that this is a good sign.

Dr Astbury comes to see Savita at 8.40 a.m.

Dr John Bates takes charge of Savita in ICU at 9 a.m. She is in septic shock, with acute respiratory distress syndrome, disseminated intravascular coagulation (DIC) secondary to sepsis and is dependent on high levels of support to keep her blood pressure at a safe level. She requires oxygen support and has a temperature of **38 degrees**. Her risk of death is now 60 per cent, medical experts would tell her inquest.

Sure that Savita will be OK, Praveen drives home again and while driving gets a call from her father. He is very worried and wants to speak to his daughter. Praveen tries to convince him she will be all right and in the end tells him he will ask Savita to call him later. He goes to bed for a few hours. He returns to the hospital at about 3 p.m. and is told that Savita is critical but stable and that youth is on her side. Savita's condition does improve slightly during the day, with her lactate levels falling from 6.5 at 3 a.m., to 4.1 at noon and 3.5 at 11 p.m. Dr Astbury sees her at 5.25 p.m. and notes some small decrease in Savita's support requirements. However her **heart rate remains elevated at 130 bpm** and her **temperature high at 38 degrees** throughout the day. The sepsis remains aggressive.

At 7 p.m. Praveen sees Dr Bates and is told that Savita is in septic shock. He does not know what this means, assuming it to be some kind of mental shock related to the miscarriage. He asks if he can speak to her and an ICU nurse tells him he can, that she can hear him but won't be able to respond. He tells her he loves her, that her father is waiting to hear from her, that everything will be all right and that they will be able to go home soon. He feels cold and goes to his car to get his jacket, then returns to ICU where he spends the night.

Friday 26 October

Savita remains critically ill through the night. She is still intubated, ventilated and requiring significant support to keep her blood pressure up. She is described as 'warm' and 'well profused' – i.e. her tissues are getting adequate oxygen.

Dr Paul Naughton, consultant anaesthetist in the intensive care unit, takes over Savita's care at 9 a.m. He notes that her body is swollen due to an accumulation of fluids, that she has a **tachycardia of 140 bpm** and a **temperature of 40 degrees**. She has normal blood pressure, but only because it is supported with infusions of noradrenalin. She has a hugely elevated white cell count of 23.5 and a C-reactive protein level of 37.2. She is moving towards multi-organ failure. Dr Naughton is concerned that perhaps they still have not found a focus of the infection and a scan is again performed to rule out retained products of conception. Savita continues to deteriorate, despite the range of supports and antibiotics, indicating that sepsis is now engulfing her body, setting off a domino effect throughout. At noon, the microbiology department identifies the E. coli bacterium as an extended spectrum beta-lactamase (ESBL) in Savita's blood cultures. The ESBL strain is a rare form of E. coli almost wholly resistant to antibiotics. Streptococcus is also isolated from the placental swab. The E. coli ESBL can be acquired in the community or in healthcare settings and though resistant to almost all antibiotics it is susceptible to the antibiotics prescribed for Savita. Commenced on these at 2 p.m. on Wednesday, she may have been started on them too late, however.

A nurse asks Praveen if he has told her parents in India that she is in intensive care. He says he has not, and she says he should tell them. They are staying with one of Savita's brothers in Bangalore and he calls them there. Speaking first to her brother, Praveen tells him about the miscarriage. He then speaks to her mother, who asks about Savita. She begins to cry and can't talk and Praveen doesn't tell her just how ill Savita is. He speaks again to her brother and tells him she is in the HDU and that they are checking for infection after the miscarriage. Praveen asks about telling her father, and her brother advises against it, saying her father 'won't be able to take it'.

He then calls his parents in Haveri and tells them about the miscarriage and the sepsis. His mother asks why he didn't tell Savita's parents while they were in Ireland and he explains that this was Savita's decision, though it was one she was not entirely happy with. She had wanted to go home to Roscam before they left, but couldn't. His mother tells him he must be strong for Savita as he is the only one here for her. She will pray for her, she says. He now starts calling friends as the nurse's advice that he should call her parents has worried him a lot. Until this point he had believed Savita would be OK.

Praveen sees Savita at 8 p.m. She is very swollen and when he holds her hand it is 'rock solid'. He asks an Indian nurse in ICU if he can get an update on Savita, and the nurse returns to tell him Savita's life 'is on a wire'. He leaves ICU to call her brother again. He tells him Savita is seriously ill and tells him all that has happened. Her brother asks if his little sister is feeling any pain and Praveen reassures him that she is sedated and not in pain.

At around 9 p.m. he calls Mrdula and she tells him to come over to her and Sunil's house in Doughiska. They discuss everything and wonder whether they should have Savita transferred to a private hospital, the Galway Clinic. So they call a GP they know, Dr Devi Chalikonda, who lives in Spiddal and whose husband works in the Galway Clinic. Dr Devi tells them she will get in touch with the ICU and find out how Savita is. Praveen returns to the ICU and finds the nurse there on the phone to Dr Chalikonda. The nurse passes the phone to him and Devi tells him that Savita is very ill but reassures him she is in the best place and says she will come and visit in the morning. Praveen goes to the hospital chapel to pray.

Savita remains 'relatively stable overnight'.

Saturday 27 October

Dr Naughton reviews her at 2 a.m. and again at 10 a.m. Savita remains critically unwell. She continues to need very high levels of support to keep her blood pressure up and her already high lactate level doubles, from 5 at 1 a.m. to 10.3 at 3 p.m.

At 11 a.m. Dr Devi Chalikonda and her husband, Dr Chalikonda Prasad, come to the ICU and a nurse gives them an update. Dr Devi sits by Savita's bed and prays for an hour or so. While her husband leaves for a work engagement, she stays, and goes with Praveen to talk to Dr Naughton, who tells them Savita is very, very ill and not responding to treatment. When they return from seeing Dr Naughton up to forty friends are in the ICU waiting area. A few go in to see Savita.

At 1 p.m. Dr Naughton starts dialysis in an attempt to correct the overproduction of acid in Savita's body.

At 4 p.m. Savita deteriorates suddenly and dramatically, becoming highly contusive and hypoxic (bruised in appearance due to her body being deprived of oxygen). She becomes cool to touch and her cardiac output falls from 6 litres per minute to less than 2 litres. Dr Naughton performs a cardiogram and finds signs of acute pulmonary embolism, which means the pulmonary artery is becoming blocked. He calls an ICU colleague, Dr Kevin Clarkson, who is at home, to discuss Savita's decline. It is clear to both that Savita is *in extremis* and Dr Clarkson offers to come in and help, but they agree that all that can be done is being done.

A shift change at 8 p.m. sees nurse Jacinta Gately take over Savita's nursing care. Her blood pressure is unrecordable, her heart rate is **150 to 155 bpm** and she remains ventilated, intubated and sedated with morphine. At 9 p.m. an arterial line is inserted and Savita's heart rate occasionally drops from its consistent 150 bpm down to 90 bpm. Her lactate levels are now 24, grossly exceeding the desirable level of 1.5. She is described as 'very oedematous, fingers flexed tightly, feet extended and very stiff'. Her abdomen is much distended.

At 10 p.m. alarms begin ringing on the ventilator. Savita is given an intravenous infusion of cisatracurium, a drug to relax her skeletal muscles in an effort to help her breathe.

At 11 p.m. Savita remains unresponsive. A system to monitor consciousness levels records her as between one and four, when 'awake' would be 100. Her lactate levels continue to rise. At 11.45 p.m. sodium bicarbonate, dextrose and insulin are infused in an effort to treat her rising potassium level and abnormal heart rhythm.

At midnight Savita is washed and her bloodstained pads are removed. When the nurses try to turn her, her heart rate increases from 140 to 190 bpm, so the nurses stop to let her heart settle.

Sunday 28 October

Between 12.30 a.m. and 12.45 a.m., nurse Gately and two other nurses are sitting by Savita's bedside when the monitor shows her heart rate becoming chaotic with a broad spectrum rhythm. Pulses are checked: none is palpable. CPR is commenced by Dr Aoife Quinn, staff nurses Veronica Rafftery, Therese Connolly, Jeurgen Schone, Áine Nic an Bheath and Gately. Within minutes nurse Gately runs out to get Praveen, who is in the waiting area with friends. She tells him Savita's heart has stopped, that they have commenced CPR, and asks if he wants to be present. He says he does. She takes his hand and asks if he understands what's happening: that they are losing her. A friend comes with him. Praveen recalls a 'big team' around Savita.

'They were pumping her heart. The doctor saw me. She came to me and said, "Do you know what is happening? Savita is dying." They were counting the compressions.' CPR continues until after 1 a.m. when a decision is made to stop.

Savita suffers a pulseless cardiac arrest.

At 1.09 a.m. Savita dies.

3

When Savita and Praveen walked anxiously into St Monica's ward in Galway University Hospital on the morning of 21 October 2012, the young Indian couple walked unwittingly into the most deeply rooted, most toxic war of wills besetting modern Irish society.

In asking for a termination in the days after she was told she was having an inevitable miscarriage, Savita was not simply requesting a medical intervention. Within the peculiar Irish context, she was also seeking self-determination, acknowledgement that she could make a just choice for herself, equality of access to healthcare with men, and recognition that the emotional, physical and spiritual life she had built over her brief thirty-one years amounted to a life worth protecting.

To the Irish, the abortion 'problem' takes in all these issues, and more. It also encompasses far more fundamental and searching questions about who we are as people, as a nation, about the role of women, how we structure our relationships – what are the informing values of our young republic, and what makes us different or similar to other nations? Savita and Praveen would have known little of the existential battles that have raged in Ireland. To this educated, worldly young couple Ireland was part of Europe and seemed to offer all that the West could. To have made it here was something to boast about back home in Karnataka. They were impressed with the Irish public healthcare system – light years ahead of the Indian public system. And they had heard Ireland was 'a good place to have a baby', Praveen would tell me.

They were not to know that twenty years previously the highest court in the land had affirmed that women and girls did have the right to an abortion where the woman's life was threatened. This Supreme Court ruling in the 1992 X case was an unforeseen and apparently contradictory consequence of a referendum nine years earlier, in which the people had voted in favour of a 'pro-life' amendment to the Constitution.

Article 40.3.3 was the result. It acknowledges the 'right to life of the unborn and . . . the equal right to life of the mother'.

Since both these landmark legal events no legislation had come to clarify what either meant. In what circumstances was an abortion permitted?

In the intervening years women and girls with crisis pregnancies had been forced into the court to seek clarity on just this issue. There had been attempts by governments to find the impossible: consensus on abortion. But none had grasped the nettle, faced down the warring sides and legislated. Since 1983 at least 100,000 women and girls had travelled from Ireland to have their pregnancies terminated, mainly in England. Those women who had the resources had been able to travel to realize the difficult decisions they had come to. Savita, however, would soon be in too much pain, and in days too ill, to travel.

That the gauntlet which had been thrown down to the legislature by the Supreme Court judgment in the 1992 X case was too toxic to take up could not excuse the fact that it hadn't been. This peculiarly Irish failure to do so, coupled with the substandard medical care she received, was to cost Savita her life.

To understand this Irish failure we need to understand the Irish State and the vision it has espoused for Irish society in general and Irish women in particular. And to understand that we need to go back to and beyond the State's foundation.

The 1937 Irish Constitution, Bunreacht na hÉireann, replaced the 1922 Constitution of the Irish Free State. Its drafting was personally supervised by the Taoiseach of the time, Eamon de Valera, and it had significant input from John Charles McQuaid, the Archbishop of Dublin, on religious, educational, family and social welfare issues. A draft of the new Constitution was presented to the Vatican for review and comment on two occasions, before its approval by the Irish people in July 1937. It was enacted in December of that year.

Its preamble, which stands today, says:

> 'In the Name of the Most Holy Trinity, from Whom is all authority and to Whom, as our final end, all actions both of men and States must be referred, We, the people of Éire, humbly acknowledging all our obligations to our Divine Lord, Jesus Christ, Who sustained our fathers through centuries of trial.
>
> 'Gratefully remembering their heroic and unremitting struggle to regain the rightful independence of our nation,
>
> 'And seeking to promote the common good, with due observance of Prudence, Justice and Charity, so that the dignity and freedom of the individual may be assured, true social order attained, the unity of our country restored, and concord established with other nations, do hereby adopt, enact, and give to ourselves this Constitution.'

Catholicism was at the very heart of the State.

Articles 41.1.1 and 41.1.2 assert that the family is the basis of order and good in society. It has natural rights superseding even man-made (positive) law:

'The State recognises the Family as the natural primary and fundamental unit group of society, and as a moral institution possessing inalienable and imprescriptible rights, antecedent and superior to all positive law', and 'The State, therefore, guarantees to protect the Family in its constitution and authority, as the necessary basis of social order and as indispensable to the welfare of the nation and the State.'

Articles 41.2.1 and 41.2.2 assert that women are the bedrock of family life:

'In particular, the State recognises that by her life within the home, woman gives to the State a support without which the common good cannot be achieved.

'The State shall, therefore, endeavour to ensure that mothers shall not be obliged by economic necessity to engage in labour to the neglect of their duties in the home.'

Perhaps one could infer from these statements that women in Ireland were regarded as having an authority and even rights superior to man-made law. Indeed it has been argued that these Articles give recognition to the unremunerated contribution homemakers (i.e. mothers) have made to Irish society, though the phrase 'neglect of their duties' gives the lie to this, reminding us that women may enjoy such veneration only as long as they know the realm in which they may enjoy it is firmly out of public life and instead within the privacy of the home. To extrapolate, once a woman became pregnant she was duty-bound to bear and rear.

These Articles stand today.

This was, and is, a Catholic Constitution for a Catholic people. It is worth looking briefly at where this (Catholic) Irish State had come from to understand just how potent was, and to some extent still is, the power of the Church over the functioning of the State.

Prior to Ireland's winning independence from Britain, the Irish Catholic Church had in effect become a parallel state, the force of authority and apparent compassion around which Irish Catholics could rally as the locus of national self-expression and self-determination. The Irish Church gradually grew stronger and more important as the institutional expression of what it was to be Irish, particularly after the hard-won Catholic Emancipation Act of 1829. That Act finally repealed the worst of British Penal Laws which had been in place since 1695 and which had prohibited Catholics from owning land, leasing land, taking up elected office, voting or in extreme times even practising as Catholics.

These laws had contributed to the rise of the British, Protestant landlord class, to the Irish hostility towards the British and to a concomitant undying loyalty to the Catholic Church. The two emotions – hostility to the British and love of the Church – went hand in glove, passed down through Irish generations. The defining attributes of Irishness were to be not British and to be Catholic.

The endless subdivision of tiny plots of land imposed by the Penal Laws and by British landlords forced Irish peasants into monoculture and potato dependency. When the staple crop failed so massively from 1845 to 1847, giving rise to the Great Famine, hatred of Britain and fealty to the Church reached un-precedented levels. The Great Hunger saw the population almost halve from 8 million to 5 million through starvation, disease and emigration. It was a watershed in Irish society and arguably did more to propel the Irish towards the War of Independence a generation later than any event before or after it.

It was a turning point for the Church. As the brightest and best left Ireland, those who remained were often among the least educated. Historian Oliver McDonagh, in an article published in *Irish Historical Studies* in 1947, titled 'The Irish Catholic Clergy and Emigration during the Great Famine', writes that 'lack of education had placed most of the people in a position of peculiar dependence upon their priests. Inevitably in these circumstances clerical guidance exceeded religious affairs. It did so particularly in a society in which poverty, tradition, politics and the fact that some priests belonged to their class, drew the clergy so close to the peasantry . . . The ordinary people in a parish usually regarded their priest as their shield against extraordinary injustice. In him they found, more or less, a focus for their inchoate purpose.'

By the time de Valera and his draftsmen were composing Bunreacht na hÉireann the Irish Catholic Church was the main focus for the Irish people and their inchoate purpose. Ireland was to declare itself a republic, though it was one which, having thrown off the yoke of British absolutism, drew about itself its own Irish, Catholic version.

As the Church of the vast majority of the population (93 per cent) it inevitably saw, and in many ways still sees, itself as both the guardian and the enforcer of the morals of *all* the people. The Irish Church is different to other nations' Catholic churches, not only by virtue of its intense relationship with the people, but also because of the central role it has had in the foundation and subsequent administration of the Irish State.

Its role in the provision of education, healthcare, social services and the alleviation of poverty predate the State's foundation. To this day it remains closely involved in managing schools, hospitals and other essential social services. The role of the local parish priest, as described by McDonagh's 1947 paper, continued well into modern Irish society, as the axis – for good or ill – of even the smallest Irish community.

The involvement of the Church at all these levels has been to the physical benefit of the people in many ways. Its concern for the poor and the marginalized in Irish society have marked it an enormous force for good. Its role here certainly suited a fledgling Irish State that could not afford to provide many of the services itself.

Remember too that at every level the State was manned by Roman Catholics, for whom Church involvement was perfectly natural. There was no reason to question it.

It would be naïve, however, to suppose the Church's intention was ever solely charitable. Its involvement has always been based on expressing and inculcating its ethos into the everyday so that its ethos appears to be 'common sense' rather than simply 'religious'. This is ideology working at its very best.

Father Kevin Doran, administrator of the Sacred Heart Parish in Donnybrook, Dublin, spoke to me in June 2013. I asked what he thought of the possibility that Catholic voluntary hospitals might be compelled to offer abortion services if soon-to-be-enacted legislation named them as places where they may be performed.

'I have no problem with the Church being significantly involved in healthcare in order to give expression to the values of the Gospel in the care of the sick,' he replied. 'But if the Church was to be involved in healthcare just for the sake of controlling the hospitals but wasn't actually able to give expression to its ethos, then I would say, "Let's get out of this and use our resources somewhere where there is a real need and we can give expression to our ethos."'

In this the Irish Catholic Church is no different to Catholic Churches anywhere. However, in Ireland where it has been almost the sole provider of schooling, hugely important in health and social services, and where it has had the loyal ear of parishioners and legislators, it has seen itself as protector not only of the Irish Catholic people's Catholic ethos but also, and far more fundamentally, of the Catholic ethos of the Irish State.

How this power was at times wielded through the formative years of the State is well documented. Those who stepped outside its moral strictures faced censure, and at times cruel punishment. Particularly at risk were those who appeared to challenge its enforcement of the 'rules' of sexual propriety.

Women were most harshly judged. Those who 'fell' (who became pregnant outside marriage, whether by rape or incest or simple lovemaking) were routinely expelled from their communities. They might be incarcerated in Magdalene laundries (institutions operated by religious originally as refuges for prostitutes but latterly as little more than prisons for thousands of women and girls across Ireland), or sent to other towns, or to England to have their babies adopted, often against their will and the cause of life-long heartache.

Children too were sent to industrial schools or orphanages, usually those of the State and again run by religious, where sexual, physical and emotional abuse existed.

David Quinn of the Iona Institute describes how this dominant 'cultural script' was 'ultra strictly enforced' from the early years of the State right up to the 1970s and even into the 1980s.

'If you didn't conform you were in trouble, big trouble. There was huge social stigma for anyone who stepped outside. The cultural script was cruelly enforced and that is why there has been the backlash against the Church in recent years. We on the conservative side are having to live with that legacy,' he told me in May 2013.

Such was the context in which the Church, through the years, fought virulently against any move by the Irish State to dilute its Catholic ethos. And there have been battles.

The first big one came in 1950 when the then Minister for Health Noel Browne proposed free medical care for all mothers and children up to the age of 16, much along the lines of the National Health Service then being rolled out across Britain. The introduction of a Bill for the Mother and Child Scheme became a major political crisis. To the Catholic bishops it was 'totalitarian in spirit' and an unacceptable interference in family life.

'We regard with the greatest apprehension the proposal to give to local medical officers the right to tell Catholic girls and women how they should behave in regard to this sphere of conduct at once so delicate and sacred. Gynaecological care may be, and in some other countries is, interpreted to include provision for birth limitation and abortion. We have no guarantee that State officials will respect Catholic principles in regard to these matters.'

The abortion battlefield was being surveyed by the Church even before it was joined.

Browne was a radical Catholic of his time, for though he was a devout observer, he advocated division of Church and State on social matters. He found little support for his scheme, however, even from the medical profession, and was forced to resign his Ministry and membership of his party, Clann na Poblachta, on 11 April 1951. His party leader, Seán MacBride, refused to back him.

The legislature and the courts would be the venues for the wars of wills, between the Church and some of its people, in coming decades. Dublin mother Mary McGee had to go all the way to the Supreme Court in 1974 to overturn the ban on the importation of contraceptives by married couples. Her success would begin to stir Ireland's incipient anti-abortion lobby into action.

In 1972 she was 27, and living in a caravan with her husband and four young children, including one set of twins. Her three pregnancies had been very close and the third had involved a series of medical complications. She was advised not to have any more children and was fitted with a cap by Dr James Loughran of the Irish Family Planning Association. The spermicidal jelly she needed, however, was not available in Ireland and so she had to import it from Britain: this was a crime. The Irish customs officials' remarkable vigilance saw the packages being seized and so Mrs McGee, encouraged by the Irish Family Planning Association (IFPA), went to court as the situation was putting her life at risk.

She asserted in the High Court in 1972 that her family's right to privacy was being violated by the ban on importation of spermicidal jelly. The court ruled against her, basing its ruling on the view that the ban on importing the contraceptive, and the assertion in the Constitution that the family had inalienable rights, were both drawn from Catholic teaching and therefore could not be incompatible. When the case went to the Supreme Court, however, the judges took an approach that was radical for the time.

Drawing on Article 34 of the Constitution, which vests in the High Court and Supreme Court powers to interpret the articles of the Constitution, the Supreme Court overturned the ruling. Part of its reasoning was, according to Chrystel Hug in her authoritative book, *The Politics of Sexual Morality in Ireland*, the growing conviction that the Constitution in its preamble gave judges the liberty to interpret the rights of citizens 'by applying their own ideas of prudence, justice and charity'.

Said one of the five justices, Justice Brian Walsh, in his judgment, 'It is natural that from time to time the prevailing ideas of these virtues may be conditioned by the passage of time; no interpretation of the Constitution is intended to be final for all time. It is given in the light of prevailing ideas and concepts.' Judge Walsh was considered the foremost authority on Irish constitutional law at the time.

In an interview with the *Irish Times*, published in May 2013, Mary McGee recounts her contention that the majority of people in Ireland in 1973 supported her battle against the contraceptive ban. 'I think we were all ready for change though. People wanted children but they also wanted a life.'

Such sentiments were of concern to those against abortion, who saw contraception and abortion as part of the same continuum. Anti-abortion unease was growing, even though abortion was illegal under the 1861 Offences Against the Person Act, which says 'every woman, being with child, who, with intent to procure her own miscarriage, shall unlawfully administer to herself any poison or other noxious thing, or shall unlawfully use

any instrument or other means whatsoever with the like intent
. . . shall be guilty of a felony'.

The McGee case came hot on the heels of Ireland's joining the
European Community in 1973. As Ireland was the only member
state where abortion was still illegal there was concern that legal
abortion might be imposed by Europe. There were also growing
concerns that judicial interpretation of marital privacy might
soon include the right to abortion. The 1973 *Roe* v. *Wade* case in
the United States had decriminalized abortion on just those
grounds. The final 'warning' came with the 1979 Health (Family
Planning) Act which allowed the sale of contraceptives on
prescription.

The Pro-Life Amendment Campaign (PLAC) was founded in
April 1981 specifically to campaign for an amendment to the
Constitution in order to protect the life of the unborn. It had
strong Catholic Church support and involvement. Both the then
Taoiseach, Charles Haughey, and the leader of the opposition,
Garret FitzGerald, were approached and both agreed that a
referendum would be put to the people. Political instability at the
time – there were four general elections between 1979 and 1982
– created an atmosphere where the two main political parties,
Fianna Fáil and Fine Gael, vied to outdo each other in winning
this pro-life vote.

The Anti-Amendment Campaign (AAC) was launched in June
1982 to fight the campaign to copper-fasten a ban on abortion
into the Constitution. Its members included doctors, lawyers,
journalists and feminists.

In November the Fianna Fáil government published its wording for an amendment: 'The State acknowledges the right to life
of the unborn and, with due regard to the equal right to life of
the mother, guarantees in its laws to respect and, as far as
practicable, by its laws to defend and vindicate that right.'

It was cautiously welcomed by the PLAC, though some did
raise concerns about the word 'unborn' as it left open the

question of when a fertilized ovum became 'unborn'. The AAC attacked the wording, saying it would threaten the lives of women, that it would endanger medical practice, that it threatened the availability of some forms of contraception and that it would further alienate Protestant unionists in Northern Ireland at a time when efforts were being made to engage them. Senator Mary Robinson commented presciently that the wording 'would throw the entire matter into the lap of the courts'.

Garret FitzGerald gave his wholehearted support to the wording and said it would be in the programme for Government after the forthcoming general election. A Fine Gael–Labour coalition was returned on 24 November 1982 and as FitzGerald had promised, the Fianna Fáil wording was accepted, without any real examination of its legal or medical implications. There was some debate about the wording and Fine Gael published its own version in March 1983: 'Nothing in this Constitution shall be invoked to invalidate any provision of a law on the ground that it prohibits abortion.' Most in Leinster House disliked it and in the end the Fianna Fáil wording was adopted on 27 April.

The campaigning for and against was fierce but in the end the Eighth Amendment to the Constitution was passed, on 7 September 1983, by a majority of two to one (66.9 in favour, 33.1 against) on a turnout of 54.1 per cent.

Emboldened, the Society for the Protection of the Unborn Child (SPUC) turned its attention to clinics providing abortion information and referral services. In October 1986 it won an injunction against Open Door Counselling (which had opened in 1978) and the Well Woman Centre (opened 1978). An appeal to the Supreme Court in 1988 failed. SPUC won on both occasions as the courts ruled that provision of non-directive counselling about and information on abortion was contrary to Article 40.3.3.

Next on their list were three students' unions and SPUC obtained a High Court injunction against their distribution of student handbooks containing addresses and phone numbers for abortion clinics in Britain. Their case went to the High Court, the Supreme Court, the European Court of Justice, back to the Supreme Court and eventually to the European Community and the European Council. As the cases progressed, any publication giving information about abortion services was hounded out of Ireland. The British women's magazines *Cosmopolitan* and *Company* were banned until they removed the ads from their Irish editions. British phone books were removed from public libraries.

In October 1992, the Irish courts' injunctions against provision of information on abortion services in other countries would be declared to be in violation of Article 10 of the European Convention on Human Rights, which guarantees freedom of expression.

The European Court of Justice would find the Irish courts' injunction against Open Door and Well Woman's receiving or imparting information on abortion services legally available in other countries disproportionate, and that it created a risk to the health of women who might seek abortion outside the State.

Also in 1992, the X case broke.

On Wednesday 12 February 1992 the *Irish Times* had as its front-page picture an image of the new Taoiseach, Albert Reynolds, receiving his seals of office from President Mary Robinson. Down the page a small piece by reporter Niall Kiely ran under the headline: 'State attempts to stop girl's abortion'.

'The State is understood to be engaged in a legal action to prevent a 14-year-old Irish girl who is allegedly the victim of a rape from having an abortion in Britain.

'An interim injunction was granted to the Attorney General following a High Court hearing held in camera late last week. This injunction restricted the teenager or her parents from procuring a termination of her pregnancy in the UK.'

By the time the order had been served the girl was already in

Britain with her mother and they had to return to Ireland without her having had the termination, to await a full hearing of the High Court.

The child in question, who lived in south County Dublin and was understood to be from a middle-class family, had been raped repeatedly by the father of a friend of hers over a two-year period. She had become withdrawn and depressed and had not spoken to her parents about the abuse until she became pregnant. Her parents, though against abortion, decided to take her to Britain to abort the pregnancy and asked the Gardai if DNA evidence from the foetus could be used in a prosecution of the alleged rapist. When the Gardai sought legal advice from the Director of Public Prosecutions, and the DPP sought advice from the Attorney General's office, the Attorney General, Harry Whelehan, took it upon himself to seek a High Court injunction preventing the abortion taking place.

As demands were made in the Dáil that Mr Whelehan publicly explain his actions, he refused, saying that to do so would be contempt of court. The outgoing Minister for Justice, Ray Burke, confirmed he had not been consulted about the case and Mr Whelehan's office confirmed he had been acting unilaterally of the Government and under powers conferred on him to take independent action as 'guardian of the public interest'.

Chairman of the Progressive Democrats party Michael McDowell insisted the general issues must be discussed as a matter of urgency. He said he believed most people 'like myself who oppose the legalisation of abortion' would nevertheless be of the opinion that there should be 'no legal jurisdiction to compel a woman or girl, who has been the victim of unlawful intercourse to allow any conception to proceed through pregnancy to birth, by preventing such a person from going abroad for a legal abortion'.

From the start the focus was immediately on the girl's right to travel. No one, from a reading of press coverage at the time, appears to have suggested that the girl might be allowed to have an abortion in Ireland. This is understandable, given the 1983 amendment and that the Attorney General's application was to prevent her travelling. However, this narrowed the debate in such a way that the eventual ruling of the Supreme Court, when published, was to cause complete consternation.

Among those supporting the 14-year-old girl's right to travel for an abortion was the leader of the Workers' Party, Proinsias De Rossa, who said he was quite sure most people who voted for the Pro-Life Amendment in 1983 'would not have envisaged that it would have led to a situation in which the Attorney General is seeking to prevent a 14-year-old rape victim from undergoing a medical procedure which is totally legal in the UK'.

Four members of the 1983 Anti-Amendment Campaign – Anne O'Donnell, Ray Kavanagh, Mary Holland and Anne Marie Hourihane – issued a statement recalling that at the time 'one of the main reasons we opposed the amendment was because we feared that individual women and girls who found themselves pregnant as a result of rape or other complex circumstances' would be prevented from travelling.

'The "pro-life" lobby rejected our fears about the possibility of Irish citizens being prevented from travelling outside the country for abortions as hysterical. They accused us of always arguing the "hard cases". Now, as predicted, we have a real, live "hard case" . . . In 1983 we believed the so-called "pro-life" amendment was nothing but an exercise in national hypocrisy. Our worst fears have been realized. How bitter it is to say, "We told you so".'

The director of the Catholic Press Office, Jim Cantwell, countered that it would be wrong ever to have an abortion following rape. 'Because rape is an act of violence, the victim has the moral right to seek medical help with a view to preventing conception. Should conception occur however a new human being then exists. This innocent human being cannot rightly be made to pay the penalty of death for the crime of another. Its right to life must be protected.'

All now awaited the ruling from Mr Justice Declan Costello in the High Court on Mr Whelehan's application. This he delivered on Monday, 17 February 1992.

His decision to uphold Whelehan's application caused total uproar. Justice Costello outlined how the girl had been subjected to sexual abuse by the man for two years and how he had heard evidence from a child clinical psychologist that the girl, on return from England, had 'coldly expressed a desire to solve matters by ending her life'.

In his report the psychologist, a State-employed expert, said: 'the psychological damage to her of carrying a child would be considerable and the damage to her mental health would be devastating'. This child, who had been repeatedly raped, now faced the prospect of being ordered, by the State of which she was a young citizen, to carry her rapist's child to term. The long-term impact on her welfare did not appear to be under consideration.

In a rigorous imposition of the 'clear rule of law' laid out in the 1983 amendment, Justice Costello ruled that whilst the threat to the life of the girl was not certain, the threat to that of the unborn would be definite were the termination in Britain to be facilitated. He put a restraining order on her from leaving the jurisdiction until the baby was born.

The Attorney General, Mr Whelehan, immediately made it clear he would advise the Government there was no need for a change in the law, while the family indicated it was unlikely to appeal to the Supreme Court.

That lunchtime there was a spontaneous protest outside Government Buildings. People carried banners with such slogans as 'Rapists 1, Women 0' and 'Ireland defends men's right to procreate by rape'. Maxine Brady, President of the Union of Students in Ireland, addressed the crowd. 'We have now witnessed the occurrence of exactly what the 1983 referendum said would never happen. We were promised this wouldn't happen.' Among the chants cried out were 'SPUC the State. SPUC the Government. SPUC off!' and 'Not the Church. Not the State. Women must decide their fate.'

Inside, in the Dáil chamber, voices called for the Eighth Amendment to be altered, or even scrapped. Fine Gael spokesman on Justice Alan Shatter said: 'There can be no doubt that there is a substantial problem presented by the constitutional amendment that must be addressed.' Former leader of Fine Gael Alan Dukes said that for the sake of rape victims and for any woman for whom pregnancy might be 'lethal' the amendment had to be changed: 'If we cannot have that, we need, and we need very quickly, a law that will curb the worst excesses of this deadly piece of misogyny.'

Fine Gael TD Nuala Fennell said the case showed that the amendment was 'seriously flawed', adding: 'There must be political commitment for the article to be amended or dropped completely.'

Anti-abortion activists were reportedly reluctant to comment on the case. Many expressed surprise at the media's focus. SPUC said: 'It is remarkable how much of this attention has focused on abortion and how little on the crime of rape and the right to life of the unborn.'

According to Des McDonnell, spokesman for Family Solidarity, nothing his organization knew about the case would cause it to review its position on abortion. In a stunning statement on the 14-year-old rape victim's case he said: 'I can't see it as being considered anything out of the ordinary. The sole purpose of the amendment was to protect the life of the unborn and I don't see anything to change that view.'

Bernadette Bonner, a leading anti-abortion activist at the time, suggested the whole case could be a 'set-up'. In an interview with RTE Radio's *News at One* programme on Tuesday, 18 February, she said: 'We have not got the information, absolute information, it . . . may be this could be a set-up. We don't know.'

Interviewer Shane Kenny asked: 'Are you suggesting this is a set-up?'

The other interviewee, Alan Dukes, then cut in: 'Is it to be suggested now that a case of this kind is a set-up? Really?'

Bonner replied: 'No, but we're saying, "Who's behind it?" The pro-abortion people have come out of the wood now, Alan, and they're all of them using this case.'

Dukes cut straight back. 'Oh no, we will not allow that lady . . . I will not allow you, Bernadette, to come along and say that pro-abortion people have come out of the wood. They tried that label in 1982. It was gross slander then and it is gross slander now.'

Ms Bonner later said she accepted the 'authenticity' of the case.

The reaction abroad was of shock. In the Netherlands parliamentarians called on their political leaders to lodge protests with their Irish counterparts. In France, *Libération* newspaper said the issue put Ireland's continued membership of the EC into question. In Australia leading senator Chris Schacht described the Irish legal situation as 'barbarous' and one which 'has taken Ireland back to the Dark Ages'. In the United States there were protests outside the Irish embassy and consulates, while in Britain there was also a protest outside the Irish embassy as the story led in the *Independent* newspaper and gave rise to editorial leaders in that paper and in *The Times* of London. The *Independent*, which also circulates in Ireland, published the phone number of the London-based Irish Women's Abortion Support Group – at that stage still a breach of Irish law.

Even anti-abortion campaigners began to voice concern, saying they had not envisaged a scenario such as the one unfolding, when they campaigned in 1983. Fianna Fáil senator Des Hanafin was asked on RTE Radio whether the PLAC had foreseen a case such as this. 'No, we didn't think this would happen and we never had any quarrel with the individual because one couldn't at that stage know the state of mind of the girl that might be travelling to England for an abortion. It was never our intention. Certainly it was our intention to stop abortion ever taking place in this country and we're successful in that.'

As protestors gathered with their candles for a vigil outside Leinster House on the night of Wednesday, 19 February, the President, Mary Robinson, intervened in the crisis. Addressing women's groups in Waterford, she said: 'I cannot but say this has been a very difficult week for women and girls in Ireland . . . Although as President I have no role in relation to either any possible constitutional or legislative changes, in a curious way as President I am very much in touch with what women and girls all over the country are feeling – and not just women because there are very many men who are as troubled and . . . I hope we [women] have the courage which we have not always had to face up to and look squarely and say we have got to [have] resolve.'

As the political agony grew, Government sources indicated to the Leinster House political correspondents that if the family of the girl wanted to appeal to the Supreme Court, all the facilities of the State would be made available; the issue of legal costs would not arise for the family. Legal advisors in the AG's office and the Department of Justice were working full-time on the case. So an extraordinary situation arose, where the Government was urging the family to appeal to the Supreme Court and would pay their costs in a case in which the State would be the opposing side.

At the same time, supporters of the original Anti-Amendment Campaign were drawing up plans for a campaign to have the Eighth Amendment repealed.

The family's acceptance the next day, Thursday the 18th, of the Government's offer was greeted with relief all round. Taoiseach Albert Reynolds was 'very pleased' the family would appeal to the Supreme Court, and went on to say that he hoped an amendment to the Constitution could be 'avoided if at all possible'. He also insisted the issue at hand was not the 'substantive' one of abortion: 'The issue is that the family was prevented from going to England for an abortion.'

In an astonishing intervention on Friday, 19 February, the Catholic hierarchy revealed its legal advice: that the constitutional protection of the life of the unborn should not have prevented the girl from travelling. 'The advice received by the Hierarchy is that the phrase "as far as practicable" needs to be further explored by the courts with particular emphasis on the question of how acceptable it is to restrict people's freedom to travel outside the country,' reported the *Irish Times*. It is surprising that the Hierarchy should take such a laid-back view of women's and girls' right to leave the country to 'directly and intentionally take the lives of the unborn' in their wombs. The issue was not whether unborn lives would be taken, but where they would be taken.

In an excoriating editorial the following day, the leader writer for the *Irish Times* said: 'Seldom – maybe never – in the recall of this newspaper has there been such widespread, seething anger: at the State, its laws, its institutions and officers . . . Here this week it is the State – safe, benign, family-loving Ireland, which has visited such cruelty on one of its own children.

'It may have been a maturing week for some in Ireland. Many who were not moved by the supposed objects of the 1983 amendment but who went along with it, believing it could do no harm, have come to a sobering realisation that they were used.' There was now a 'palpable hope', the writer noted, that the Supreme Court would take a different view to that of Justice Costello. Failing that, there was the hope, said the writer, that the family might just defy Ireland and take off for England.

'And it is in this that we encounter what is perhaps the most depressing aspect of everything that has emerged this week. That which would be wrong in Ireland may be deemed to be somehow less wrong if the unfortunate child is transported to London. An Irish child is raped in an Irish city. The case is investigated by

Irish police officers and will be dealt with, in time, by an Irish court. But the dirty business we will leave to England.'

All eyes now turned to the Supreme Court which would hear the case on 24–25 February.

On Wednesday the 26th, the Supreme Court overturned the High Court ruling.

To a surprised court, Chief Justice Mr Thomas Finlay said the appeal was allowed and the High Court order, which had the effect of preventing the girl's abortion, would be set aside. The Taoiseach was 'delighted' the appeal had been upheld. 'The family is now free to take whatever action they wish,' he said. It was also welcomed by pro-choice and anti-abortion groups alike. Expressing 'delight and relief', the Council for the Status of Women said it hoped the family and girl would now be left in peace. Pro-choice groups to a one said the Eighth Amendment now needed to be repealed.

Anti-abortion campaigners said the judgment showed that the 1983 amendment had never been intended to stop women and girls travelling; Dr Mary Luccy, spokeswoman for SPUC, said the organization had not wanted that and did not think the judiciary had in any way given a green light for abortion. According to Des McDonnell of Family Solidarity, those who supported the 1983 amendment had been proved correct. 'We are not moral policemen and we acknowledge the right to travel,' he said. Senator Hanafin said the people had always wanted the girl to have the right to travel and he expressed his relief that she now had it. 'The amendment had proved now to be a good amendment, a compassionate amendment, sympathetic and it obviously only deals with these shores within this State,' said Senator Hanafin.

Regius Professor of Laws at Trinity College and supporter of the Pro-life Campaign William Binchy, in a piece for the *Irish Times* on Thursday, 27 February, said: 'Those who sought the amendment have been vindicated by the Supreme Court in their interpretation of every relevant legal principle.'

Everyone was relieved and all talk at political level about another amendment or the scrapping of the Pro-Life Amendment dissipated.

The texts of the rulings of the five Supreme Court justices were published the following week and outraged the anti-abortion lobby. The judgments did not overturn Justice Costello's opinion that the girl should be restrained from travelling for an abortion. Three of the judges upheld this point of law in situations where there was no right to an abortion.

Radically, by a majority of 4 to 1, the judges considered the threat to the girl's life by suicide to be sufficiently 'real and substantial' for her to be legally entitled to an abortion. Abortion was now legal in Ireland, albeit in narrowly limited circumstances: where there was a 'real and substantial risk to the life, as distinct from the health, of the mother', including the risk of suicide. The girl was thus legally entitled to an abortion and so could travel to Britain for one.

The judgment has been described variously as 'flawed', 'wrong', 'dangerous' and 'out of touch with the Irish people' by anti-abortion campaigners ever since.

Four of the judges did not take a 'face value' approach to the Eighth Amendment. Radically, they interpreted and indeed developed its meaning. Their approach echoed that of Justice Walsh in the McGee contraceptive case ten years previously.

Justice C. J. Finlay said in his judgment that a harmonious interpretation of the Constitution involved a consideration of the rights and obligations of the unborn, of the mother and also of the interrelation of these rights with those of other people. The court must also be concerned 'with the position of the mother within a family group, with persons on whom she is dependent, with in other instances, persons who are dependent on her and her interaction with other citizens and members of society in the areas in which her activities occur'.

He said the threat of suicide could not be monitored constantly through a pregnancy in the way the progression of a physical illness could and so it might be impossible to prevent the girl committing suicide if she was intent on it. The threat to her life thus did not have to be immediate or inevitable, as this would insufficiently vindicate her right to life.

'I am therefore satisfied . . . as a matter of probability that there is a real and substantial risk to the life of the mother by self-destruction which can only be avoided by termination of her pregnancy.'

Justice Niall McCarthy in his ruling spoke of the girl having a right not just to a physical life, but to her 'life in being'. And in taking this meaning for the word 'life' he said: 'If the right to life of the mother is threatened by the pregnancy and it is practicable to vindicate that right, then because of the due regard which must be paid to the equal right to life of the mother, it may not be practicable to vindicate the right to life of the unborn.'

He continued: 'It is not a question of balancing the life of the unborn against the life of the mother; if it were, the life of the unborn would virtually always have to be preserved . . . In my view the true construction of the Amendment, bearing in mind the other provisions of Article 40 and the fundamental rights of the family guaranteed by Article 41, is that paying due regard to the equal right to life of the mother when there is a real and substantial risk attached to her survival not merely at the time of application but in contemplation at least throughout the pregnancy, then it may not be practicable to vindicate the right to life of the unborn. It is not a question of a risk of a different order of magnitude; it can never be otherwise than a risk of a different order of magnitude.'

In other words, when the pregnancy itself is threatening the mental and emotional life of the mother throughout the course of the pregnancy, and her physical life too is threatened by the possibility of her committing suicide, the risk to her life is of an altogether greater magnitude than the threat to the physical life of the unborn posed by termination.

As already said, the judgment has been attacked since as 'flawed' by anti-abortion campaigners because the evidence given to the High Court as to the girl's mental distress was from a non-medical psychologist rather than a psychiatrist. If it was flawed by anything, suggests Rhona Mahony, Master of the National Maternity Hospital, in an interview in June 2013, it was flawed with compassion. 'Everyone should read those Supreme Court judgments. They are full of humanity and compassion,' she says.

Former Supreme Court Justice Catherine McGuinness, addressing the Oireachtas Health Committee in January 2012, said of the X judgment: 'The Court made a genuine effort to reach the huge human dilemma put before it rather than simply approaching it from a theoretical point of view. It made excellent arguments with regard to the way in which the Constitution should be interpreted.'

In this, one might say, the Supreme Court ruling put right, in some way, the impact of a flawed Eighth Amendment. It could be cogently argued also that had the Supreme Court not overturned the Costello judgment and the girl had been forced to bear her rapist's child, the pressure to abandon the Eighth Amendment would have proved irresistible. As things stood, this pressure waned and the Government was off the hook as regards a referendum on the 'substantive issue' of abortion.

Justice McCarthy was scathing in his comments about the in-action of the legislature since 1983. 'I think it reasonable, however, to hold that the People when enacting the Amendment were entitled to believe that legislation would be introduced so as to regulate the manner in which the right to life of the unborn and the right to life of the mother could be reconciled.'

The continued failure to legislate, he said, was 'no longer just unfortunate; it is inexcusable. What are pregnant women to do? What are the parents of a pregnant girl underage to do? What are the medical profession to do? They have no guidelines save what may be gleaned from the judgments in this case. What additional considerations are there? Is the victim of rape, statutory or otherwise, or the victim of incest, finding herself pregnant, to be assessed in a manner different from others? The Amendment, born of public disquiet, historically divisive of our people, guaranteeing in its laws to respect and by its laws to defend the right to life of the unborn, remains bare of legislative direction.'

The anti-abortion lobby, when successfully fighting for the Eighth Amendment, had not wanted legislative guidance on what it meant. That would negate entirely its point, but here now was legislation being demanded by the supreme legal authority in the land.

For the first time Ireland now heard its politicians speak openly about the possibility of abortion being carried out in Ireland. Mary Harney, Minister of State at the Department of the Environment, commented on national television: 'If it is morally wrong in Dublin I cannot see why it is morally right in London.'

Despite Justice McCarthy's criticism of the State, and Albert Reynolds declaring after the judgment that he did not want to govern in a police state, the 'substantive' issue was sidestepped as three referendums – the possible Twelfth, Thirteenth and Fourteenth amendments – were put to the people on 25 November 1992. These were to address a number of arising issues – the right of pregnant women to travel; the right of Irish women to information on abortion services abroad and of clinics to provide it; and, following anti-abortion disquiet after the Supreme Court ruling, a proposal to remove suicidality as a grounds for abortion.

The Twelfth Amendment proposing that the possibility of suicide was not a sufficient threat to justify an abortion was rejected by 65 per cent to 35 per cent.

The Thirteenth Amendment proposal that the prohibition of

abortion would not limit freedom of travel from Ireland to other countries where a person might legally obtain an abortion was approved, by 62 per cent to 38 per cent.

The Fourteenth Amendment proposal that Irish citizens should have the freedom to pursue and learn about abortion services in other countries was approved by 60 per cent to 40 per cent.

The right to information about, and freedom to travel for, abortions *outside* the State seemed assured for all. The right to travel, however, was to be tested five years later, in another 'crisis' case.

In August 1997 a 13-year-old girl from the Travelling community was raped while being driven home by her attacker. She had been babysitting for him and his wife. She was to become known as Miss C. She became pregnant and was taken into temporary care by the Eastern Health Board because of the rape. In November she indicated that she wanted to have an abortion. As she was in state care, the EHB was advised it could not facilitate her going to Britain for an abortion. The only solution appeared to be that she would have to go back into the care of her parents. An agreement to this effect was in train and due to be formalized at the Children's Court in Dublin on 19 November 1997.

Again, the Dáil was faced with an appalling human tragedy involving a minor, raped, wishing to have an abortion, and the State, in the form of the EHB, standing in her way. The Minister for Health, Brian Cowen, said there would have to be either another referendum, though he did not say to what purpose, or legislation.

The case did come before the court, which heard the father had changed his mind and now did not consent to his daughter travelling for an abortion. According to the report in the *Irish Times*: 'His change of mind coincided with the appearance at the court of prominent anti-abortion campaigners, including Mr

Peter Scully of Family and Life and Una Bean Mhic Mhathúna. The girl's parents arrived in court in the company of anti-abortion campaigners who stayed with them until the case was heard.'

The case came back to the Children's Court two days later. Following an eight-hour hearing the judge ruled that the girl was entitled to travel as she was likely to take her own life if forced to carry on with the pregnancy. She was to stay in the care of the EHB and not return to her parents. The case went immediately to the High Court. In a special late-evening sitting it put a stay on the Children's Court ruling, to allow the parents time to appeal.

That evening, Taoiseach Bertie Ahern, speaking in Luxembourg, said: 'I believe we have an obligation to prepare the legislation [on abortion].' He said the legal limbo since 1992 could not continue.

On 27 November Justice Hugh Geoghegan in the High Court upheld the Children's Court ruling that as Miss C was likely to take her own life if forced to continue with the pregnancy, she was entitled to an abortion. Though she could legally now have had the abortion in Ireland, the EHB social workers took her to Britain.

With another crisis averted through the good offices of the courts, the Government did not move hastily to legislate, but opened up a national discussion on what to do about abortion. A Green Paper would be drawn up to 'stimulate and to facilitate informed public discussion on the options in relation to the issue of abortion in the light of the range of constitutional, legal, medical, moral, social and ethical issues involved'. An inter-departmental working group would be established to draw up such a discussion document under the auspices of a Cabinet committee chaired by Minister Cowen.

In September 1999, the Green Paper was published, setting out seven options. These were: an absolute constitutional ban on abortion; amendment of the Constitution to remove suicide as grounds for abortion; retention of the status quo; retention of the status quo along with legislation to restate the prohibition on abortion, which would make it more difficult to obtain abortion on the grounds of suicidality; legislation in line with the X case; deletion of Article 40.3.3 and reversion to the pre-1983 position; and allowing abortion in circumstances beyond X. It was roundly welcomed as an authoritative and considered piece of work underlining the complexities of the Irish abortion issue.

The all-party Oireachtas Committee on the Constitution then began hearings on the issues. It was chaired by the late Brian Lenihan and fourteen months later in November 2000 it published a 700-page report without reaching agreement on what to do about the legal issues of abortion. It offered three options for consideration: a referendum on a bill to reverse the X case ruling; the establishment of a Crisis Pregnancy Agency (CPA) to reduce the number of crisis pregnancies; and/or legislation to give effect to X. The report was sent for the consideration of a Cabinet subcommittee chaired by Minister for Health Micheál Martin. The subcommittee was split between the legislative and the referendum options, though agreed on the establishment of a CPA. This was set up the following year.

On 3 October 2001 the Government announced it would hold a referendum the following year, in which voters would be asked to either accept or reject the Protection of Human Life in Pregnancy Bill, which would remove threat of suicide as grounds for abortion and increase the penalties for helping a woman have an abortion.

The referendum campaign confused voters enormously, with both pro-choice and extreme anti-abortion campaigners urging a 'No' vote. While choice campaigners objected to the removal of suicide as grounds for abortion, those on the extreme right railed against the fact that the Bill defined the unborn life as starting at conception rather than at fertilization. In the end just 43 per cent of the electorate turned out; 50.4 per cent of them voted against, with 49.6 per cent voting in favour. The electorate, by the slimmest of margins, had again rejected the proposal to remove suicidality as grounds for abortion.

Over the next decade there were further crisis cases before the courts, both in Ireland and in Europe.

In 2005 a Dublin mother, Deirdre Conroy – known at the time as D – took a case to the European Court of Human Rights. She had been pregnant with twins but decided to terminate her pregnancy after learning that one of the unborn had died in the womb and the other had developed a foetal anomaly. She argued that her rights had been violated as she had been unable to access an abortion in Ireland. Significantly, Gerard Hogan SC, acting for the Irish State, argued that had D taken a case in the Irish courts, she would have been allowed an abortion in Ireland. He said that although Article 40.3.3 excluded a liberal abortion regime, 'the courts were nonetheless unlikely to interpret the provision with remorseless logic, especially when the facts were exceptional' and that there was an 'at least tenable' argument that the foetus could be seen by the Irish courts as not in need of having its life protected as it had no prospect of having a life. Accepting this argument, the court ruled that D had not exhausted all domestic avenues and ruled against her.

In May 2007 a 17-year-old known as Miss D, who was in the care of the State, discovered she had an anencephalic pregnancy and wished to terminate it. She refused to say she was suicidal and so could not 'fit' into the X rubric. The Health Service Executive (HSE) wrote to the police asking that they arrest Miss D if she attempted to leave the country, and also asked the Passport Office to refuse to issue her with a passport. She was thus forced into the High Court to obtain permission to travel. Mr Justice Liam McKechnie ruled that she had a right to travel and he criticized the HSE for failing to put the 17-year-old girl in its care at the heart of its decision-making.

In December 2010, the most important case in this list came to a conclusion. It was so important because the ruling went against the State and came from a European Court whose rulings were binding.

In the case of *A, B and C* v. *Ireland*, the Grand Chamber of the European Court of Human Rights (ECHR) unanimously ruled that Ireland's failure to clarify when and how the existing right to an abortion, when a woman's life was at risk, could be accessed had violated Applicant C's right to a private life.

C, a Lithuanian woman resident in Ireland, had had to have chemotherapy while pregnant and had had to travel to England for an abortion before commencing the cancer treatment. The ECHR found in C's favour, ruling that, because of the failure of the State to legislate for the constitutional right to an abortion where her life was at risk, she realistically could not avail of either appropriate medical consultation or legal options to establish her right to a lawful abortion.

The Court said the blanket ban on abortion in the 1861 Offences Against the Person Act had a 'chilling effect' and was a source of legal uncertainty which inhibited both doctors and pregnant women.

The Government accepted the ruling as binding and committed to acting on it. Whether that would be through legislation, regulation or otherwise had yet to be decided. But it would act.

The following June (2011), the Government announced it would establish an Expert Group to gather opinion and report back to Government with options on how to act on the ECHR ruling. (This vital report would be delayed a number of times and was eventually submitted to Government the night before the news of Savita's death broke.)

With 2012 came the 20th anniversary of the X case ruling and renewed vigour on both 'sides' of the debate. The report from the Government's Expert Group was also anticipated in the summer.

In January a number of pro-choice activists came together to found Action on X, 'to put some pressure on the Government', recalls pro-choice activist Sinead Kennedy.

In March and April a group of women went public about their experiences of abortion. They had had to travel for abortions when they found that the foetuses they were carrying had fatal anomalies. They spoke out first in the *Irish Times*, then to parliamentarians in Leinster House, and some days later on RTE's *Late Late Show*. They had a powerful impact, as they were ordinary women speaking openly about the pain and anger they felt at having been forced to leave the country they called home to seek out a service they believed passionately should be available in their own country.

Through the summer there was ongoing discussion at political level about whether members of the Irish parliament or Dáil, TDs, should be allowed a 'free vote' if and when there might be legislation on abortion following the awaited recommendations from the Expert Group.

In June and July Youth Defence unveiled a national campaign that enraged thousands and brought many young people into pro-choice activism for the first time. The 'Abortion Tears Her Life Apart' campaign involved large ads on billboards and on buses depicting torn scans of an 18-week foetus and of sad-looking women, with the messages 'There is always a better answer' and 'No More Shame'. Many people found the ads offensive and there were hundreds of complaints to the Advertising Standards Authority. However, it was unable to take action against Youth Defence as it was not advertising a product. Numerous pro-choice activists interviewed for this book pointed to this campaign as a seminal moment. The Youth Defence campaign had backfired, drawing a new generation of young activists to the pro-choice cause.

At the end of July the Irish Choice Network was founded to build a strategy towards and beyond the much-anticipated

Expert Group report. Meetings around the country were attended by both veteran activists and the thousands of new young faces who were getting involved in choice politics for the first time. A new group, Galway Pro-choice, was established in the summer. One of its founder members, student Sarah McCarthy, recalls 'a really amazing new energy in that group'.

'We started setting up the basics – got an email account set up. We had a public meeting in the Harbour Hotel that Clare Daly [Independent TD] spoke at, in early September. We called that "Beyond the X-case. A woman's right to choose". The reception at that was incredible. So for a couple of months after that we held stalls on Shop Street. We just kept organizing and had another public meeting. It was very embryonic but people began to know we existed and it just grew.'

In August, Catholic Primate of All-Ireland Cardinal Seán Brady warned that if the Expert Group recommended legislation there would be an all-out campaign by the Church against it. As to the form this campaign would take, Church sources told the *Irish Times*, priests would be equipped with ample, high-quality 'pro-life' material for preaching and personal contact with parishioners.

On 29 September 2012, to mark the International Day for the Decriminalization of Abortion, several thousand took part in a March for Choice in Dublin, calling for X case legislation. It was planned as a major mobilization of pro-choice activists as the issue came increasingly to the fore.

A month later, Savita walked into Galway University Hospital.

4

Praveen's immediate response to Savita's death was to collapse. As the intensive care staff stepped back from her bed, Praveen's friend Laxmish helped him out to the waiting area where up to forty of his and Savita's friends had been arriving, praying and being together since morning.

Praveen vomited in the waiting area, and was unable to speak to anyone. When Garda Mark Kerrisk from Mill Street Garda Station arrived at about 1.50 a.m. to witness Praveen identify his wife's body, Praveen had to be supported by two friends. 'He couldn't even stand, couldn't speak,' recalls his friend, Dr Chalikonda Prasad. 'He was exhausted too, and just went catatonic. Shock and total exhaustion.'

He didn't go home to Roscam that night. He has never slept again in the house he and Savita shared at 123 Ros Caoin. He stayed instead with a friend who lived near the hospital, and while Savita's body remained in the hospital for post-mortem and certification, he hardly ate.

'He didn't speak or talk to anyone for most of the next two days,' recalls Dr Prasad. 'No one could get through to him. So, well, we all began making the arrangements.'

First they had to find an undertaker who could arrange to have Savita's remains brought home to Belgaum. After some phoning, they found a Monaghan-based undertaker, Wards, which had expertise in repatriating remains. Among the documents they had to gather in order to be granted the certificate was a declaration that Savita had no debts in Ireland. 'Praveen had to give an undertaking that Savita didn't owe money to anybody and if there were any monies owed that he would be responsible. Savita didn't even have a bank account,' says Dr Prasad. 'We thought "How are we going to ask Praveen to do this letter?", but after a few days he came through, began to communicate, and we got him to sign the letter.'

Monday was a bank holiday so the post-mortem was carried out the next day, by Dr Grace Callagy, pathologist at the hospital.

That evening, Praveen met a solicitor, a contact of his friend Dr Prasad. That solicitor, Gerard O'Donnell of O'Donnell Waters solicitors in Galway, recalls how he first met Praveen.

'On bank holiday Monday evening, the day after she died, Prasad rang me at home to tell me about a friend of his whose wife had died, and that she had died needlessly, at Galway University Hospital. He asked if perhaps I might meet him the following night. So, I did. I met him the following evening in the Ardilaun Hotel.

'When I met him first he was somebody who was just completely numb, shocked. And of course I was not prepared for the type of story he was going to tell me. What I knew from the details Prasad had told me was that he had lost his wife, she had been miscarrying and that they had asked for a termination, it had been refused and she had died. Praveen then outlined it all to me. We went through the story for about two hours. It was quite shocking and sad, what had happened. My thoughts were that we would get the medical notes and find out whether or not he wanted to bring an action for medical negligence. That was what I thought might have been the focus of his attention. But it wasn't. What he really wanted was to find out why this had happened. I knew he was going back to India, so I said we'd have the medical notes by the time he got back. We'd see where we'd go from there.'

Savita's body was released on Tuesday night. She was laid out at a funeral home in Mervue, not far from Roscam, on Wednesday evening. Their friends as well as colleagues from Boston Scientific came to sympathize. Praveen began his final journey home to Belgaum with Savita on Thursday. Friends, worried about Praveen and his ability to cope with the seventeen-hour journey, insisted that someone accompany him.

'We weren't sure about Praveen's condition,' says Dr Prasad. 'Some people thought he might be suicidal or self-harm. He was in a very bad way. So we thought about sending someone with him, to watch him. He said he didn't want that. He said he had had so many visitors and friends in the past week and when he got to India there would be another barrage of family and friends, that he wanted the time on the flight just for him. He was exhausted and totally drained, but we were very concerned about him. So, we talked about it again and talked to him again. We said he could sit at the front of the plane and a friend could sit at the back, and he wouldn't even know he was there. So then he agreed.

'His company Boston Scientific were very good. They bought a ticket for his friend, Raj, he's in the restaurant business, and he went with him.'

With Praveen and Savita on their way home, their friends then began to address what had happened. They were horrified and they were angry; as they saw it, Savita had been denied standard medical treatment – and had died as a result. In their view her treatment in the hospital had been criminally negligent. Said Dr Prasad to me some months later: 'If it had happened in an Indian hospital the doctor would have been arrested.'

Many have said in recent months that there were three sides to the abortion debate – the anti-abortion, the pro-choice and the majority middle ground. The reaction of Galway's Indian community represents a fourth side: a 'new-Irish' side perhaps representing a completely fresh – for Ireland at any rate – perspective on the abortion issue. Savita and Praveen's friends did not regard the denial of a termination to Savita as a women's rights issue or as a choice issue, but as a fundamental issue of basic medical treatment. The denial to Savita of the termination she had sought was a denial of her right to her health – and, ultimately, to her life.

Before Praveen left, Dr Prasad and another friend sat him down and made him tell the whole story. 'What had happened was completely wrong, so we wanted to make a record of it. We said to him, "You know in time you just might forget details", so a friend put an iPhone in front of him and just recorded. Also we were not sure that he would come back. We thought, once he goes it would be too traumatic to come back and as far as we were concerned a crime had been done to Savita. So we were going to have to do something about it.'

Praveen arrived in Bangalore in the early hours of Friday, 2 November 2012, at the airport where he had arrived many times when coming to see Savita during their courtship and when he and Savita had come home every summer for a month to see family. Savita's brother Santosh was there to meet Praveen. Together the two men took Savita on the final leg of her journey home to Belgaum.

Her funeral, the following day, was a small, private service. No one beyond her family and friends had yet heard of Savita Halappanavar. Unlike other Hindus, Lingayats do not cremate their dead, but return them to the earth. Savita was buried, her hands interlocked, her feet crossed, as in meditation. Her ishtalinga was placed in her left hand and she was laid to rest in the quiet Kalmath graveyard, in the Sadashiv Nagar district, about a ten-minute drive from her home.

It was now, her friends in Galway believed, appropriate to act and they met to discuss what to do next.

'After the funeral there was a meeting. About twenty of us met and it looked to us like it was more than a civil matter,' says Dr Prasad. 'We wanted to ask the Guards to go and take the statements before it all blew over and people forgot details. We wanted to press criminal charges. We had to have something done. We had to get answers.'

They had difficulty in contacting the Garda who had come to the hospital to identify Savita the night she died, and there was confusion about his name. Several days later a group of about five of them decided to go in person to Mill Street Garda Station, the main police station in the city.

When the five members of the Indian community started to talk to a garda in the public concourse about what they saw as a criminal matter, recalls Dr Prasad, 'He actually brought us out of the Garda station. I don't know why.' They asked when they could expect the Garda investigation to begin and when statements would be taken. Given that the coroner had not yet directed that the Gardai take statements, as he had not yet decided whether an inquest would be held, this garda was not in a position to help.

'He said it could all take one and a half or even two years. He said, "Things happen slowly. We just have to wait for the coroner to give the go-ahead to take statements." He said that's how the system works. So then we were thinking what to do now. How to get these statements from the staff, how to get the ball rolling? We had many meetings. We didn't know what to do.'

It was anti-abortion campaign group Youth Defence who gave Dr Prasad an answer. 'I was watching the news on the Saturday evening and there was this big pro-life rally in Castlebar, in Enda Kenny's home town. I think about 2,000 people were there and it was big on the news. I saw all these banners in the report about the people being anti-abortion. So I thought the other side, the pro-choice people, might be able to give us some information about abortion in Ireland.

'A day later we were having another meeting, in the Clybaun Hotel, internet surfing and we found Galway Pro-choice. It had a mobile number and it was for Sarah. So Laxmish, he called the number and it was Sarah who answered the phone.'

Sarah McCarthy, a student at the National University of Ireland, Galway, had been one of the founders of Galway Pro-choice just four months previously; this was largely in response to the national 'Abortion Tears Her Life Apart' billboard campaign by Youth Defence. She was getting ready to go to Dublin, on Sunday, 4 November 2012, when she got the phone call from Laxmish.

'He said, "I want to speak to you about a tragedy at UCHG." I said "OK". Remember now, I'm 21 and I was pretty un-prepared for what he was about to tell me. He said, "Someone has died because they were not given an abortion." He started to tell me a bit but I asked him if he would be comfortable sending me an email outlining the details.'

A few hours later the following email arrived:

Dear Sarah,
Prochoice
We are friends of Savita Praveen [traditionally in India married women take their husband's first name as a first surname and are known by this, though they also take the husband's surname as an official married name] who is a 31 year old woman who lost her life on 28th October 2012 at 1.09 a.m. She was 17 weeks pregnant and attended University Hospital Galway at about 9 a.m. on 21st October. She was admitted after repeated demands in view of her condition. She went in with pre-mature labour pains and her water had already broken. She was told that her cervix was fully open and that they would not be able to save the pregnancy. She passed away a week after her admission.

We believe that her life could have been saved but for denying her a timely medical termination of pregnancy.

We look forward to meeting your organisation in helping
future mothers' lives.

We look forward to meeting you in advance of the next meeting to discuss further details.

Kind Regards

Friends of Savita

'Basically,' says Dr Prasad who had helped write the email,
'we wanted information from them. We didn't want them to
go and do a big demonstration or anything like that. We wanted
information. What else could we do? We weren't getting
anywhere with the Guards, or with the coroner. The hospital
said they'd do some inquiry but we didn't think it was
good enough. So, we just wanted to have a chat about it,
find out what the position was. We saw Galway Pro-choice
as an information group where we could get advice on what to
do.'

And so it was that, having got nowhere with any of the obvious
agencies of the State, Savita and Praveen's friends, members of
Galway's Indian community, found themselves sitting in the
lobby of the Meyrick Hotel in Eyre Square with two young local
pro-choice activists. McCarthy recalls arriving at around 7 p.m.,
on Tuesday, 6 November, with another member of the group,
John Walshe.

'There were doctors and nurses among the people waiting for
us and they knew what they were talking about. We just sat down
and asked them to step-by-step go through everything that
happened. Before we met I was concerned the details would be
wrong or that we wouldn't be able to handle it. I was really
worried that it wasn't going to be clear-cut and we weren't going
to be able to do much to help them. Then, as they went through
it all, it became clear that this was serious and that it had to do
with our laws on abortion.'

Dr Prasad says that about twenty of Praveen and Savita's friends came to the meeting.

'We told the story. They were just shocked and John kept saying "I apologize on behalf of our country". He said women should have a choice. If a man has a prostate cancer he discusses it with the doctor, the doctor gives options and the man chooses what he wants. That choice is not there for women. He said: "That's what this organization is about".'

McCarthy says they told her and John about the recording they had of Praveen's account. 'They said that they had tried to lodge a complaint with the hospital. They had tried to get in touch with the HSE, the Guards and basically he said, "No one is talking to us. Everyone is shutting us down. No one will give us answers and we want to get the story out there".'

'We said the story could be told anonymously,' says McCarthy. 'They actually said, "No, we want her face out there. We want people to know Savita as a person".'

Dr Prasad says, 'We weren't worried about a journalist knowing. We thought we need to bring this to public attention one way or the other. We didn't expect it would be front page of a broadsheet. We thought hopefully it will be in some small section, get a little bit of attention.'

Dette McLoughlin, a pro-choice activist for over twenty years and member of Galway Pro-choice, unable to attend the meeting, got a message from Walshe about it later that night. McCarthy and Walshe were considering putting out a general press release to all media if Praveen approved. McLoughlin cautioned against it.

'I was concerned that it be handled properly. I just thought "Gosh if it gets into the wrong hands . . ." I was worried for the dead woman's family.'

McLoughlin called a veteran pro-choice activist and occasional journalist she knows. 'She said it would be best if it went to one journalist. So I put that to the group. I reminded them that when the story of the X case came out it was because one journalist ran with it and it was clearly focused from the outset. It wasn't splashed in bits across every paper.'

I was at home in Dublin, getting ready to go to bed on Wednesday, 7 November, when a call came telling me of a 'tragedy' in Galway, involving an Indian woman who had died after being refused an abortion. The caller knew little more than that stark detail – apart from the fact that someone from Galway Pro-choice was said to have seen an email from a group 'called Friends of Savita, or Sabita or something like that'.

The following morning, I told my news editor, Roddy O'Sullivan, of the tip-off and we mused how to check the story out. I sat down at my desk and turned first to Google and started hopefully typing in key words. I tried 'Sabita and Galway'. Nothing. Then 'Sinita and Galway'. Finally I typed in 'Savita and Galway'. There was one listing. On the Irish death-notice website RIP.ie was a listing, published on 30 October:

> The death has occurred of Savita PRAVEEN HALAPPANAVAR 123 Ros Caoin, Roscam, Galway City, Galway
>
> Sunday, October 28th, suddenly at the University Hospital Galway. Reposing at the Holy Family Funeral Home, Mervue from 5pm on Wednesday afternoon until removal at 6.30pm to Wards Funeral Home, Ballybay, Co. Monaghan, to await Burial in India.

I had found her. I searched for her home address in Galway on Google Earth. Up came a picture of her house. As I sat at my desk, looking at the screen, at the modest, suburban house where this young woman had lived with her husband, I knew I had to go there. I told O'Sullivan I had found the death notice and said: 'It may be a wild goose chase, but I want to go to Galway. I can be there by lunchtime.' He turned down the radio news, and nodded. 'Go. Stay in touch.'

I looked up Galway Pro-choice on Facebook and messaged a few members, telling them that I was on my way to Galway and invited them to phone me. About an hour into the journey, just outside Athlone, my phone rang. It was John Walshe, the pro-choice activist who had met Savita's friends a few days earlier. Agreeing to meet me, he expressed concerns about telling the story before Praveen got back from India. Praveen was due back on 8 December. It was now 9 November.

'I can absolutely understand that,' I told him. 'But this story will not hold until December the 8th. People will be talking about it in the hospital and around Galway and this will get out. I would just suggest,' I said, 'that if her family and friends want to have some control over how it gets out they should probably consider talking to one journalist they trust, now.'

When I got to Galway I made my way to Roscam, a relatively new residential area, to the east of Galway city and just off the main road in from Dublin. The house, at 123 Ros Caoin, was empty of any sign that anyone had lived there. I knocked on nearby doors. Few neighbours were aware a young Indian couple had been living there and only one, an older woman babysitting a grandchild, knew that a woman had died. Her son, she said, worked with the husband and had known him to say hello to.

'My son was at the funeral home in Mervue before her body was brought back to India. It's very sad. Seemingly she died because she refused treatment in the hospital,' she said, clearly believing Savita had refused to accept medical treatment.

I went to the campus at NUI where Walshe and Sarah McCarthy had agreed to meet me. Earlier that morning, they had heard from Praveen's friends that he was happy to talk to a journalist. They had called Praveen himself in India themselves to discuss it. Again they talked through the story and gave me a number for Praveen's friend, Dr Prasad.

Dr Prasad was on his way home from work at the Galway

Clinic when I called him. He said he could speak to me over the phone or meet me at his home in Spiddal, a village about 10 miles outside Galway city, in an hour. I drove out with McCarthy and Walshe to meet Dr Prasad. He went over the story yet again, and gave me Praveen's mobile number in India. The three left the room so that I could call Praveen.

It was about 1 a.m. in Belgaum, Karnataka, in the south-west of India, when I got through. I told Praveen how sorry I was to hear what had happened and said, given how late it was, I could call him the following morning.

'No,' he said, 'it's fine. I will talk to you now.' A quiet, gentle man, he told me the story, of how he had brought his young wife to the hospital with severe back pain on the morning of 21 October, of how they had been told she was miscarrying and that it would all be over in a few hours, of how she went on to endure almost four days of physical and emotional 'agony'.

He told of how his and her requests for a termination were refused because the foetal heartbeat was present and of how it was explained to them that it could not be done because 'this is a Catholic country'. The foetal heartbeat finally stopped on the afternoon of Wednesday, 24 October, the womb contents were removed and Savita was moved first to the high dependency unit and then to intensive care where, having contracted septicaemia and E. coli ESBL, she went into multi-organ failure and died at nine minutes past 1 a.m., on Sunday, 28 October.

'What is the use in being angry?' he asked. 'I have lost her. I'm talking about this because it shouldn't happen to anyone else. It was all in their hands and they just let her go. How can you let a young woman go to save a baby who will die anyway? Savita could have had more babies.' I sympathized with him, thanked him for talking to me and told him I was certain the story would be published in the *Irish Times* within the next week. 'Perfect,' he said.

As I was putting away my notes and thanking Dr Prasad, he asked me whether I thought it would be a story. 'Will the *Irish Times* really be interested?' I assured him the newsdesk would be interested. I asked about a photograph of Savita and he said he'd arrange to have one sent up. He showed me a copy of the post-mortem findings, a photograph of which he had on his phone, showing her cause of death. We discussed the role of religion in medical practice. I said I would be in touch.

When I stopped for petrol outside Galway, I called my news editor O'Sullivan to tell him I had spoken to Praveen in India, to his friend Dr Prasad, who had confirmed the details, and that as far as I could establish the story appeared to be true. Obviously I would have to put the allegations to the hospital, I said, and agreed to write a first draft over the weekend.

It was a story that 'wrote itself', as journalists sometimes say. It was a straightforward tragedy, to be told chronologically in the words of the husband. Apart from a hospital response and some context, no more was needed. I emailed it to O'Sullivan, so he could read it and send it on to the newspaper's solicitors.

On the morning of Monday the 12th, my colleague health correspondent Paul Cullen came on board to put the story to the hospital and to Dr Katherine Astbury, the consultant obstetrician who had treated Savita. Meanwhile, I got in contact with another of Savita's friends in Galway, Mrdula Vaseali, asking for any memories she might have of Savita and reminding her of the need for a photograph.

'If you had a good, clear close-up that would be great,' I said.

She wrote back later: 'Savita had completed her bachelor's degree in dentistry in India and worked a few years there before moving to Ireland after marrying Praveen in 2008. With ambitions to continue and fulfil her future in dentistry she cleared the dental exams in Ireland, which allows her to work here. She was academically high achiever [*sic*] and was looking forward to contribute to Ireland with her services in dentistry.

'She was also an accomplished dancer. She had performed at international dance festival April 2009 at Radisson Blu Hotel, Galway. She also worked as cultural secretary for the Galway Indian community and played major role in introducing Indian culture and dancing forms to children both Indian and Irish origin. She was also looking forward to start a dance school to train Indian dance forms as hobby in the near future. Her social nature enabled her to develop friends quickly in Ireland and [she] was known to extend her hand for any kind of assistance for her friends.'

Attached to the email was a jpeg, a photograph of Savita which Mrdula said she hoped would be OK. It was that photograph, the image that was to accompany the story on the *Irish Times* front page and travel around the world. A dazzlingly beautiful young woman, resplendent in her traditional dress for the Diwali festival the previous year, beaming to the camera.

Dr Katherine Astbury, who had gone on leave the day before Savita's death, was still on holiday and could not be contacted, the hospital's press spokesman told us. At 6.07 p.m., however, we received a response from the hospital:

> Firstly, the Galway Roscommon University Hospitals Group wishes to extend its sympathy to the family and friends of Ms Halappanavar. As you will be aware we cannot discuss the details of an individual patient with the media. In general sudden deaths are reported to the coroner. Galway Roscommon University Hospitals Group (GRUHG) cooperates fully with coroners' inquests.
>
> In general in the case of a maternal death, a number of pro-cedures are followed including a risk review of the case and the completion of a maternal death notification form. External experts are involved in the review and the family of the deceased are consulted on the terms of reference, are inter-viewed by the review team and given a copy of the final report.

This final paragraph warned:

> In general in relation to media enquiries about issues where there may be onward legal action, we must reserve our position on what action we may take if assertions about a patient's care are published and we cannot speak for individual doctors or other medical professionals if a report were to name of [*sic*] identify any.

Having received this statement, both Paul and I believed the story would run the following morning. It was a source of enormous frustration when O'Sullivan said the story would be held for another day, for further legal consideration. 'We could be slaughtered in the courts if Dr Astbury was to claim she was given no chance to respond.'

On the following morning, Tuesday, I set about trying to contact Dr Astbury. I told the hospital switchboard operator I was with the *Irish Times*, that we were planning to run a story the following day involving Dr Astbury, and advised her that Dr Astbury should be contacted, despite the fact she was on leave, so that she could have the opportunity to comment.

Later, editor Kevin O'Sullivan called a meeting in his office. Deputy editor Denis Staunton, news editor Roddy O'Sullivan, assistant news editor Eithne Donnellan, Paul Cullen and I combed through the story as written so far, discussing it line by line and examining the background material again. We had her death notice, an interview with her husband, a corroborating interview with Dr Prasad and a statement from the hospital. I mentioned I had briefly seen a copy of the post-mortem report from pathologist Grace Callagy, which Dr Prasad had in his possession. I agreed I should try to get a copy of this from Dr Prasad and rework the opening paragraph of the story.

I also explained that I had left urgent messages with the switchboard at the hospital and was hopeful of getting to talk to

Dr Astbury. It was important not just from a legal point of view to do all we could to seek comment from Dr Astbury, but also to be scrupulously fair to her. I called the hospital yet again seeking Dr Astbury, while Paul pursued her through the hospital public relations officer. I stressed to the switchboard operator that I had to make contact with her. She agreed to phone Dr Astbury on her mobile, while I hung on the other line. She came back to me.

'She is on leave and can't make any comment.' I asked her to call Dr Astbury once more and put it to her that she had told Savita Halappanavar, a patient of hers, that she could not have a termination as this was a Catholic country. She did call the doctor again, and again came back to me. 'She says the case is part of a legal process now and she just can't comment. She said you should contact the press office.'

Dr Prasad emailed the post-mortem results to me. We were happy we had done all within our power to obtain a comment from Dr Astbury. Interestingly, the solicitors were also reassured because a corroborating account of the story had come from a consultant surgeon – Dr Prasad. 'He's a person of standing. Being a senior doctor, he would have a lot to lose if it came out that he wasn't telling the truth.'

I then set about reworking the introductory paragraph. Though the request for a termination was obviously a critical plank of the story, it was felt it should not be in the first line. I was also careful throughout the copy to make it clear we had Savita's loved ones' account only and no confirmation of the details in the hospital response.

The page was being laid out on screen as I left that evening, at about 6.30. The chief subeditor asked me to check over it before I left, to approve the headline and the subhead. The following morning, Wednesday, 14 November, the story appeared on the front page. Savita's face radiated, almost incongruously, across four columns.

'Woman "denied a termination" dies in hospital' ran the headline.

'Two investigations are under way into the death of a woman who was 17 weeks pregnant, at University Hospital Galway last month.

'Savita Halappanavar (31), a dentist, presented with back pain at the hospital on October 21st, was found to be miscarrying, and died of septicaemia a week later.

'Her husband, Praveen Halappanavar (34), an engineer at Boston Scientific in Galway, says she asked several times over a three-day period that the pregnancy be terminated. He says that, having been told she was miscarrying, and after one day in severe pain, Ms Halappanavar asked for a medical termination.

'This was refused, he says, because the foetal heartbeat was still present and they were told, "this is a Catholic country".

'She spent a further 2½ days "in agony" until the foetal heartbeat stopped.

'The dead foetus was removed and Savita was taken to the high dependency unit and then the intensive care unit, where she died of septicaemia on the 28th.

'An autopsy carried out by Dr Grace Callagy two days later found she died of septicaemia "documented ante-mortem" and E. coli ESBL.

'A hospital spokesman confirmed the Health Service Executive had begun an investigation while the hospital had also instigated an internal investigation. He said the hospital extended its sympathy to the family and friends of Ms Halappanavar but could not discuss the details of any individual case.

'Speaking from Belgaum in the Karnataka region of southwest India, Mr Halappanavar said an internal examination was performed when she first presented.

'"The doctor told us the cervix was fully dilated, amniotic fluid was leaking and unfortunately the baby wouldn't survive." The doctor, he says, said it should be over in a few hours. There followed three days, he says, of the foetal heartbeat being checked several times a day.

'"Savita was really in agony. She was very upset, but she accepted she was losing the baby. When the consultant came on the ward rounds on Monday morning Savita asked if they could not save the baby could they induce to end the pregnancy. The consultant said, 'As long as there is a foetal heartbeat we can't do anything.'

'"Again on Tuesday morning, the ward rounds and the same discussion. The consultant said it was the law, that this is a Catholic country. Savita [a Hindu] said: 'I am neither Irish nor Catholic' but they said there was nothing they could do.

'"That evening she developed shakes and shivering and she was vomiting. She went to use the toilet and she collapsed. There were big alarms and a doctor took bloods and started her on antibiotics.

'"The next morning I said she was so sick and asked again that they just end it, but they said they couldn't."

'At lunchtime the foetal heart had stopped and Ms Halappanavar was brought to theatre to have the womb contents removed. "When she came out she was talking okay but she was very sick. That's the last time I spoke to her."

'At 11 p.m. he got a call from the hospital. "They said they were shifting her to intensive care. Her heart and pulse were low, her temperature was high. She was sedated and critical but stable. She stayed stable on Friday but by 7pm on Saturday they said her heart, kidneys and liver weren't functioning. She was critically ill. That night, we lost her."

'Mr Halappanavar took his wife's body home on Thursday, November 1st, where she was cremated [*sic*] and laid to rest on November 3rd.

'The hospital spokesman said that in general sudden hospital deaths were reported to the coroner. In the case of maternal deaths, a risk review of the case was carried out.

'External experts were involved in this review and the family consulted on the terms of reference. They were also interviewed by the review team and given a copy of the report.'

The story broke that night.

5

The *Tonight* show with Vincent Browne on TV3 that Tuesday night was due to discuss delays in the processing of student grant applications. Browne opened the programme with the news that a story was breaking about the death of a woman in Galway University Hospital, who had been refused an abortion. Fifty minutes later the show closed, as always, with a preview of the next day's newspapers. The *Irish Times* front page, dominated by Savita's picture, flashed on to the screen. The show's always busy Twitter hashtag, #vinb, went into overdrive. The image of the story and Savita's photograph were rapidly tweeted and retweeted, the comments of those tweeting united in shock and horror.

The first call came just before 6 a.m., from the national radio station Newstalk 106, seeking an interview for their breakfast programme 'about the Galway situation'.

Shortly after, RTE's morning radio-news programme *Morning Ireland* called. Then Today FM, Galway Bay FM, Highland Radio, TV3, UTV and BBC Northern Ireland. It was a big Irish story, as was to be expected.

What wasn't expected, at least by me, were the calls which quickly began to pour in from CNN, the BBC World Service, *Channel 4 News*, Sky News, the *Telegraph*, France 24, Al Jazeera,

El País . . . Most were seeking interviews. Almost all asked for Praveen's phone number in India, which I was not in a position to share: he had agreed that I pass it on only to RTE. One international news organization offered to pay me 'generously' if I gave them the number. The story was leading news bulletins in Ireland from early morning and by mid-morning was the lead on the BBC, Sky News and CNN as well as being covered on news websites across Europe.

At the *Irish Times* website irishtimes.com, the story was viewed 880,000 times – by far the most read story in the seventeen-year history of the site; traffic that day exceeded 2 million page impressions for the first time. Traffic was also disproportionately international at the height of the story, another first, with the usual 60–40 divide in favour of domestic traffic reversed.

Many news outlets were already speculating as to the political ramifications for the Irish State. Sky News, available in more than 100 million homes across 115 countries, said: 'Her death is expected to spark a backlash against the Irish Government, criticized by left-wing members of parliament for failing to introduce new laws to permit abortion in life-threatening circumstances.'

The *Guardian* published an online story headlined 'Scandal in Ireland as woman dies in Galway "after being denied abortion"'. Commentary on the story also led the sites at the *Mirror*, the *Huffington Post* UK, the *Telegraph* and the *Belfast Telegraph*. In Britain popular feminist commentators Caitlin Moran and India Knight were tweeting the news to their tens of thousands of followers, while the *New Statesman* published a comment piece by Sarah Ditum, saying, 'For too long, Irish women have been the victims of cruel politics and heartless zealots. It is time to listen to the campaigners who speak for the simple truth that women's lives matter.'

By morning in North America, the story had crossed the Atlantic. The *New York Times* carried it under the headline:

'Hospital Death in Ireland Renews Fight over Abortion'. The *Washington Post* reported: 'Abortion flares in Ireland over death of critically ill woman denied quick termination'. The website Jezebel.com's post 'Woman denied abortion dies in agony at hospital' gave rise to an influx of angry comments. The *Toronto Star* reported: 'Savita Halappanavar was in agony but her doctors remained obstinate'. *Time* magazine said Savita's death 'prompts soul-searching'. CNN reported: 'Death of woman denied an abortion causes uproar in Ireland'. Fox News ran an opinion piece titled, 'How bureaucracy killed a woman'.

At lunchtime, Praveen spoke from India to Sean O'Rourke on RTE Radio's *News at One*. He recounted the story just as he had in the *Irish Times*. He spoke of his and Savita's requests for a termination and the explanation they had been given for its refusal, that 'it was a Catholic country'. It was the first occasion Irish people had heard his voice.

Towards the end of the interview, which lasted almost ten minutes, he told of Savita's last minutes. 'That night [Sunday 28 October] at around one o'clock, the nurse came running. I was just standing outside ICU. She, she just told me to pray and she took me near Savita and she said, "Will you be OK to be there during her last few minutes?" I said, "Yes, I want to." I was holding her hand. They were trying to pump her heart. There was a big team around, and the doctor just told me, they just lost her.'

His calm, steady and tender account affected everyone listening.

'There would be very few women, and men, in Ireland who wouldn't have been very moved by the account of her death,' recalls retired Fianna Fáil government minister and Senator, Mary O'Rourke. 'It was just so, so sad.'

Praveen was, commented Dette McLoughlin of Galway Pro-choice after hearing the RTE interview, 'such a hero. You just knew that all he wanted was justice, justice for Savita. He wasn't f-ing and blinding or calling for people to be hung, drawn and quartered, which would be many people's natural reaction. He was just being so unbelievably just right. So sensitive and dignified. I think he just touched everybody.'

'Praveen changed everything,' says Orla O'Connor, chief executive of the National Women's Council. 'He was so clear and so public and so powerful. He said that they had requested an abortion, and she had died. That affected a lot of men as well as women. That morning there were just so many calls into the Council ... it was a feeling of outrage. One of the marked differences was the number of men calling the NWC, phoning to say it was absolutely awful. It could have been their wife, it could have been someone in their family and they wanted to do something about it ... You could really sense things were changing fast, but then there was an anger. "Why does something like this have to happen to make people wake up to the issue of abortion?"'

In an ironic twist, the Council was publishing a report on gender mainstreaming in access to health services that morning, with the junior Minister for Health, Kathleen Lynch, and a number of senior HSE staff in attendance. 'So when we went to have the launch in the Ashling Hotel, it was full of media and all they wanted to ask about was Savita,' recalls O'Connor. 'The Minister, on the day, she said yes it was clear they, the Government, they had to do something about this.'

Two weeks earlier the Council had launched a campaign, to mark the 20th anniversary of the X case, encouraging people to send an email from its website to their local TD calling for abortion legislation in line with the 1992 Supreme Court judgment. On the day of the campaign launch, 1,549 emails were sent. Thereafter, the number fell to an average of about 75 a day. On the day the story broke, 45,431 'legislate for X' emails were sent.

In the Dáil, fourteen TDs asked to speak on the issue, among them Clare Daly of the United Left Alliance who seven months earlier had unsuccessfully introduced a bill to legalize abortion where the life of the woman was at risk. The Government's junior coalition partner, the Labour Party, had voted against her bill – some of its TDs, including Ciara Conway and Anne Ferris, claiming that the reason they couldn't support the Bill was that it didn't go far enough.

When Daly rose to her feet, she was apoplectic. 'I am boiling mad. This beautiful young woman is dead as a result only of political cowardice. The failure of successive Governments, including this Government, to provide for a woman's constitutional right to an abortion where her life is in danger is absolutely outrageous.'

Richard Boyd Barrett of People Before Profit and Joe Higgins of the Socialist Party were equally enraged.

The speeches by pro-choice TDs were, perhaps, predictable. In the view of anti-abortion campaigners they were triumphalist and manipulative. Marc Coleman said he felt huge anger that 'a death arising from such complex and delicate and humanly sensitive circumstances was so quickly, clinically and cynically manipulated to push an agenda'.

Less predictable was the impact the story had on anti-abortion TDs within Fine Gael. Many who spoke to the *Irish Times* political correspondent Harry McGee the day after the story broke said they were 'reconsidering' their views, or that their views were 'evolving'. Regina Doherty, TD for Meath East, said, 'I am anti-abortion and pro-life but I am pro my life and the lives of my children . . . It's something on which the medical profession deserves clarity. Women deserve clarity around when is my life at risk and what medical intervention is legal in that scenario. If I am to be honest, we have had this conversation. Given the result of the X case, the State should act.'

Wicklow TD Simon Harris said: 'In the past I've said I didn't see the need to legislate. Let me assure you today I am reconsidering. There can be no grey areas.' The comments were echoed by Fine Gael party chairman and TD for Laois–Offaly, Charles Flanagan and the Taoiseach's constituency colleague in Mayo, John O'Mahony.

The Minister for Health, James Reilly, counselled caution in the Dáil debate, urging deputies not to prejudge the outcome of investigations into what happened. It also emerged during the debate that, by almost bizarre timing, the Government had just the previous night received the long-awaited report from its Expert Group on how best to implement a 2010 judgment from the European Court of Human Rights demanding clarity for Irish women as to when they could access an abortion in Ireland.

Almost everyone interviewed for this book said they knew immediately upon hearing the story that the abortion issue would explode again. Recalls political commentator Noel Whelan: 'I thought, "This poor country, tortured as it is with economic woes, is now going to tear itself up over abortion."' 'The minute I heard it, I knew immediately that it was going to become the central point of a huge row over abortion,' says O'Rourke. 'I knew it would stir things. It seemed to make it very clear that the 1983 amendment was out of kilter. There are times when you have to decide between the life of the mother and the child.'

Aodhán Ó Ríordáin, Labour Party TD (Dublin North Central) said that as soon as he heard it he knew 'something big' had happened.

'I think the fact that she wasn't Irish possibly for a lot of people made it more poignant because she was a victim of Irish law. When the story broke I remember instinctively knowing this was going to be a big deal . . . I do think that what the tragedy did was to change the nature of the conversation, because we were talking about an actual case, about an actual person who had made a real request for an abortion. It was denied her. Obviously Savita wanted that baby with her husband Praveen. Only in the most desperate of situations would she have wanted to have an abortion. I think what it did was make people realize there was a constitutional situation that had to be sorted out.'

The story, as O'Connor of the Women's Council had said, woke people up to the abortion issue in a way no pro-choice campaign ever could. What had 'woken' them quite so dramatically and evoked such instinctive horror was of course the fact that they knew who Savita was. This had been Praveen's wish – that people knew who his wife was and how she had died. We had had the X case, the C case, the Miss D case, the *D* v. *Ireland* case, the *A, B and C* v. *Ireland* case. All had involved real women in unspeakable circumstances, but they had all been anonymous. This time we knew Savita's name, her face. She was a person with whom we women could identify and Praveen a man with whom husbands, partners, brothers, fathers could all identify.

The Well Woman Centre in Dublin, which provides health services, saw the number of women coming for post-termination counselling increase dramatically in the immediate wake of the story. The average number of women seeking such counselling at the Centre is usually about 25 per quarter. In the last three months of 2012 that number shot up to over 80.

'There was a whole different feel to the counselling world in those last three months,' said Alison Begas, its chief executive, in May 2013. 'People were angry about Savita. There was a sense again that Ireland was closing in, the illegality of it came to the fore again and people who had had abortions were suddenly struck with all this sense of judgement. Some who came in had had an abortion twenty years ago. It's a secret women hold, whether they had an abortion five years ago or twenty years ago and often they still won't have told their nearest and dearest. Then when you get these extraordinary extremes of jargon, "pro-life" and "pro-choice" and it's just they want to, need to talk about how they are and where they're at in themselves. Women's experience of being pregnant and of abortion is intensely personal.'

The use of the term 'Catholic country' obviously had an

enormous impact. These two words transformed the story from one of medical treatment denied to one of medical treatment ideologically denied. They horrified people because Ireland in 2012 was supposed to have left behind blind adherence to religious dogma. They dislodged the comfortable notion that Ireland was now a worldly country that could act on the international stage unquestioned, could invite the best and the brightest young things to live and work here, people like Savita and Praveen, and show them a life as good as anywhere else.

To people in their twenties and thirties who had come to adulthood in times of prosperity and who knew Ireland as a place of Google and Pfizer, of gap years in Australia and Erasmus years in Paris, the story seemed to suggest that it was not in fact the all-modern society they had thought, that there was something dysfunctional at its heart. And that was something many had never before confronted.

That Wednesday afternoon, the national public broadcaster RTE had to give over almost the entirety of its popular afternoon phone-in radio show, *Liveline*, to Savita's story, as woman after woman phoned to tell their own stories of having been denied abortions or of having difficult miscarriages in Irish hospitals. Their calls filled the programme for the following two days as they publicly and openly told their stories in a way that had never been heard in Ireland before. Some women had had to travel for abortions, after a diagnosis that their babies had fatal foetal abnormalities and no prospect of life after birth. They expressed the sense of isolation they had felt, the fear of people finding out, the lies they had had to tell, and the almost total lack of support within Ireland.

One woman, who gave her name as Carolyn, told a story bearing a disturbing resemblance to that of Savita. It had happened twenty-seven years earlier. She had been 16 weeks pregnant when she realized she was having a third miscarriage and presented at a hospital in the south of the country. When she was scanned, a foetal heartbeat was found.

'It was made clear to me nothing could be done until I had been seen by a gynaecologist. I tried to tell them what needed to be done. I was in extreme pain, much more so than in my first and second miscarriages. I did try to say what was needed now was a D and C [dilation and curettage]. I had had one at my first and second miscarriages, which took place in London. I was told I'd have to wait. I was brought to a ward and I remember it was the first time in my life when really I'd lost control. I was in so much pain I was wailing and terribly distressed. I think I asked for pain relief and I was told it couldn't be administered because of the fact there was a baby.

'While I was lying there, the hard, cold reality of my situation dawned on me. It was the mid-1980s and the Society for the Protection of the Unborn Child was quite prominent and it just dawned on me that this was probably down to me or the baby. I realized very clearly that I might die and that was what I felt more than anything. The fear I felt was indescribable – that I might die.' Her gynaecologist arrived some hours later and performed a D and C.

'He saved my life and I was enormously grateful. When I woke up this morning and heard this story of this girl in Galway, the thought that crossed my mind was that twenty-seven years later this kind of thing could actually still happen. I had clearly believed that in the interim more enlightened legislation [was in place].'

India, five to six hours ahead, found its voice the following day. CNN and the BBC World Service were clamouring to cover the story, given their huge audiences in South East Asia and the sub-continent. There were calls to the *Irish Times* newsroom from the *Hindu* newspaper, New Delhi TV, the *Times of India* as well as from smaller news organizations around Bangalore and Goa in the south-west of India from where Savita and Praveen had come.

Much of the coverage in India was angry. The indiatimes.com site, which describes itself as the most popular in the world for Indian readers, ran the headline, 'Ireland murders pregnant Indian dentist'. There were protests outside the Irish embassy in New Delhi and in towns and cities across Karnataka province.

Savita's parents were widely quoted accusing Ireland of having 'murdered' their only daughter. To the Irish audience, this appeared wildly over the top, sensationalist hyperbole. However, according to Savita's friends, this to most in India was not an issue of women's rights or a woman's right to choose. It was a question of basic medical care denied and, in effect, the wilful neglect of a young Indian woman.

Abortion was decriminalized in India in 1971 in response to a combination of the large numbers of women dying as a result of illegal abortions, and the rapidly growing population. It is permitted in a range of situations, including where the woman's physical or mental health is endangered, in cases of foetal abnormality, and where the pregnancy is the result of rape, and is regarded as a standard gynaecological intervention when the pregnant woman's welfare is at risk.

In Karnataka itself the Chief Minister, Jagadish Shettar, wrote to Savita's parents expressing his shock. 'I was pained to know a precious life was lost because proper medical care was refused,' he was reported as having written.

Speaking to reporters in Bangalore, the state capital, on Friday, 16 November, he said: 'Humanity precedes legality. The Irish hospital should have considered abortion as a humanitarian consideration. This is a serious issue. There is a lot of public anger and protest. To ensure justice to the victim, we are taking up the issue with Ireland through the government of India,' he said.

Belgaum Deputy Commissioner Anbu Kumar visited Savita's parents at their home in Sri Nagar to convey his condolences and offer any help they might need. Andanappa was reported in the

Times of India as having said to Mr Kumar: 'If the Irish law on abortion is changed, I would think my daughter has been sacrificed for a good cause.'

Loveena Tandon, the London-based Europe correspondent of the publishing and broadcasting organization India Today, was sent to Dublin and Galway to report over a two-day period.

'It just did not make sense to people that a woman could die in Ireland because she couldn't get a termination. I remember my sister asking me, "Are you serious? Isn't Ireland meant to be a developed country?"

'Of course in India abortion gives rise to other issues, such as female foeticide, but as a procedure it is taken for granted.

'To Indians it was just bewildering . . . In India a doctor would have just done the abortion because it would be the best care they could give.'

Rahul Joglekar, London-based reporter for New Delhi TV and the BBC World Service, had read the story on the irishtimes.com site and knew immediately it would be 'huge' in India. There was also a class dimension that was fascinating to the Indian audience.

'The media is very much focused on the "aspirational classes", the elite,' he said speaking to me in June 2013. 'India for so many decades had been the "sick man of Asia", so poor. Economic reforms in the early 1990s were a watershed, opening up India to economic investment, to foreign investment and the West. A lot of people left poverty behind and there is a huge interest still in this "new India" and the classes leading that. So, Savita ticked boxes. She was successful, educated and living in Europe.

'Those young Indians who leave India to establish lives in Europe or North America are regarded as having "made it". You're doing well for yourself. If that success story doesn't go right, that is interesting for people at home. This story though was very big for other reasons too.

'The religion issue fascinated people . . . It sparked a lot of debate in India, with people from the Catholic minority running from television studio to studio, explaining the rules. And that is a debate that is not really had in India . . .

'Also, of course it was a very emotional story, a young couple expecting their first child. It was just so sad. So there were many elements to it.'

Reaction in Ireland would consist of innumerable elements too, the first emerging even before the story broke.

6

Some in pro-choice activism had been aware at an early stage of the death of a woman in the Galway hospital and that a 'denied abortion' was allegedly a factor in it. Among these was founder of Choice Ireland and chair of the Labour Party's Women's Committee, Sinéad Ahern.

'I got an email the week before the story broke . . . from a member of the Indian community in Galway, just asking for information on Ireland's abortion law. The email made reference to the fact that a friend of theirs had passed away having been refused an abortion. It was from a group calling themselves Friends of Savita . . . just wanting to understand why what had happened had happened, wanting to know what was the legal situation.

'We were very cautious about what we did with that information, very aware it was from friends, not family, and we didn't know what the family wanted. We didn't advise them in any way on what to do except to say they had every right to query what happened with the hospital.'

The following weekend she was at a pro-choice activist meeting in Belfast, at which she told me there were 'rumours a story was going to break similar to the X case. Then I heard you had spoken to the family, and then it broke on Vincent Browne. I had heard it would be mentioned so I was watching out for it on Vinnie Browne.'

Though she knew that the story was about to come out, when it did she felt shattered. 'I remember that night after Vincent Browne, standing out at the back of my house with a cigarette and finding myself collapsing into tears, and crying. It just hit me, that after all the years of campaigning and fighting and pickets and leaflets and postering and meetings and rallies and marches, and just trying so hard, we didn't get there in time, and a woman had died. I couldn't sleep. I felt guilt and genuinely felt we had fucked up.'

Another pro-choice activist, Sinead Kennedy, also at the Belfast rally, heard rumours of a story about to break:

'I was completely shocked though when I read the piece in the *Irish Times*. I couldn't quite believe it . . . what I had always thought was that if you were actually dying that, unofficially, doctors felt they could operate in the best interests of a woman, that there wouldn't be that much hesitation, that there was if you like "wriggle room" to protect women's lives.'

Though little legally had changed since 1983, with regard to women's access to abortion in Ireland, like many she assumed that culturally, medically, something had, and that the logical conclusion of the 1983 pro-life amendment to the Constitution wouldn't actually be reached. That it now had, she said, 'really shocked people'.

It echoed the death almost thirty years previously of Sheila Hodgers. The story of her death was broken in the *Irish Times* in September 1983, the day before the 'pro-life referendum', by journalist Padraig Yeates.

Sheila Hodgers, a young, married Dundalk mother of two, had died in agony at Our Lady of Lourdes Hospital in Drogheda the previous March, two days after giving birth to a premature baby girl. She had become pregnant while receiving treatment for a recurrent cancer. The hospital had refused to continue the treatment because of the pregnancy. Her husband, Brendan, had asked variously for an abortion, early delivery of the baby or a Caesarean section. All were refused.

The baby girl, Gemma, delivered at seven months' gestation, died a few hours after birth. 'By then Sheila had tumours everywhere: on her neck, her legs, her spine,' Hodgers told Yeates. Like Savita, Sheila died days after her daughter. As Emily O'Reilly, now European Ombudsman, wrote about the Hodgers case in her seminal 1992 text *Masterminds of the Right*: 'The rights of both could not have been more finely balanced. Mother and baby had died.'

'I suppose I did always fear something like Sheila Hodgers could happen again,' says Kennedy, 'and it was probably always on the cards. But that it had happened, that was a real shock. I think that reality stunned people.'

She put up a Facebook post that morning: 'No more shame. Irish women demand the right to choose. Protest Savita's Death, 6 p.m. at the Dáil.' Word spread on Twitter and Facebook. People spoke of checking their Twitter accounts as they left work and of finding themselves outside Leinster House an hour later, mourning Savita.

They arrived in their thousands, in the dark and on a cold evening in November, carrying candles and hastily fashioned placards with such slogans as 'I have a heartbeat too' and 'I am here to apologize for my country'.

The tone was one of sadness, even of shame.

In a live link from the vigil at about 6.10 p.m. on RTE television news, Sandra Hurley reported: 'The crowd is swelling all the time as people are coming out of work . . . One woman I spoke to said she had been on the streets twenty years ago for the X case and she couldn't believe here she is again. Other people I spoke to said they had, in fact, never been on a protest but they felt so, so strongly about the situation that they had to come here tonight.'

Kennedy, MC at the vigil, recalls: 'It was very quiet. People were crying. People were holding candles, pictures of Savita. It had a really sombre, sad, shocked tone. It felt almost like being at a funeral.'

Ahern was walking around the crowd before she addressed the vigil, helping to give out candles.

'There were just so many people there who I think had no intention of going to a rally that evening but had gone, on their way home, just to be there. There was a spectrum of people . . . It was people in suits who had come down from their office to take a few minutes. And it was eerily quiet, and it was eerie how quietly people dispersed afterwards. That picture of her looking so full of life – so many people had that picture and it was so beautiful. Everyone was just very aware it was important to be there and I think people felt that huge weight of responsibility.'

She had agreed that morning to speak but found it difficult when the time came. 'I was standing there and all I could think of to say was, "Sorry".'

A minute's silence was called and people began to sit on the ground, some closing their eyes, others crying.

After the vigil dispersed, about thirty pro-choice activists met in Buswells Hotel, just across the road from Leinster House, to organize a national protest in the city for that weekend – three days later.

'We knew we had to pull a march together by Saturday,' says long-time pro-choice activist Anthea McTeirnan.

'We divided up the tasks and we organized the march in forty-eight hours. We had no money. I organized the speakers. Other people gave us the truck. It was hard work. People were so upset. And we literally did beg, borrow and steal . . . But we didn't beg, borrow or steal the people who came, in their thousands and thousands, who just needed to say sorry.'

It became known as the March for Savita. It was to begin at 4 p.m. at the Garden of Remembrance in Parnell Square, followed by a march to Government Buildings on Merrion Square, passing Leinster House on Kildare Street on the way, ending with speeches and a candlelit vigil.

From 3.30 p.m., the only direction in Dublin seemed to be towards Parnell Square. One garda standing in the square was heard to comment, 'They just keep coming and coming.' 'Yes,' said his colleague, 'it's great to see.' There were teenagers with their classmates, mothers who had come from outside Dublin, bringing their children with them.

The mood had palpably changed since Wednesday, from profound shock and sadness to anger.

As the march moved off the rain was driving down and the crowd kept swelling. Among those at its head were university lecturer Goretti Horgan from Derry, reproductive rights campaigner Anthea McTeirnan from Dublin, writer Suzanne Lee from the United States, abortion support worker Ann Rossiter from London carrying a long, white banner, the words NEVER AGAIN across it in black, and the picture of Savita that had been on the front page of the *Irish Times*. The women led the crowd with cries of 'Never again. Never again. Never again.'

There was no music, no sloganeering and for much of the time the marchers walked in silence, some carrying home-made placards, some pushing children in buggies. Others had brought their dogs on leads or carried lighted candles. Many had never been on any kind of march before.

Placards read 'Woman up and legislate', 'Will I be doing this again when I'm 50?' and – on one carried by a young man in a bobbly hat – 'My mother is a woman'. News reports quoted marchers explaining why they were there. 'We were here twenty years ago when my daughter Fiona was a baby, and I cannot believe my daughter has to live in a world where they do not prioritize women's health,' said one woman in her fifties.

Chelsea Uddo, quoted in the *Irish Times*, said: 'I woke up this morning and I just couldn't believe it. I felt like crying all day. I

couldn't stop thinking, "That could be me. It could be anyone".'
'I'm here because I feel ashamed to be Irish,' said Kate Dunne.
There were calls for emergency legislation to 'sort this out'.

Veteran feminist activist Ailbhe Smith on Trade Union TV
was moved to tears as she spoke of why she was there. 'We really
have no way of beginning to calculate the damage, the suffering,
the hurt, the injury, the shame of this country . . .'

RTE news reporter Conor Hunt described the march: 'It's a
sight that's usually associated with decades past, but the death of
Savita Halappanavar has brought the issue of abortion back out
on to Irish streets.'

Sinead Kennedy, a veteran of protests, was among the speakers
at the end of the march. 'Up on the van all I could see was a sea
of faces. People just kept coming . . . It was different to
Wednesday. It was moving and sombre and respectful, but there
was a huge amount of anger. You could feel it. It was winter and
so it was dark by the time we got to Merrion Square. There was
a rawness and a disbelief that this is the country we live in. It was
equally men and women there, a lot very young and a lot of
people there with their children. People didn't see this as an issue
against having children. It was about human rights and women's
well-being. It was very different to any pro-choice event before in
this country.'

Ahern addressed the thousands: 'Today we march and today
we stand, in solidarity with our brothers and sisters who are
expressing their grief and expressing their sorrow, in Ennis, in
Galway, in City West, in Limerick, in San Francisco, in New
York, in Brussels, in Kilkenny, in Carlow, in Wexford, in towns
and cities across the world.'

Clare Daly derided Taoiseach Enda Kenny for saying he would
not be 'rushed' into introducing legislation. Almost screaming to
be heard above the crowd booing their rage, she thundered: 'This
political pygmy has sat in Dáil Éireann for over thirty years while
150,000 Irish women have been exported out of here.'

There were accusations from anti-abortion activists that the march was triumphalist and that pro-choice activists had 'hijacked' Savita's death to further their agenda. Rejecting this, Kennedy says: 'Savita's family, and in particular her husband Praveen, had come out and had gone public. That must have been a very difficult thing for him to do. He had told the world, forcing Ireland to take a look at itself and its reality. I felt we had an enormous responsibility to back him up, to do something about it. He had done it, he said, because he didn't want it to happen to another woman. He had done his part. He had gone public and we, the Irish people, had to be public. Now it was up to us and part of that was getting people out on the streets.'

'I wasn't pleased with [the march], because I didn't want it to happen,' says McTeirnan. 'I was gratified to see people cared, but that's where it stopped. There was no triumphalism. There was anger and sadness and upset. I reject any of the other side's calls to stop jumping on bandwagons. We were just saying sorry and I am sure there were people on the other side on that march, with basic humanity, who just had to be there too, to say, "We're really sorry about this".'

About the same time, about a thousand people gathered in Galway's Eyre Square for a vigil in remembrance of Savita. Sarah McCarthy of Galway pro-choice found it 'very moving, very powerful'.

Journalist Loveena Tandon, covering the Galway vigil for India Today, 'loved how the Irish expressed their solidarity that day.

'It was amazing to see how people felt the pain and felt responsible to look after this woman. I honestly tell you I was in tears.

'I remember saying that in my report, that the death of this beautiful Indian woman might just be the last push needed to bring about change. I know too the family in India were very appreciative of that vigil in Galway and they had no problem with the Irish people. It was the whole dilemma of the Irish system.'

It was a disaster for the anti-abortion lobby. The argument that there was no need for abortion in Ireland to save women's lives appeared to have been blown out of the water. The need for legislation for the X case seemed irrefutable. The assertion that Irish doctors had all the guidance and freedom they needed in order to act in the best interests of the mother seemed patently untrue. Claims that there was no demand for abortion in Irish hospitals had been exposed as, at best, mistaken.

We had had a suicidal child seeking permission to travel for an abortion. We had had mothers carrying foetuses with fatal anomalies forced to travel overseas because the Irish State didn't want to know. We had had young women in care who had to go to court to vindicate their right to travel. This time, we had a young woman, in her first much-wanted pregnancy, who, in her own husband's words, had died because she had been refused an abortion.

It was the greatest crisis in the history of anti-abortionism in Ireland. There was an immediate rush to contain it.

7

The Irish anti-abortion lobby knew the reaction to Savita's death would be explosive, and the demand for legislation to clarify when an abortion was legal in Ireland irresistible.

The lobby was desperate to halt this momentum, for as soon as there was legislation to clarify when abortion was legal, the ground would shift irrevocably. No longer would the debate be about whether abortion should be legal, but about in what circumstances it should be legal. Legislation would mean an absolute and existential defeat. Every argument in their arsenal would be employed in their cause.

The anti-abortion lobby has many compelling arguments.

Breda O'Brien, patron of the conservative Catholic think tank the Iona Institute and weekly columnist with the *Irish Times*, spoke to me at length in late May 2013 of her deep concerns. Her vision of a society where no woman or girl should ever be forced to choose *not* to carry a pregnancy to term is compelling.

Neo-liberal Western society has become so preoccupied with ensuring everyone is available for the marketplace, she says, that the uniquely female thing that women do – have babies – is not supported. Abortion, she says, is put to women as a solution when it is not. In this way it is deeply damaging not only to women but to society.

'The worst possible reason for having an abortion is because you don't have enough money. That's an indictment of society. We need to change and be idealistic,' says O'Brien, who describes herself as a pro-life feminist. 'To me this is all part of the battle for the recognition of what it is to be a woman. The baby is not the enemy; the enemy is the man who raped her. The enemy is the society which says she cannot choose to have a baby. Getting beyond that is the real strength of a woman.'

'Everything is privatized and we have privatized our decision-making. It lets the rest of us off the hook. It kills me when I hear students travelling to have an abortion because a baby will affect their degree. I think, "Get the university to facilitate you, support you." Women have babies. Get over it. Do something about it. It's not going to solve the problem of universities making it difficult for pregnant students to continue their studies. It's not going to solve the problem of sexist workplaces, or abusive relationships.'

Her colleague in the Iona Institute, David Quinn, argues that modern society is not nurturing people in a community, but atomizing them. There are 'cultural drivers' behind the demand for abortion, drivers that are not being questioned.

'Everyone is looking for happiness and self-fulfilment,' he told me in an interview in May 2013. Modern society values above all else, he argues, 'adult freedom', but no one is questioning whether it's making us happy.

'One of the drivers is: "I've got to be single and not just single but unattached right through my twenties, with maybe the odd boyfriend here or there, and if suddenly there's a baby, I want to be unencumbered, so the baby dies." This is all about adult freedom. The guy is thinking I don't want a baby so the baby dies. The woman is saying I want to be free as well so she goes off to the abortion clinic. I don't see how a culture that sets such a premium on the freedom of adults is pro-child. We're so attached to our freedom that we sacrifice kids in its name. The cultural script says put off all your big responsibilities until you are in your thirties.'

Both Quinn and O'Brien were generous with their time and cogent in their arguments. Father Kevin Doran, administrator of the Sacred Heart parish in Donnybrook, was also engaging and interesting. Marc Coleman, anti-abortion writer and broadcaster, corresponded at length by email.

Those against abortion to whom I spoke voiced sincere concerns that it was a human rights issue; central to this was their view that the unborn life was of equal value to that of the woman carrying it. Their ideal world is one where abortion was never necessary. It appeared, however, that for them the idea that a woman or girl could freely choose to end a pregnancy was unimaginable. They spoke of women being put under pressure to have a termination, of not being supported by society to keep their pregnancy, of being misguided or not fully appreciating what they were doing. There was also a sense that they viewed abortion as something some women who just couldn't be bothered to be pregnant did. An assumption of thoughtlessness, on the part of women and of society, on the abortion issue, came through in all the interviews.

O'Brien, for example, in questioning the high premium Western society puts on individual choice, was implying that people needed societal protection from the 'bad' choices they might make.

'To me choice has become the dominant ideology and I have big problems with that. Choice is not the ultimate value. Choice is hugely important to be a human being, because freedom is very important, but choice also requires that you can make bad choices. I think the ideology of choice says that once you've made a choice it must be honoured regardless, and there's a negative impact from that. It's not a communitarian point of view, it's a radically individualized point of view – if you make your choice live with it, and I don't think that's good for society.

'I think it erodes a sense of caring for each other. To me the ultimate value is life.' She spoke of the 'tyranny of choice'.

'It's the triumph of consumer capitalism that all hinges on choice. The right to choose is not the ultimate value. The right to live will give you the right to make choices.'

The right to make a choice must be circumscribed once pregnancy comes into a woman's or girl's life, because of the life of the foetus within her. And the society for which she argues must, I inferred, if not impose these values for the greater good, certainly espouse them.

'I'm totally in favour of people planning their families, but once the family is already started then I think your planning has to be of a different nature. If a woman is not financially secure and set up, well to me [because] she is already pregnant [society must support her].'

Quinn argues that once children – or pregnancy – come into one's life, some freedoms must be sacrificed, while Father Doran asserts that while the Church 'wouldn't say a pregnant woman gives up some rights . . . certainly we would feel that when one exercises rights they should not ignore the rights of others. We believe fundamentally in the dignity of human life from the point of conception.'

The main groups in Ireland's anti-abortion vanguard are Youth Defence, the Life Institute, the Pro-life Campaign, the Iona Institute and Family and Life.

Youth Defence in particular is associated with 'American-style' campaigning characterized by aggressive lobbying, personalized attacks on anyone who contradicts their beliefs and displaying pictures of dead foetuses at campaign rallies and stalls. The Life Institute shares an office with Youth Defence and was founded by Niamh Uí Bhriain who had founded Youth Defence.

The Pro-Life Campaign was founded in 1992 in response to the X case. Among its founding members were Fianna Fáil Senator Des Hanafin and Regius Professor of Laws at Trinity

College William Binchy, both of whom were involved in the 1983 pro-life amendment campaign. Its primary spokespeople are William Binchy and Caroline Simons, solicitor.

The Iona Institute is a conservative, Catholic lobby group, founded in 2007 by religious commentator David Quinn. Its strong focus is on traditional family values and it promotes heterosexual marriage, heterosexual parenting and state-funded denominational schooling. Though it is anti-abortion, the issue is not central to its campaigns. Nevertheless it has engaged in the post-Savita debate, Quinn explaining that it had to, in order to 'share the burden' with its anti-abortion colleagues, such was the media demand for their voices.

Family and Life is a registered company and charity, based at 26 Mountjoy Square, Dublin 1. It 'believes in a total life ethic which requires a commitment to oppose all attempts to undermine the inalienable and imprescriptible nature of human life'. Its volunteers take life-size models of foetuses into Catholic primary schools, to 'help students to understand the development of the unborn child and also to instil a sense of respect for life at its most vulnerable stages'. Family and Life plays a major role in organizing mass events such as the annual National Novena in Defence of Life, as well as the Vigil for Life of January 2013, held in Dublin, which was attended by about 20,000 people. It is also involved in pro-life projects in Poland and Russia, with a sister Polish organization, Friends of Human Life.

When news of Savita's death broke on 14 November 2012, the first, most urgent task for the anti-abortion lobby was to shoot the messenger.

The *Irish Times*, within hours, was accused of deliberately creating hysteria by publishing the story 'under the most sensationalist headline you could possibly imagine' and of using 'screaming headlines' to flog the story all over the world. The headline on the front page that morning was carefully written to capture the facts as told as well as the concerns of our main source for the story, Savita's husband Praveen. It was written by the chief subeditor on duty that night and was approved by both the editor Kevin O'Sullivan and news editor Roddy O'Sullivan. I was asked to approve it too before I left work on the evening of Tuesday the 13th. Needless to say, it was also sent to the newspaper's solicitor, Andy O'Rorke, for his approval. Rarely had a headline been so carefully worded.

'Woman "denied a termination" dies in hospital' it said. A woman had died in hospital; her husband said she had been denied a termination. The headline was correct in fact and in spirit.

According to anti-abortion groups the *Irish Times* was also in cahoots with the pro-choice lobby, an allegation apparently borne out by the manner in which pro-choice activists were, they said, capitalizing on it.

A new website, savitatruth.com, which appeared in the days after the story broke, said: 'Abortion advocates are using the tragic death of Dr Savita Halappanavar to promote abortion in Ireland through fear and error'.

'Know the Tragedy, Know the Facts' exhorted its home page and among its first 'facts' was that between 28 October when Savita died and 14 November when the story broke the 'media wait[ed] to publish the story'.

'If only they knew,' sighed Paul Cullen and I at one point, as we mused over our frustration in those days before publication at its being repeatedly held for further legal consideration and to esure fairness to the hospital and doctors.

The savitatruth site said: 'Dr Savita's [*sic*] husband and the media are silent for over two weeks about her death. Abortion advocates know the story is going to break at least three days ahead of time and co-ordinate a media strategy exploiting the death to promote their long-standing campaigns to legalize abortion in Ireland.'

The source cited for this was an article in the *Sunday Independent* published on 18 November under the headline: 'Campaigners had heard of Savita's death three days before story broke'.

'Abortion campaigners, including two left-wing political researchers in Leinster House, were aware of the Savita Halappanavar case at least three days before her death became public knowledge,' wrote the reporter. 'Pro-choice activists held an emergency meeting last Monday night in Dublin city centre to plan how they would proceed after the details emerged publicly about the death at University Hospital Galway of 31-year-old Mrs Halappanavar whose death is now the subject of two separate investigations.'

Emails sent between pro-choice activists, which 'show they were aware last Sunday, and probably earlier, that a "denial of abortion" story was about to break' were cited.

Pro-choice activists were aware of the story before it broke in much the same way as any source for any story is aware of it before it breaks. One could hazard a guess that there were also some in the anti-abortion lobby aware of the *Sunday Independent*'s story before it broke, and who stayed silent while they co-ordinated their media strategy.

Some said the story had been used to 'manufacture' pro-abortion madness across the land. In January 2013 Niamh Uí Bhriain (née Nic Mhathúna), former chairwoman of Youth Defence and founder of the Life Institute, appeared on the *Huckabee* show – a primetime talk show hosted by former governor of Arkansas and Baptist pastor Mike Huckabee on the Fox News Network. 'What's happening in Ireland is that this huge global hysteria, that was manufactured by abortion campaigners, they're putting enormous pressure on the Government to legalize abortion,' she said.

The contention that the *Irish Times* was working conspiratorially with pro-choice campaigners is ridiculous. Apart from being dangerous professionally for any news reporter to 'get into bed' with any one 'side' in a debate – let alone on an issue as contentious as abortion – it would be insane to leak a story when trying your best to ensure it doesn't break before your publisher is ready to publish. After meeting John Walshe and Sarah McCarthy of Galway Pro-choice in Galway on Friday 9 November, I had no further contact with them until interviewing for this book.

The suggestion on one anti-abortion website that Praveen was involved in an ideologically motivated media campaign is of course offensive to both him and his love for Savita.

David Quinn is more realistic about how the story played out. 'Obviously the pro-choice side used the story to advance their point of view, but I wouldn't begrudge them that, because from their point of view . . . she died because of the law. Rightly or wrongly it's what they believe so it's fair enough that they should use it to campaign for a change in the law. And if the opposite had happened in some way, shape or form then it would be very unusual for the pro-life side to say sorry that's what happens when you allow x, y or z or don't allow x, y or z, so of course pro-choice are going to use it to vindicate their position. So, it's not exploitation per se. It's what happens.'

Breda O'Brien is also more reflective. She too 'regretted very much' the original headline and the 'way the story was framed from the beginning'. The focus on the repeated requests for the termination, she says, 'made the debate incredibly difficult to have'. She would have liked to have seen a far greater emphasis in the original story on Savita's sepsis, and this issue got lost. However, from Savita's husband's point of view and that of her community in Galway who first brought the story out, the debate had to be about abortion and the legal situation that seemed to have denied Savita one. Their interpretation framed the debate. It was their interpretation that many, including leading obstetricians, doctors, lawyers and ordinary people, agreed with.

And there can be no denying that if Savita had had the abortion she asked for on Monday or Tuesday, no debate at all would have arisen and no one outside her circle would have ever heard the name Savita Halappanavar.

There were the predictable attacks on the bona fides of the reporting journalist.

Among other facts on the savitatruth site is the following: 'The original *Irish Times* story is written by the daughter of two noted abortion activists.' The 'noted abortion activists' presumably are journalist Mary Holland, who died in June 2004, and journalist Eamonn McCann. Mary Holland was best known for her work over four decades covering the Northern Irish Troubles. She was also a feminist, trade unionist and founder member of the 1983 Anti-Amendment Campaign. Eamonn McCann is a journalist, human rights campaigner, and is pro-choice. This comment on parentage was repeated and repeated on anti-abortion sites and blogs across the world. How it should detract from the facts of the story has yet to be explained. One Irish anti-abortion site featured the particularly vile comment: 'she must have caught the virus coming through the mother's birth canal'.

A key moment for the global anti-abortion lobby was an interview on Newstalk radio, hosted by Marc Coleman. *Coleman At Large* is a current affairs programme with a right-wing bent. In the interview he asked about variations in Praveen's account, in different interviews, of when Savita had been started on antibiotics during her week in hospital. In one interview Praveen had spoken of antibiotics being administered on Sunday 21 October; in another, of them being administered on Tuesday the 23rd. We now know Savita was started on several antibiotics during the week. When asked about these differences I said, 'All one can surmise is that his recollection of events, you know, the actual timeline and days, may be a little muddled.'

I also said at a later point, when asked about the fact that there was no record in Savita's medical notes of her repeated requests for a termination: 'Who knows what will come out in that inquiry?' In relation to the HSE inquiry into her death, I said: 'They may come back and say she came in with a disease she caught from something outside the hospital before she even arrived in, and there was no request for termination.'

The word 'muddled' was seized upon, as was the speculative conversation, initiated by Coleman, about why Savita's requests for a termination were not recorded. We now know there is evidence that at least one discussion about a termination was not recorded in Savita's notes. The Life Institute was first out with a press release, four days after the interview was broadcast: 'In an astonishing interview with Marc Coleman on Newstalk 106, Kitty Holland, the *Irish Times* journalist who broke the story of Savita Halappanavar's tragic death, now says that the story may be "muddled" and that it may be found that there was "no request for a termination".' It was an astonishing stretch of what was said in the interview. Uí Bhriain said: 'But Holland and the rest of the Irish and international journalists never referred to any "muddled" recollections or to the possibility that there "was no request for a termination" when abortion campaigners were shrieking that Savita had died because she couldn't get an abortion. This has been the most cynical and deplorable exploitation of a tragedy by abortion campaigners that I have ever witnessed in my lifetime.'

The release was not followed up to any great extent in the mainstream media, though anti-abortion sites across the world gave it great space.

Lifesitenews.com in the United States reported: 'The *Irish Times* reporter who broke the story about the death of Savita Halappanavar that launched a global crusade against Ireland's pro-life laws, has admitted that the story of Mrs. Halappanavar asking for an abortion may have been a little bit "muddled" in the retelling.' A blog on another US site, consciencelaws.org, publishes what it claims is a transcript of the interview, into which innumerable 'ah' 'em' 'mmm' 'unintelligible' and so on are inserted, inaccurately, into my contributions.

Cristina Odone, former editor of the *Catholic Herald* in Britain, in her blog posted on the *Telegraph* site, described the original story as a 'tale' and repeated Uí Bhriain's description of the Coleman interview as 'astonishing'. 'In their rush to make a pro-abortion point, journalists and editors did not check their facts,' she stated.

I was grateful in the following few days for the messages of support from other journalists and my union, the National Union of Journalists. Justine McCarthy, journalist with the *Sunday Times*, wrote in her column of 9 December 2012 of the attacks she had received over the years, from elements within the anti-abortion lobby. She described a man in County Meath telling her she had been 'rejoicing in Savita's death' so she could argue for 'abortion on demand'; a woman who had followed her into the Four Courts some years ago, shouting abuse at her because a newspaper she had once worked for had made an out-of-court settlement with Niamh Nic Mhathúna/Uí Bhriain of the Life Institute nine years after she had written about her in a piece about the thirteen-year-old rape victim, Miss C.

'One of you followed me all the way upstairs, still holding your placard depicting aborted foetuses as you harangued me. Were you aware that, in the courtroom, the woman you wedged your-self in beside was the distraught mother of Miss D, the girl with an unviable pregnancy whom the Health Service Executive had brought to court to stop her travelling to England for an abortion?' asked McCarthy. She said she knew she was not the only journalist who had been vilified by some of the anti-abortion lobby, in their attempts to intimidate.

A more repugnant line of offence was to deny the story itself, effectively denying Praveen's account.

The argument was that Savita's death had nothing to do with abortion; her death was due to sepsis and miscarriage only; the doctors in Galway were free to intervene and should have – a possibly libellous assertion that to my knowledge has not been pursued by Dr Astbury or her colleagues. In fact, said the anti-abortion lobby, all doctors were free to intervene to save a mother's life even if this meant the loss of the unborn: it was always clear when they should do so, and doctors knew this. Furthermore, if Savita's pregnancy had been terminated, it would not have been abortion at all. Besides, Ireland, in their view, was the safest place in the world to have a baby, since abortion, in their view, never took place here.

The anti-abortion strategy was and is multi-pronged, slick and brilliantly executed. No opportunity is missed. Most of its spokespeople look great and present their cause as reasonable and rational.

'Let's be very clear on this,' says Noel Whelan, barrister and political commentator. 'There is a very sophisticated co-ordinated strategy going on on the pro-life side in response to this. Everything you see happening at their end, these are all the logical things you would do if you were organizing a campaign. None of this is spontaneous.'

And so, in a well-planned fashion, the anti-abortion lobby made a series of contentions.

They said, **Savita's death was due to sepsis and a mismanaged miscarriage, and that is all.**

It would be important to await the findings of investigations before commenting, said Uí Bhriain in a statement the afternoon the story broke. She was sufficiently confident of her facts, however, to declare: 'the loss of Ms Halappanavar's life was not caused by Ireland's ban on abortion'. The campaigners were focused on separating Savita's case from the lack of legal clarity on abortion.

That night Caroline Simons, legal advisor to the Pro-Life Campaign, was on the panel of the *Tonight* show, with Vincent Browne. Having discussed Savita's death, and dwelling on death rates from sepsis, she said: 'We're talking about a miscarriage. In a case of a miscarriage, doctors expedite delivery. We really don't know what has happened in this case.' Doctors in Ireland don't expedite delivery if there is a foetal heart unless there is a threat to the life of the mother.

When asked about failure to legislate on the X case she sat back in her chair and said: 'Now that is an entirely different question. Now let's just realize we have finished discussing the Galway case that dealt with a miscarriage and now you are asking me whether the Oireachtas should legislate to implement the terms of the X case.'

She said in a case like Savita's it was 'absolutely clear . . . the doctors had the freedom to intervene, including to terminate the pregnancy'.

On this she and other anti-abortion campaigners rely on the guidelines on abortion set out by the Irish Medical Council, the regulatory body for doctors. According to its *Guide to Professional Conduct and Ethics for Registered Medical Practitioners*:

> Abortion is illegal in Ireland except where there is a real and substantial risk to the life (as distinct from the health) of the mother. Under current legal precedent, this exception includes where there is a clear and substantial risk to the life of the mother arising from a threat of suicide. You should under-take a full assessment of any such risk in light of the clinical research on this issue.

They continue:

> In current obstetrical practice, rare complications can arise where therapeutic intervention (including termination of a pregnancy) is required at a stage when, due to extreme immaturity of the baby, there may be little or no hope of the baby surviving. In these exceptional circumstances, it may be

necessary to intervene to terminate the pregnancy to protect the life of the mother, while making every effort to preserve the life of the baby.

Simons later contradicted herself when co-panellist, consultant obstetrician and gynaecologist Dr David Walsh argued that there was a lack of clarity for him and his colleagues in these guidelines. Dr Walsh said: 'If you look at the Medical Council guidelines. [Imagine] you have to read this at two o'clock in the morning, there's a sick patient who is bleeding or with an infection, and the first thing it says is "Abortion is illegal in Ireland". Then, you should undertake a full assessment in light of the clinical research. So you have to be a barrister, you have to be a clinical researcher. This is the most, it's not very helpful. It's certainly not explicit. The problem is you are dealing with uncertainty.'

'Absolutely,' nodded Simons.

'That is where true expertise is manifest.'

'Absolutely.'

'Any idiot can tell you when there's an obvious infection or not. But the difficulty is in that transition from one to the other. You get the wrong side of the equation and you get . . .' said Dr Walsh.

'That's right. I agree,' said Simons.

The following night, on the same programme, Dr Berry Kiely, also of the Pro-Life Campaign, said: 'There are two things to distinguish here. One is the management of miscarriage. The other is abortion.' The next night, on RTE's *Late Late Show*, Simons was again on air, telling host Ryan Tubridy: 'There isn't a person in this country who hasn't been deeply, deeply shocked, deeply worried and who might now be very afraid about what treatment they're entitled to when they're pregnant.' She warned, however, that we must not rush to conclude that the law on access to abortion services should be clarified. 'I think if there was a poll tomorrow they would say "Yes" to absolutely anything if they thought it would have saved Savita Halappanavar's life in this awful case in Galway.' Nevertheless, 'This was a case which concerned management of miscarriage.'

Speaking on the US Fox News network's *Huckabee* show in January 2013, Uí Bhriain told the host: 'What got lost in all the hysteria about the tragic death of Savita was that this was nothing to do with abortion at all . . . The facts are now starting to emerge and they tell a totally different story.' This was some months before the inquest into Savita's death opened in April. 'Savita Halappanavar very sadly lost her life to septicaemia . . . Abortion is not a treatment for septicaemia. It's not a treatment for miscarriage. These facts became completely drowned out in the hysteria that was created by abortion campaigners and by the media, and they were doing that in order to try to push abortion on Ireland.'

The anti-abortion lobby chose to view Savita's requests for a termination as irrelevant, in much the same way as the law had. Consistently the anti-abortion lobby determined to reduce a highly complex, rapidly unfolding obstetric emergency to simple black and white certainties. Praveen was, however, equally certain and equally consistent. His wife had been having a miscarriage and the way he and Savita had wanted it to be managed was with a timely abortion.

They said **the law was clear and doctors know exactly when to intervene to save the life of the mother, even if this results in the death of the unborn**.

On this, as related earlier, Simons had spoken somewhat confusedly the night the story broke. The following night on the same programme Uí Bhriain said there was 'no evidence [obstetricians] are confused'. Despite an interview that morning, on RTE Radio's *Morning Ireland*, on which one of Ireland's most respected obstetricians and gynaecologists and former Master of the National Maternity Hospital, Dr Peter Boylan, had said obstetricians had 'no clarity' and 'the current situation is like a Sword of Damocles hanging over us', Uí Bhriain argued on.

She told the host: 'The All-Party Oireachtas Committee on Health actually reviewed practice in Ireland specifically in relation to this issue and they found that there was no evidence that women in Ireland were being denied medical treatment because of our ban on abortion. That's really important. It's really important to look at what's actually happening statistically. Women in Ireland are not dying because they can't access life-saving treatment.'

Simons, on the *Late Late Show*, the following night, said there was in the Irish Constitution an 'inbuilt appreciation in the right to life section [Article 40.3.3] which shows it is not always practicable to defend and vindicate the life of the unborn. And doctors in this country do always look after the mother as a priority. They have to make judgement calls and they have to have the freedom and space in critical situations that can involve terminating a pregnancy. That's legal and it's ethical . . . I'm very thankful for the standard of medical care that we have.'

The following Wednesday night, 21 November, Dr Berry Kiely was on the RTE television current affairs programme *Primetime*. Having told co-panellist Dr Boylan he was 'judging' the Galway doctors involved in Savita's care for 'being incorrect in what they did' without knowing the full facts, Kiely said: 'There is nothing in ethics, there is nothing in law, in this country which impedes a doctor from treating this case be it conser-vatively, medically or surgically . . . There would be nothing preventing that doctor inducing labour.'

Dr Boylan, interjecting, told Dr Kiely he specifically had not commented on the Galway case, adding, however, that if a doctor had terminated a living foetus at 17 weeks' gestation when the mother's life was not at risk, they would have been breaking the law. 'If the mother's life is not at risk, you cannot terminate a pregnancy where the baby is alive. There is no argument about that. If the mother's life is at risk, you can.'

The Irish Medical Council guidelines were just that. Guidelines. They lacked the force of law, in a way that the 1861 Offences Against the Person Act criminalizing abortion and making it punishable by life in prison certainly did not. As Professor Kieran Murphy, President of the Council, told the Oireachtas Health Committee on 17 May 2013 during its hearings on the abortion legislation: 'While doctors are expected to adhere to the IMC's guide in their professional practice, it is important to note that it is not a legal code.'

They said, **when doctors did intervene ethically to save the life of the mother and ended up killing the foetus, this was not actually abortion. So, abortion is never necessary to save a woman's life**.

Asked her views on this proposition, Dr Rhona Mahony, Master of the National Maternity Hospital, said: 'This is pure semantics. It's an attempt to evade reality and it has no place in medicine. [When] facing sometimes tragic reality, clarity is central to the job. It's silly. It's unhelpful. Of course it's never the deliberate destruction of the baby. It's saving the mother's life, but a termination of pregnancy is a termination of pregnancy. The mother deserves to know one will be performed if necessary to save her life. They deserve to know absolutely that their lives will be guarded.'

This anti-abortion argument was set out most forcefully in the so-called 'Dublin Declaration' drawn up at a symposium on maternal health in September 2012 held in the King's Inns in Dublin. It was promoted by the Irish Catholic Doctors Association, and its keynote speaker was Professor Eamon O'Dwyer, Emeritus Professor of Gynaecology and Obstetrics at National University of Ireland Galway and avowedly anti-abortion.

The Declaration says:

As experienced practitioners and researchers in Obstetrics and Gynaecology, we affirm that direct abortion – the purposeful destruction of the unborn in the termination of pregnancy – is not medically necessary to save the life of a woman. We uphold that there is a fundamental difference between abortion, and necessary medical treatments that are carried out to save the life of the mother, even if such treatments result in the loss of life of her unborn child. We confirm that the prohibition of abortion does not affect, in any way, the availability of optimal care to a pregnant woman.

Dr Mahony says of the Convention: 'I don't acknowledge it. I don't recognize it. It means nothing to me. I would go so far as to say I deeply resent the name Dublin being part of it. This symposium was an offshoot group. This was a group of people who have a certain ideology, who are politically motivated, who had a meeting and I know from many people who went to that meeting that there was no such consensus, but they published this at the end claiming this was some kind of expert consensus. It's irrelevant. Is it true? No. It is sometimes necessary, of course it is, to terminate a pregnancy to save a life. I do it several times a year. Always be wary of the word "never". There is no such thing as the word "never" in medicine. It's not credible.'

This is a central tenet of the anti-abortion lobby: that the abortion of a pregnancy is not an abortion if the intention is to save the mother's life. It apparently enables the lobby to argue that because abortion is never needed to save a woman's life – because that is not actually an abortion – then legislation to clarify when an abortion may be carried out is not necessary. It is a complex argument that sometimes confuses people.

Professor John Bonnar, former chair of the Institute of Obstetricians and Gynaecologists, is a keen advocate of the thinking that underpins the Dublin Declaration. Speaking on RTE's *Primetime*, on 19 April 2013, he said he would have no problem with terminating a pregnancy regardless of the presence of a foetal heartbeat. 'I've had to undertake terminations of pregnancy mainly for problems such as uterine or cervical cancer or ovarian cancer and the fact that there was a foetal heart there never stopped me providing the appropriate care for the mother,' he said. 'We meet other emergencies like ectopic pregnancies, abdominal pregnancy. The fact that there is a foetal heart there would not be an issue in my view in treating the mother if she is seriously ill.' In fact in some cases he would terminate even if the mother was well: 'In an ectopic pregnancy there can be a foetal heart, the mother is perfectly well. She is not seriously ill but I know she is going to be in serious difficulty,' he said.

The difference, he maintains, is that in such situations this is not the 'direct and intentional killing' of the unborn but a side effect of administering life-saving treatment to the woman. It is, in theological parlance, a 'double effect' termination, where treatment has the good effect of saving the mother and the second, unfortunate, effect of killing the unborn.

This approach, known as the 'principle of double effect', was formulated by Thomas Aquinas in the thirteenth century. According to this principle, Christians are not morally culpable for an action which would normally be sinful, when it is the un-intended effect of a morally legitimate action. It has been contested since the seventeenth century as, in short, it allows Christians to 'have their cake and eat it'. In states where abortion is illegal, such as Britain before 1967 or Ireland at the time of Savita's death, it does at least permit doctors to abort pregnancies in clear-cut cases such as those mentioned by Professor Bonnar. However, in cases which are less clear it is, arguably, confusing and lacks the necessary clarity for medical practice. As Desmond Clarke, Emeritus Professor of Philosophy at University College Cork, wrote in the *Irish Times* on 7 June 2013, the principle of double effect is 'unreliable' in the medical context.

Dr Boylan, on the same *Primetime* programme with Professor

Bonnar, said: 'The problem with Savita was that when she was seriously ill she progressed rapidly. What she needed was treatment before she became seriously ill, and that's the brinkmanship I'm talking about. This is nothing to do with ectopic pregnancy or the treatment of cancer, which is completely irrelevant in this context.'

They said **Ireland is the safest place in the world to have a baby so abortion is not necessary here**.

The day the story broke, the Pro-Life Campaign declared that Ireland was 'recognized as a world leader in protecting women in pregnancy by the UN and World Health Organization'. Niamh Uí Bhriain, speaking at a fundraiser at the Chicago Irish American Center in January 2013, said: 'Ireland is currently the safest place in the world to have a baby – without recourse to abortion.'

This is neither true nor relevant.

The anti-abortion lobby has based this claim on the 2005 maternal mortality estimates of the World Health Organization, UNICEF, the UN Population Fund and the World Bank. These showed Ireland's maternal mortality rate to be just one per 100,000 live births, compared to an average of nine per 100,000 in the developed world. The data on which this claim is made, the civil registry of deaths in each country, are recognized as unreliable for fully measuring maternal deaths.

The Confidential Maternal Death Enquiry (CMDE) in Ireland, which issued its first report in 2011, uses a data-reporting method pioneered in Britain in 1952, in which hospitals, social workers, obstetricians, midwives and anyone else capable of recognizing and recording a maternal death, reports to the Enquiry. According to its *Report for the Triennium 2009–2011*, the Irish maternal death rate was eight per 100,000. Dr Michael O'Hare, consultant obstetrician at Daisy Hill Hospital in Newry, Co. Tyrone, and chairman of the MDE group, says the higher rate comes from more thorough data-gathering, and also from the fact that a death up to a year after pregnancy is now recorded as a maternal death, whereas the previous system had included only deaths up to six weeks post-partum.

Ireland still has a lower maternal death rate than Britain's 11 per 100,000 live births. However, the Scandinavian nations of Norway and Sweden, which also have liberal abortion regimes, do better, with seven maternal deaths per 100,000 births in Norway and five per 100,000 in Sweden – both in 2008. Taken in the round, said Dr O'Hare in the *Irish Times* on 4 December 2012, the figures made it difficult to use maternal mortality rates to argue for or against abortion services. 'I have serious doubts about the validity of the arguments. If you look at Britain which it is acknowledged has fairly liberal abortion legislation, they are not doing any better than us, while the Scandinavian countries which are doing better also have liberal provision,' he said.

The question of maternal mortality rates in the developed world *is* related to access to abortion services. Among the reasons why Ireland has so few maternal deaths (and no deaths caused by illegal or backstreet abortions) is its proximity to Britain, to which numerous women whose health or lives are at risk due to their pregnancy go in unknown numbers each year.

Nowhere, in the anti-abortion lobby's arguments, is the issue of the pregnant woman's wishes considered.

On Tuesday, 4 December, almost three weeks after the story broke, an anti-abortion rally was held outside Leinster House. Organized by the Pro-Life Campaign, Youth Defence, the Life Institute, and Family and Life, it was attended by four bishops and archbishops – the Archbishop of Tuam, Michael Neary; the Bishop of Kilmore, Leo O'Reilly; the Bishop of Killaloe, Kieran O'Reilly; and the Bishop of Ossory, Seamus Freeman – along with about 7,000 others.

People held placards, candles and posters calling on Fine Gael to 'keep [their] pro-life promises'. Uí Bhriain addressed the crowd, saying: 'We are not for turning and we will not yield. We are proud to be a pro-life nation. We are here to tell the politicians in Dáil Éireann that they have destroyed our economy but we will never let them kill our children. The lives of our children are worth fighting for and the mothers who are driven to abortion in fear are worth fighting for and the pro-life ethos in this country is worth fighting for.'

Caroline Simons announced a mass Unite for Life vigil, to be held in Dublin after Christmas.

In the following weeks, the Catholic bishops asked the priests in their dioceses to urge parishioners to get to Dublin for the Unite for Life vigil on Saturday, 19 January.

'Wow!' commented colour writer, Miriam Lord, in her *Irish Times* report on the January rally. 'Now that's the way to organize a vigil.'

Over a hundred buses were laid on across the island from early morning to get supporters up to Dublin. An impressive sea of people filled one side of Merrion Square, the majority carrying either pink placards with a picture of a young woman cuddling a baby, saying 'Love them Both', or yellow ones saying 'Vote Pro-life'. There were none of the home-made scrawls of independent, quirky opinion on show at the March for Savita in November. And where the speakers at that march had had to make do with the back of a borrowed truck, for this there was a rock-concert-size stage, complete with mixer desk and a huge screen called, apparently, a Jumbotron, so that speakers could be seen from a distance. Between 20,000 and 30,000 people were there in bitterly cold weather and, judging by the TV footage, they were disproportionately young.

According to Lord's report: 'A small group of disgruntled men stood outside the barrier. Forbidden signs which they were carrying included some large "Abortion Kills" placards, along with another saying "men abandon, women abort, State abrogates – thou shalt not kill."'

'We asked why, given it was a public protest, people were not allowed to join in with their own banners. "There are four or five signs that have been agreed and it's been agreed by the right-to-life committee and that's it. There are no unauthorized signs," said the steward, who declined to give his name.'

RTE reporter Sinead Hussey, on that evening's six o'clock news, spoke to some of the people who had come to Dublin to voice their concern about the Government's stated commitment to introduce legislation on abortion. A man in his later thirties, carrying a child on his shoulders, said: 'I have come from Castlebar just to try and make some kind of difference. We have to choose between life and hope or death and despair.' A woman in her late forties, wearing a red rain-mac, had come from Cork. 'I'm very disappointed with the Government, especially the Fine Gael Government,' she said.

David Manly of Family and Life told the crowd that a different culture was emerging – 'a culture which debases and dehumanizes the unborn child and his or her mother'. Tyrone GAA manager Mickey Harte said he was 'most concerned that this Government proposes to legislate for abortion' and there was 'no point in saving the economy if a child's right to life is compromised or forgotten'. Uí Bhriain, to rapturous applause, came on to the stage. In true showbiz style she greeted the crowd, 'Hello Dublin! And every other county that's here today. We are the pro-life majority and we will not accept abortion – not now, not ever, not in our country and not in our name.'

Organizers of the vigil said afterwards that they were 'thrilled' with the turnout. Attendance probably did outnumber the March for Savita in November, though only just, and some reports, including that by Lord in the *Irish Times*, said numbers were equal at each.

The big pro-life rallies since Savita's death have consistently attracted about 20,000 people or more. That was the estimated number at the January 2013 Vigil for Life, and at the National Vigil for Life, also in Dublin, on 8 June. There were about 35,000 at the final pro-life rally on 6 July, 6 days before X case legislation was passed in the Dáil the following Thursday, 11 July. However, 1.2 million turned out to greet Pope John Paul II when he visited Ireland in 1979. Given the enormous resources and organization put into these rallies, given the exhortations from every Catholic pulpit in the land in the weeks running up to them, it might be expected that they would attract crowds nearer 100,000 to 150,000.

Among those at the 6 July protest was a contingent from the conservative Catholic Irish American organization, the Ancient Order of Hibernians. Also there were many hundreds of anti-abortion sympathizers from the United States who had flown in to support the final push against the legislation. The ideological links between the Irish anti-abortion lobby and the US are well known. Hard evidence of financial support flowing from the US pro-life coffers into the Irish is almost impossible to produce, given the reluctance of such organizations as Youth Defence and the Life Institute – which have the strongest US links – to allow scrutiny of their funding streams. The issue is important. The suspicion that large sums of money are flowing from the US into one side of an Irish debate with huge implications for Irish women gives rise to concerns about undue external influence.

Among those who have examined the audiences for some of the anti-abortion lobby is Geoff Lillis, a Dublin-based IT systems administrator who researches the social media accounts of the most influential Irish anti-abortion organizations. A techie fanatic, he has a fascinating blog, Geoffsshorts, and was inspired by a piece on broadsheet.ie in July 2012, which found that 80 per cent of Youth Defence's Facebook 'Likes' were from people in the United States.

'I thought "I wonder if I can do something similar with Twitter?" and I was curious about who follows their Twitter account,' he explains. He built a programme to 'mine' the Twitter accounts of Youth Defence, the Life Institute, the

Pro-Life Campaign, David Quinn, Independent Senator Ronan Mullen and Ireland Stand Up. Looking at the 'stated location' of followers as well as the time zones from which they tweet, he was able to establish where their followers were based. All sites had majority US and Canadian followers.

In the case of Youth Defence, in September 2012, he was able to 'pin down' all but 13 per cent of its 1,339 followers. Some 59 per cent were based in the USA or Canada and just 14 per cent were Irish. The rest were in Europe, the Philippines, Ecuador and Australia.

The Pro-Life Campaign, in November 2012, had 5,410 followers of its @ProLifeCampaign account. Some 70 per cent were based in the US, 11 per cent in the UK, 10 per cent in Ireland, 2 per cent in each of Canada and the Philippines and the rest in Mexico, South Africa, Australia and Europe.

'I also found myself wondering who and what the Youth Defence followers followed. So I pulled out stats on every group followed by everyone who follows Youth Defence.'

He found that 50.3 per cent of Youth Defence's followers also follow LifeSiteNews, a US based website established in 1997, 'dedicated to issues of culture, life, and family'. It is anti-abortion, anti-gay-rights, anti-feminism and hosts such campaigners as controversial Canadian conservative Bill Whatcott who seeks to have both abortion and homosexuality, or 'homofascism' as he calls it, criminalized.

Uí Bhriain is described by LifeSiteNews's communications manager as a 'dear friend' and has written on numerous occasions for the site. Some 45 per cent of Youth Defence's followers follow the account of Lila Rose, an American pro-life activist, born in 1988, who founded the anti-abortion Live Action campaign when she was fifteen. Over 32 per cent of YD followers also follow the account of the American Life League, 20 per cent follow Sarah Palin's account and 19 per cent follow Fox News.

Ireland's apparently 'abortion-free' status is extremely important to anti-abortion campaigners in the United States, and the encouragement of the US campaigners is clearly important to the Irish.

Writing in May 2012, Kate Bryan, communications director of US anti-abortion activist group Live Action, said: 'Although Ireland is small, it is a nation that has become one of the pro-life movement's most precious jewels. We must stand with Ireland and make sure that this "jewel" is guarded and that life is protected. And then we will add more jewels to this crown and polish them to make them shine brighter than ever before. We will win this battle; Ireland continues to give us hope every day in this battle for life. For many years, Ireland has fought to keep Ireland abortion-free, and I am happy to say that today will be another day without abortion in Ireland. And remember when you are out celebrating to raise a glass in honor of the 100,000 lives that have been saved because of Ireland's ban on abortion, and remember that there is hope for our great nation – that one day, America will be ABORTION-FREE!'

Uí Bhriain, in her January 2013 appearance on Fox News channel's *Huckabee* show, appealed to American anti-abortion sympathizers for support. She agreed with another guest, Lila Rose, who had said: 'Planned Parenthood has been fighting to push abortion into Ireland. They had cases that they brought before the European Court, some of them which were thrown out. They were false cases, again trying to manufacture facts, trick people, mislead people and it's happening all over again in Ireland.' She was, it seems, referring to the *A, B and C v. Ireland* case which came before the European Court of Human Rights in 2010, in which the three women were supported by the Irish Family Planning Association, which is affiliated to the International Planned Parenthood Federation.

Uí Bhriain said the reason Ireland mattered 'so much' to 'global abortion campaigners' was 'because Ireland is like the proof, the scientific evidence that you can ban abortion and keep your mothers absolutely safe. In Ireland the people decided thirty years ago that we can offer better answers to women than abortion, that we can protect our mothers and our babies. That has made Ireland like a safe haven for mothers and babies. And now Planned Parenthood . . . are raising global hysteria to try and force Ireland to legalize abortion. And as young women, the Irish pro-life movement is rising up and saying, "Not on our watch".'

The lesson was 'clear', said Rose.

'America looks to you as an inspiration to take back our own country and re-institute the right to life in our own nation . . . We should praise Ireland and we should be standing with Ireland right now.'

Within weeks of the news of Savita's death, dramatic statements were made by a stellar line-up of Irish anti-abortion activists on another US television network. A series of 'program shorts' titled 'Life Crisis in Ireland' were made for the Alabama-based Eternal Word Television Network. EWTN is a Catholic radio, television, multimedia and multi-platform publishing organization with services available in English, German and Spanish.

In one program short, the camera moves between activists in different locations, each saying a few lines, and builds towards an appeal to viewers to support anti-abortion work in Ireland. Caroline Simons of the Pro-Life Campaign tells viewers: 'In recent times there has literally been a tsunami hitting Ireland.'

'A tsunami of the culture of death,' continues *Irish Times* columnist John Waters. 'This has put Ireland's pro-life culture under very serious threat of death indeed.'

Wendy Grace, of Catholic Comment Ireland, says: 'But one thing we do know and doctors tell us, there is never a case where abortion is necessary to save the life of a mother.'

Former MEP Kathy Sinnott, standing in a field, says:

'Referendum after referendum has demonstrated the pro-life position of the Irish people.' The truth of this statement is questionable, given the outcomes of the 1992 and 2002 referendums, which copper-fastened the right to travel for abortion, the right to information on abortion and the right to abortion in cases where the woman's life is at risk by suicide.

Referring to the 2010 ECHR judgment, Sinnott says, 'This is how abortion was legislated for in Britain and the United States – primarily under the guise of so-called exceptional circumstances.'

'This must not happen in Ireland. For the sake of our children, let's not make the same mistake,' warns Patrick Carr of Family and Life Ireland.

Ide Nic Mhathúna (Niamh Uí Bhriain's sister) of Youth Defence says: 'We need to stand together right now, more than ever before against the culture of death that is pressing down on our nation,' while Patrick McCrystal of Human Life International warns, 'This battle can only be won if we are on our knees' (praying, one assumes).

David Quinn, of the Iona Institute, appeals for support for those fighting legislation on abortion. 'We need to help if we can by pledging our resources by taking their lead in this crisis.'

When asked about her involvement in the EWTN short, at the Oireachtas Health Committee in January 2013, Simons said: 'In relation to EWTN, I don't know what you're talking about. I'm sorry I can't help you with that one. I wasn't aware that I was on it. I don't know any agents of the culture of death, I hope. Certainly they haven't introduced themselves to me.'

In another short in the EWTN series, 'Prayer to the Immaculate Heart', Father Owen Gorman of the Diocese of Clogher, tells viewers: 'In Ireland right now we are facing a serious crisis. The agents of the culture of death are attempting to have abortion legalized in our country. We cannot allow this to happen. In these moments we are asking the EWTN family to join with us in prayer.' He then bows his head and says: 'This day we consecrate to your heart, this country and all its people. Intercede for the cause of life that is now so threatened in our land. Soften the hearts of those who oppose life. Give us love for our enemies and healing for all your daughters, who in fear and trembling rejected the gift of life within them. May they know the peace and forgiveness of your son, Jesus.'

Youth Defence and the Life Institute seem particular darlings of wealthy US anti-abortion campaigners. In an article in the *Sunday Business Post* in December 2012, Joseph Scheidler, president of the Chicago-based Pro-Life Action League, was quoted as saying that Youth Defence was a primary recipient of its funding. 'They need the money for publicity. Abortion is about conversion and it's very hard to convert people in masses, and that is why people like Youth Defence go out into the street.'

In a recorded interview with Alyson Henry, a journalism Master's student at Dublin City University, in June 2013 – which I have heard – Scheidler explained the close relationship between the Pro-Life Action League and Youth Defence. 'We work almost exclusively with Youth Defence. They're the people that we see doing the type of work that we do.' He told Henry the League was 'activist orientated . . . we go to the abortion clinics; we go to the places where politicians are speaking. Anything to do with abortion we try to be there to have a vigil, an image of those who support life and who oppose abortion so that keeps us very, very busy.'

The League, like Youth Defence, is known for displaying pictures of aborted foetuses at stalls and rallies. Scheidler told Henry: 'We believe very firmly that people have to see what abortion does to an unborn child because unless you see the victim you don't understand the problem.'

He said that while the League did not 'work alongside' Youth Defence, he and family members do come to Ireland to help out. He was evasive when asked about funding Youth Defence, saying: 'I'm not very much into the funding business . . . I know that once in a while somebody here in the States will invite one of the members usually of Youth Defence over and they will try to raise some money for them but I have no idea how successful that has been,' he told Henry.

'It's one of the only European countries that doesn't have a liberal abortion law. We see that as a real plus for Ireland and a real encouragement for Americans, especially Americans of Irish descent who realize their country does not condone abortion.'

There is a strong Irish-American presence in the US anti-abortion lobby and the image of the fighting Irish facing down the cruel oppression of reproductive rights has strong appeal.

In June 2012, just as Uí Bhriain was about to arrive in the US for a fund-raising blitz she was interviewed by journalist Sheila Gribben Liaugminas for *Crisis* magazine. Liaugminas reflects on Ireland's reputation as a beacon of scholarly good works during the Dark Ages. 'Times are pretty dark right now in the West, and Ireland once again remains unfallen to anti-life barbarians. Might the Irish save civilization again?' she asks.

Uí Bhriain, it seems, had the fund-raising answers. 'Two decades of persistent public engagement and education [by the Life Institute and YD, one assumes] has maintained Ireland's pro-life majority and in that time abortion campaigners have failed to win the necessary public support to build momentum for abortion legislation,' says Uí Bhriain. 'But they are now openly availing themselves of the massive global funding being made available to efforts to overturn Ireland's pro-life laws. As in many other jurisdictions, since they [pro-choice activists] cannot get the people to agree with abortion, they want to use the courts and the massive wealth and power of a tiny elite minority to foist abortion on the nation.'

On the trip, Uí Bhriain spoke at a fundraiser in Chicago which according to the American *Catholic World Report* site was 'quickly organized to respond to the current pro-life crisis in

Ireland'. The 'current pro-life crisis' was the 20th anniversary of the X case which saw a burgeoning of pro-choice activity through the spring and summer.

People at the Chicago fundraiser were told of a 'David and Goliath' fight under way in Ireland. Uí Bhriain delivered the keynote address and told of the tireless work of the Life Institute. The next speaker was Tom Brehona, senior counsel of the Thomas More Society – a national law firm which exists 'to restore respect in law for life, marriage, and religious liberty'. Its website explains it is anti-abortion, anti-gay marriage and pro the right to pray and protest outside clinics providing abortion services. According to coverage in the *Catholic World Report*, Brehona 'spoke about . . . the disparity of funding between the pro-life side (which has public support but which receives relatively little funding) and the pro-abortion side (which has little public support in Ireland but which receives funding from donors with deep pockets) and the absolute need to help Ireland right now.'

Life House Ireland, based in Frederick, Maryland, was founded in 2011 by Scott Schittl, who studied politics in Trinity College, Dublin, worked with the Dublin Simon Community between 1998 and 2003 and in 2005 gained Irish citizenship. The Life House Ireland website tells us he 'care[s] deeply about life issues, and as a dual citizen of both the US and Ireland [is] proud to be able to tell everyone about Ireland's pro-life ethos.' Life House Ireland is an 'American, tax-exempt organization . . . [whose] purpose is to help make sure Ireland remains pro-life and abortion-free – and make it easier for Americans to support Ireland's pro-life success story.' Schittl was heavily involved in Youth Defence when he lived in Ireland.

Youth Defence and the Life Institute make no secret of their engagement with the US anti-abortion lobby, and clearly both engage energetically in the Irish political debate on abortion. They describe themselves as speaking for the Irish 'pro-life majority', but the majority of their followers are based in the US. One might reasonably infer that a good proportion of their funding also comes from the United States.

The Irish Standards in Public Office Commission (SiPO) initiated an investigation into the two organizations in December 2012. Under the terms of the 1997 Electoral Act any third party which raises funds for political purposes and which receives a donation in excess of €126.97 must register with SiPO. The third party must make a statutory declaration that all funds for political purposes are channelled through a bank account. In addition third parties may not accept a donation from an individual in excess of €6,348.69 or a donation of value from a person outside the State who is not an Irish citizen. Schittl's dual citizenship is a potential boon here.

Neither the Life Institute nor Youth Defence is registered as a political third party. Both argue that their work is not political but educational. According to a spokeswoman for SiPO in July 2013, the Commission was of the view that both Youth Defence and the Life Institute were organizations that engaged in political lobbying. She said the Commission had written on seven occasions since November 2012 asking them to reconsider their view that they did not need to register as third parties for political purposes. Both replied just once, in February, saying that they considered themselves not political but educational organizations.

She expressed the Commission's frustration at its inability to compel organizations to register and comply with SiPO's rules laid out for third parties. She said that SiPO had written to the Minister for the Environment, under whose remit it operates, seeking greater powers to compel compliance. Legislation is awaited. Until then it remains impossible to ascertain just where these organizations get their money.

Early in the afternoon of 18 November, as the battle over the Savita narrative raged, Praveen Halappanavar, a member of no political or educational organization, walked quietly through the arrivals gates at Dublin airport's Terminal 2.

It would be his calm and resolute ownership of her story in the coming days and months that would command the attention of the moral majority and have a more enduring impact than any dollar-funded advertising or billboard campaign ever could. What he needed now were answers.

Right: Savita, aged three.

Below: Six-year-old Savita Yalagi at home in Bagalkot, dancing before going with family to a cultural event.

Bottom: Savita, front centre, aged eight, on a family holiday.

Right: Savita on her graduation from secondary school.

Below: Savita, front, with fellow dentistry students at the KLE University, Belgaum, Karnataka, circa 2001.

Left: Savita, on the occasion of her graduation from KLE University, 2004.

Savita at home in Belgaum with her mother, Akhmedevi, during a family birthday celebration (**above left**); and with her father, Andanappa, circa 2000 (**above right**).

Below: Savita, relaxed in the living room of the family home in Sri Nagar, Belgaum, circa 2008.

Above: Savita with her best friend Smita in April 2008, on a trip to Mumbai shortly after her wedding and before she moved to Galway.

Below: Savita and Praveen celebrate Praveen's thirty-fourth birthday at their home in Galway, October 2012, shortly before her death.

Above: Praveen, in the kitchen of a friend's home in Doughiska, Galway, with a photograph of Savita in the background. This photograph was taken the evening after he arrived back in Galway after Savita's funeral in November 2012.

Left: Thousands attend the 'March for Savita' in Dublin, November 17, 2012, three days after her death became public.

Right: Thousands attend an anti-abortion rally in Dublin, June 8, 2013.

Key figures at the inquest into Savita's death at Galway Courthouse, April 2013: Solicitor Gerry O'Donnell and Praveen Halappanavar (**above**); Galway coroner Dr Ciaran McLoughlin (**right**); Dr Katherine Astbury (**below left**); and midwife Ann Maria Burke (**below right**).

Above: Dr Peter Boylan, former Master of the National Maternity Hospital and expert witness at the inquest into Savita's death, leaving the hearings after making his deposition, April, 2013.

Left: Dr Rhona Mahony, Master of the National Maternity Hospital, leaving the Oireachtas Health Committee hearings, January, 2013.

Below: Professor Sir Sabaratnam Arulkumaran (*left*), Chairperson, and Dr Philip Crowley, National Director for Quality and Patient Safety, at the publication of the Health Service Executive (HSE) clinical review report into the death of Savita Halappanavar in June 2013.

8

As soon as he began the drive home from Dublin airport, thoughts of Savita came crowding in.

'It was my first time travelling back without her. I was feeling so lonely,' recalled Praveen the following day – Monday, 19 November. Sitting in the front living room of a friend's house in the Doughiska area of Galway, he said that all he wanted now was to find out the truth of what happened to his wife, and why. Just over two weeks earlier, she had been buried in her home city, Belgaum. Four years before that, they had married.

'I haven't a clue who is at fault. I just want to know the truth. After Savita passed away I checked with friends, who said if the mother's health is at risk they can terminate the baby, but it is too late now.' Perhaps he had been misinformed, or had misunderstood, but a pregnancy could not be terminated in Ireland if it was only the mother's health (rather than her life) which was at risk.

Praveen had thought an intervention to save Savita would have been allowed. 'We didn't know what the law was. We didn't know we would come across this scenario ourselves. We knew that abortion is illegal . . . [but] this would be a medical necessity to save a bigger life because they knew they couldn't save a baby.'

He had come back to Ireland earlier than planned, because of the furore around the story and because he believed that as a result there was now wide support for a full public inquiry. There had been a chance Praveen would not return to Ireland at all. 'We had grave doubts about whether he'd come back,' recalls Dr Prasad. 'At least in India he has family. There's a lot of buzz and noise in India. But . . . when he saw all the attention the story was getting here, he knew he had to come back and fight.'

Praveen arrived back in Galway late Sunday afternoon. He spent much of Monday with his solicitor, Gerard O'Donnell. Before Praveen had returned to Ireland O'Donnell had had contact from the hospital about Savita's medical notes.

'I had written to the hospital on maybe the 1st or 2nd of November for the notes. Normally notes from any hospital take a bit of time to come through, but what had happened of course was in the meantime Praveen had made contact with you, the story was published on November 14th and the following day I got a phone call from the hospital to say the notes would be made available to me. Then all hell broke loose, as we know. Then the hospital wanted to drop the notes down to me, which would be very unusual for them to deliver notes to a solicitor's office, I can assure you, but I went up to the hospital to collect them. They were keen to be as co-operative as possible, to be seen to be doing the right thing.'

On the evening of Friday, 16 November, the then director of Galway University Hospital, David O'Keeffe, faxed a copy of the terms of reference of the inquiry the HSE was proposing to establish into Savita's death, recalls O'Donnell.

'So I got a contact then from Dr Philip Crowley [HSE's national director of quality and patient safety] at home on Saturday and I said I had looked at the terms and said I couldn't comment until I got instruction from my client. But I said I didn't imagine my client would be happy with the HSE conducting an inquiry into their own management of Savita, but I would take instructions and come back to him.

'Then on Monday morning I got a phone call from the HSE to say they were moving ahead with their appointment of the chairperson, and as it so happened the person they intended to nominate was coincidentally in Dublin they were going to nominate this person. It was just a fait accompli. They asked me had I any comment about it and I said I had none at all.'

In his discussions with Praveen later that morning O'Donnell found that Praveen didn't want the hospital or the HSE running an inquiry; nor did Savita's parents. In Dublin, apparently in response to the furore around the story, the HSE was announcing additions to its 'incident management review' of Savita's death.

As soon as her death became a major news story, however, it was clear this would not be enough. The Executive promised to 'strengthen' the investigation and to appoint 'an independent external expert in obstetrics and gynaecology'. The new expert and proposed chair of the inquiry was presented at a hastily convened press conference: Professor Sir Sabaratnam Arulkumaran, head of obstetrics and gynaecology at St George's University in London. Though the team's terms of reference had not yet been finalized and a time frame not yet been set, Dr Crowley told the press conference that the inquiry would be methodical and fair and would be concluded in 'the shortest possible time'. Also on the inquiry team would be Cora McCaughan, co-chair of the HSE's national incident management team, and Geraldine Keohane, director of midwifery and nursing at Cork University Hospital. In line with standard practice, a number of staff from the hospital where the death had taken place were also included: Professor John J. Morrison, consultant in obstetrics and gynaecology, Dr Catherine Fleming, consultant in infectious diseases, and Dr Brian Harte, consultant in intensive care and anaesthesia.

However, Praveen told the *Irish Times* on Monday evening that he could have no faith in an inquiry which included staff from

Galway University Hospital. They would be investigating themselves, he said. It was all disappointing.

'It does bother me that there are people from Galway Hospital on the inquiry. I will request that there be no one from the Galway Hospital on it. The main reason to have internal people involved is not to give specific directions but to find out about their standards and practices.' He had no faith in the HSE or the hospital, surmising that if the story of Savita's death had not been told worldwide, the two institutions would never have initiated an inquiry such as this. 'I was in India for nearly two weeks and I never heard from the hospital. I don't think there would be any inquiry if there had been no public pressure. I think there would have been an inquest and no one would have known this happened. It is a pity because I thought Ireland would care more for someone so young who died. That let me down.'

The following day, the three members of the Galway Hospital staff were removed and replaced by Professor James Walker, professor and honorary consultant of obstetrics and gynaecology at St James's Hospital in Leeds, Dr Brian Marsh, consultant in intensive care medicine at the Mater Hospital, Dublin, and Professor Mary Horgan, consultant physician in Cork University Hospital. The changes had come in response not just to Praveen's concerns but to wider political opinion. As commentator and barrister Noel Whelan put it: 'An inquiry must be unbiased and must be seen to be unbiased.'

It appears to have been assumed by the authorities that Praveen would now take part in Professor Arulkumaran's inquiry, enabling the Government to say it was handling the crisis competently and well. But Praveen held hard to his conviction that an investigation established by a body that had been involved in Savita's care – whatever its composition – would be inherently flawed. He wanted a public, sworn inquiry. He told the *Irish Times* on Tuesday, 20 November: 'I am not happy with the HSE. The HSE are the ones who messed up Savita's care.'

In an interview with RTE's Miriam O'Callaghan, broadcast the next day, he said he had 'no confidence the HSE will do justice' to an investigation into the death.

That morning, the Taoiseach Enda Kenny insisted in the Dáil that a public inquiry would take too long, and suggested it was Praveen's legal advisors rather than Praveen himself who wanted one: 'The chairman of the investigation team is not being allowed to sit down with Mr Halappanavar because, apparently, his legal team is saying that it wants a full public sworn inquiry.'

Kenny said he wanted to speak directly to Praveen, over the head of his legal representative, and urged him to meet Professor Arulkumaran. 'I would appeal directly to Praveen Halappanavar, who is a decent man, to meet the chairperson of the investigating team, without prejudice, because it is very necessary that the truth of these circumstances be found out . . . All of the documentation and all of the contracts in this public hospital are within the structure of the HSE.'

Kenny, it should be remembered, was appealing to a man who had come to Ireland six years previously, aged twenty-eight, having grown up in a country where corruption is endemic and where many in civil society have little trust in government bodies. Those who characterized Praveen's genuine concerns as obduracy showed a surprising lack of appreciation of who he was and of the values he carried.

There were fears that the type of inquiry Praveen sought would turn into a tribunal along the lines of the Moriarty Tribunal into political corruption: that had lasted more than ten years and cost upwards of €100 million. The Smithwick Tribunal into allegations of Garda collusion with the IRA had opened in 2005 and was still hearing evidence. Despite this concern, Praveen's calls for a sworn public inquiry were backed by Labour Senator Ivana Bacik and Fianna Fáil leader Micheál Martin. The United Left Alliance pointed out that Praveen and Savita's family were legally entitled to such an inquiry under the

European Convention on Human Rights. 'The attempts by James Reilly and Enda Kenny to browbeat Praveen into accepting an HSE inquiry must stop immediately,' said the Alliance.

That Wednesday evening, in an extraordinary move, President Michael D. Higgins intervened in what was beginning to become a major political row. Speaking to reporters in London, the President said any inquiry into Savita's death must 'meet the needs of her family as well as the State'. He added that the investigation must ensure 'above all else' that women would be safer and have access to all medical treatment necessary during pregnancy.

It is not entirely clear why the inquiry which Praveen wanted was not established. Perhaps cost was the decisive factor. It is possible, too, that the Government did not want to set a precedent for other families whose loved ones had died in hospital – though given the enormity of the public, political and constitutional interest in what exactly had happened at Galway hospital, Savita's case was arguably of 'uniquely urgent public' concern.

Neither Taoiseach Enda Kenny nor Minister for Health James Reilly made any attempt to contact Praveen throughout this period, a failure described by Micheál Martin as 'inexplicable and beyond acceptable' at Leaders' Questions on that Wednesday, 21 November. Kenny countered that Government representatives were right not to meet Praveen because, if they did, 'a different construction would be put on it'.

'No,' countered Martin, 'there would not.'

Minister Reilly, in Galway on the following day for a separate engagement, did briefly meet Praveen in the company of his solicitor, Gerard O'Donnell.

The Taoiseach and his Minister, says Noel Whelan, handled this phase, the immediate fallout, terribly. 'Bertie Ahern [former Taoiseach and leader of Fianna Fáil] in that scenario would have found someone local, on the ground in Galway and he'd have sent them straight around to Praveen, to talk to him and say, "What do you need? What can we do?" James Reilly sits, waiting over a week, before fitting him into his schedule for a few minutes . . .'

O'Rourke agrees. 'Oh immediately, immediately someone would have been sent to see Praveen [under a Fianna Fáil government]. Sure that's basic manners apart from anything else and no one would have thought bad of you if you did that.'

'As for the Galway staff on the inquiry,' says Whelan, 'that straight away goes against the principle in law that an inquiry must be unbiased and must be seen to be unbiased . . . The normal process with an investigation is that there'll be a couple of people on the ground, someone from outside and an expert of some kind chairing it. The mistake here was not to realize that this was a whole different case, this was of a different magnitude. How Reilly let that go, how it crossed his desk . . . well perhaps that was down to his political inexperience.'

Disappointed by the HSE and by the political processes, Praveen did have faith in the coronial process. Under the Irish system, the local coroner will call an inquest in cases of sudden, unexplained, unnatural or violent death. The purpose is not to attribute blame or liability but to ascertain the circumstances of the death – classically the 'who, when, where and how', but not necessarily the why. The coroner is an independent official with medical or legal training, and ideally both.

Galway coroner Dr Ciaran McLoughlin has both legal and medical degrees and practises as a GP in the small town of Clifden, Connemara, in Co. Galway. He had assured Praveen that his inquest would 'get to the truth' and would satisfy some of his and Savita's parents' need for a public, independent and sworn inquiry.

Praveen had been in touch with him from India, and, though initially concerned that there would be a delay before the inquest, was reassured when Dr McLoughlin told him the Gardai would begin taking statements immediately, before details were forgotten.

McLoughlin recalls his contact with Praveen in India. 'He said she had died and somebody had to be accountable, and somebody should be suspended. I think he thought I had far greater powers than I have. I couldn't engage with him on that, but I told him we would certainly hold an inquiry. I told him it would be April and he raised some reservations about that, said people would have forgotten the sequence of events.

'I said, "Well, the Guards are quite quick about getting the statements and would do it very professionally." As well as that I told him the veracity of the statements would be tested in public at the inquiry.' The necessity for Praveen himself to make a statement, as well as Dr McLoughlin's assurance that a sworn process would be under way within days, hastened Praveen's return to Ireland.

Two days after his return, on Tuesday, 20 November, Praveen went with his solicitor, O'Donnell, to Oranmore Garda Station, just outside Galway. O'Donnell recalls a harrowing day. 'There was an inspector, a garda who had also been a midwife, and we were there over eight hours, giving a very, very detailed statement to the Gardai. We were all exhausted after it. He was quiet but determined. An incredible memory for detail of all the events that had happened. It was very difficult for him. He had to relive all those last days and hours with Savita.'

In an apparent attempt to appease Praveen's concerns about the independence of its inquiry, the HSE asked the Health Information and Quality Authority (HIQA), the independent authority which monitors compliance with best practice in hospitals and care facilities, to carry out its own inquiry into Savita's care. The Government denied that this amounted to a U-turn. On Friday the 23rd, the HIQA board confirmed it would investigate the care and treatment Savita had received. Praveen did consider participating in the HIQA inquiry but in the end declined the invitation – again because it was to be neither in public nor sworn.

All through this period there were cries that abortion should not be politicized, that this was an issue of conscience and beyond party point-scoring. Emotional speeches became commonplace. TDs spoke of their personal views 'evolving' and 'crystallizing' and changing in nuance. Though abortion for individuals might well be above politics, what to do about the immediate issue was clearly party-political.

A week after the story broke, Sinn Féin tabled a motion in the Dáil calling for X case legislation. Some nineteen TDs spoke to the motion over two days. SF's Mary Lou McDonald said it offered an opportunity to 'deputies of all political parties and none' to bring clarity to the law. 'This motion does not come down on either side of that broader and ongoing debate on the extension of abortion rights. It simply asks that what is already lawful and constitutional be defined and guided by legislation. In the words of Dr Rhona Mahony, Master of the National Maternity Hospital at Holles Street, everybody needs to be protected. The women of Ireland must be protected and the doctors giving health care must know they are also protected in their ability to do the job.' She criticized both Government parties and Fianna Fáil, accusing them of running for cover, of hiding and fudging on the issue, castigating them for 'twenty years of inaction and delay'.

All nineteen speakers to the motion expressed their sympathy to Praveen and Savita's family, before moving on to the politics at hand.

Ciara Conway, TD, of the Labour Party was quick to get back at Sinn Féin on its record. 'A party that prides itself on being an all-Ireland party, and is in power in the North under the leadership of Martin McGuinness, has resisted attempts to bring any part of the UK abortion law to Northern Ireland. Five of the Sinn Féin Deputies abstained on the vote on Deputy Clare Daly's Bill [in February].

'The Labour Party is the only party to have asked for legislation to end this inequality and mistreatment of women's health.'

Her party colleague Robert Dowds reminded everyone that the Labour Party had been criticized for seeking clarification on abortion in its election manifesto. '[We] stated we would legislate in accordance with the Supreme Court judgment and the ruling of the European Court of Human Rights, and we got plenty of stick for this. The reality is that if Britain was not on our doorstep, we would have had to introduce abortion legislation years ago to avoid women dying from having backstreet abortions.'

Billy Kelleher, Fianna Fáil's spokesman on health, defended his party's record on the issue. 'Some people might say nothing was done but while nothing was achieved, we tried to do things. They may not have met with universal approval in this Chamber and they certainly did not meet with universal approval outside it, but efforts were made and unfortunately they did not succeed in addressing any of the concerns that are being expressed in the context of what is required now to bring clarity to the issue.'

Fine Gael speakers were unanimous that the motion was ill-timed and ill-thought-out and argued that TDs should await the report of the Expert Group. Billy Timmins, who some months later would defy his party leadership on the issue and vote against it, praised his party leader: 'I commend the Taoiseach and the Minister for Health on their handling of this issue. I hope we will all have an opportunity to deal with the upcoming report and what course of action should be taken because a course of action must be taken in a calm and considered way.'

The Sinn Féin motion was defeated the following evening. A Government amendment that the Dáil should await the Expert Group report, which had reported on the Government's options in addressing the 2010 ECHR ruling in the *A, B and C* v. *Ireland* abortion case – due for publication a week later – passed comfortably.

There were many who criticized the Labour Party in particular for voting against the Sinn Féin legislation, just as there had been when they voted against similar legislation that had been introduced in April 2012, by United Left Alliance TD Clare Daly. The Labour Party was the only political party which had had a commitment to legislate for the 1992 X case ruling in their general election manifesto and yet here they were, again, voting such legislation down.

Labour Party TD Aodhán Ó Ríordáin (Dublin North Central), who was on the March for Savita with party colleague Ged Nash on 17 November, recalls being jeered and told they had Savita's blood on their hands. 'There were taunts from one of the political groups also marching, abuse and saying, "Labour shame, shame on Labour".'

He is adamant that his party did the right thing in voting against the legislation each time.

'On both occasions, the Expert Group had yet to report. There was a process under way and, speaking very coldly, the process in politics is what you have to stick with if you want to get things done, if you really want to change things. People say it's as easy as going in and voting for a private member's motion. It's not. If it was that simple we [Labour] would have all walked in and done it,' he says. 'We could have. But guess what? Fine Gael wouldn't have. So what's the point? It's all very well sloganeering but if you're really serious about your politics and getting things enacted, you have to respect the process.'

The highly charged reaction to Savita's death was a turning point. Where during the general election in 2011 his party's commitment to legislating for X made canvassing difficult at times, with people accusing him of being 'pro-abortion', immediately following Savita's death he had hundreds of contacts from constituents asking 'Why has this happened?' –

because, he explains, 'everyone has a sister; everyone has a niece or someone they love . . . And for the first time I had a huge number of communications from people who had never been in touch with a politician before who were minded to contact. I got 700 or 800 emails from people and they were genuine people living in my constituency saying, "This can't happen again. Please act on X case legislation." So I think what it did was allow people like me to be a little bit braver, a little more vocal and to not shy away from what we believe in.'

However, Ó Ríordáin says it would have been foolhardy to rush to legislate following Savita's death. He was worried when the news broke that the anti-abortion lobby would exploit any chink they could find in the story. If the anti-abortion lobby were to succeed in this, anyone who had 'hung their hat' on the story as a basis for legislating would lose the argument, he says.

'The Savita Halappanavar case definitely shifted public opinion but the constitutional imperative was unchanged and it wasn't going to change. But it certainly softened the mindset of some in the public and some in the Oireachtas as to the necessity for this.'

The following week saw a plethora of demands that the Government move quickly to legislate once the report was published. This, said a range of commentators, was an 'emergency' that required swift action. Women's lives were at risk. Some in Government spoke to the mood. That weekend Minister for Public Expenditure and Reform Brendan Howlin said Government would act 'speedily' once the report had been considered by Cabinet.

Speaking in Cardiff, on Monday the 26th, after a meeting of the British–Irish Council, the Taoiseach said the Expert Group report would be published the next day and legislation would follow 'as soon as is practicable to do so'. He did not want to see the process 'drifting on interminably'.

At this point, there seems little doubt that public and the

majority of political opinion would have backed speedy legislation. In an opinion piece in the *Irish Times*, published on Saturday, 24 November, political editor Stephen Collins wrote: 'If the Coalition seizes the opportunity and moves to deal with the issue early in the new year, it can be assured of broad public support for a solution that provides legal underpinning for current medical practice in situations where a mother's life is in danger.' Predicting which of the Expert Group's recommendations the Government would be most likely to take up – primary legislation to give effect to X, plus guidelines – Collins said that while this would, for different reasons, displease some in both Fine Gael and in Labour, it could 'provide a basis for consensus'.

Praveen, in an interview with the *Irish Times*, said he would like to see the law on abortion clarified. 'The law has to change,' he said. 'Maybe Savita was born to change the law here.'

The Expert Group's report was published after Cabinet discussion on Tuesday the 27th. It outlined four options: non-statutory guidelines; statutory regulations giving the Minister for Health power to regulate the area by statutory instrument; legislation alone; or legislation plus regulations. It recommended the second or fourth option, appearing to favour the fourth, saying that it met the requirements of the judgment of the European Court of Human Rights, would provide checks and balances between the powers of the legislature and the executive, and would allow flexibility in the event of clinical and scientific advances.

Kenny had a tightrope to walk. Having gathered his nerves after the debacle of his public appeal to Praveen's 'decency', the failure to make personal contact with him and the row over the HSE inquiry, he steeled himself to deal with what was the most contentious issue in Irish politics. As well as getting either regulations or legislation on abortion on to the books, he had to keep his Government in power. Commentators were wondering aloud if this was the issue on which Labour would 'walk'. The

Labour Party badly needed a policy win after two bruising Budgets that had hit low-paid workers and some social welfare recipients hard. It was the only political party in the general election to have committed to legislating for X in its manifesto. For many Labour backbenchers, including Aodhán Ó Ríordáin, Ciara Conway and Anne Ferris as well as Senator Ivana Bacik, legislating for X was a core commitment on which there could be no compromise.

Within Fine Gael were an unknown number of avowedly anti-abortion backbenchers who were not minded to support any change. Four months previously, in July, a group of fifteen of the party's TDs had warned they would resist any liberalization. They sought a 'cast-iron' guarantee from Minister Reilly that they would be consulted when the Expert Group report – wrongly rumoured as about to be published – was released. Among the fifteen had been Charlie Flanagan (Laois), John Deasy (Waterford), Simon Harris (Wicklow), James Bannon (Longford–Westmeath), John O'Mahony (Mayo), Regina Doherty (Meath East), Patrick O'Donovan (Limerick), Jerry Buttimer (Cork South Central) and – most worryingly for the Taoiseach – Minister of State for European Affairs Lucinda Creighton. While Kenny knew that he could afford to lose a few overboard, loss of fifteen to twenty TDs could well lose him not just the legislation but his leadership.

Despite having told journalist Vincent Browne some years previously that he would 'never' legislate for abortion, Kenny kept his counsel, nailing his colours to no mast. His party had not made any 'pro-life promise' before the general election in 2011, despite the claims of anti-abortion campaigners. The 2011 Fine Gael election manifesto, 'Let's Get Ireland Working', refers to abortion only once, under the heading 'Children, Older People and the Family'. The party would, it said, 'establish an all-party committee with access to medical and legal expertise, to consider the implications of the recent ruling of the ECHR and to make recommendations. Such a process would, wc believe, be the best way of examining the issues in a way that respects the range of sincerely held views on this matter.'

This had been the extent of the party's manifesto commitment, and the commitment had been honoured.

In his remarks in Cardiff on the eve of publication of the Expert Group report, Kenny set out the parameters of the discussion he was going to engage in. Central, he said, was the European Court of Human Rights ruling that required clarity on the circumstances and conditions in which a termination could be carried out in Ireland. 'That is what we are going to deal with and that is what we will do,' he said. Perhaps speaking to his own backbenchers, he continued: 'I want this to be a sensitive, comprehensive, pragmatic and understanding discussion. I know there are very polarized views on this matter and have been in Ireland for the past twenty-five years. We had this in the '80s and before, but we do need to provide for legal certainty in the appropriate circumstances from a medic's perspective to deal with this.'

The Government would decide which option to go with before Christmas, he said. He also reminded any who needed reminding that Fine Gael had clear rules and any TD who stepped outside the rules would have to accept the consequences. 'People who are elected to the party that I lead . . . act and vote in accordance with party decisions. And that is the way that it will be. We are dealing with a very different generation of politicians; our country has moved to a different space.' Appealing to the 'middle ground', he said: 'The vast majority of people understand what needs to be done here, but they do not want to move to a position where you have abortion on demand in the country.' So the party whip would be applied. In the meantime, everyone would have an opportunity to have their say.

Kenny was plain from the outset where his primary responsibilities lay and he has been widely praised for this. His stance should have come as no surprise. In July 2011 he set down a clear marker to the Catholic Church – and to anyone who might expect him to be its loyal servant – when he gave his response to a government investigation into clerical sexual abuse of children in the diocese of Cloyne. The Cloyne Report, he told the Dáil, 'excavates the dysfunction, disconnection, elitism . . . the narcissism that dominate the culture of the Vatican to this day.

'The rape and torture of children were downplayed or "managed" to uphold, instead, the primacy of the institution, its power, standing and "reputation". Far from listening to evidence of humiliation and betrayal with St Benedict's "ear of the heart" . . . the Vatican's reaction was to parse and analyse it with the gimlet eye of a canon lawyer,' said Kenny. In a long speech, he said Ireland, 'thankfully', was not Rome.

'Nor is it industrial-school or Magdalene Ireland, where the swish of a soutane smothered conscience and humanity and the swing of a thurible ruled the Irish-Catholic world.

'This is the "Republic" of Ireland 2011.

'A Republic of laws, of rights and responsibilities, of proper civic order.'

He concluded: 'Cardinal Josef Ratzinger said, "Standards of conduct appropriate to civil society or the workings of a democracy cannot be purely and simply applied to the Church." As the Holy See prepares its considered response to the Cloyne Report, I want to make it clear, as Taoiseach, that when it comes to the protection of the children of this State, the standards of conduct which the Church deems appropriate to itself, cannot, and will not, be applied to the workings of democracy and civil society in this republic.

'Not purely, or simply or otherwise. Because children have to be, and will be, put first.'

It was a devastating speech, which made headlines across the world. It made Kenny's view on the Church's credibility on moral matters clear. He would have no truck with them. The irony resonates still when looking now at the dogged effort the Church invests in rallying for the welfare of *unborn* children.

On the day of publication of the Expert Group's report, the Taoiseach's Minister for Health made an apparent slip of the tongue when he said the Government would implement 'through legislation' its decision on which option to follow. Later he said that he had 'misspoke', an explanation not accepted by the increasingly fractious anti-abortion section of the party.

Foolishly perhaps, the Labour Minister for Communications, Pat Rabbitte, exacerbated the Taoiseach's difficulty when he declared that the report tallied with the Labour Party position of many years. 'The long-standing position of the Labour Party . . . is that legislation will prove necessary. And I think it's the case, isn't it, that the Expert Group recommends that legislation is the safe way forward, perhaps requiring some finessing by way of regulation thereafter, but that primary legislation will be necessary.' The statement might have been designed to raise the hackles of the anti-abortion element among his partners in Government. Certainly, it must have hugely irritated a Taoiseach now facing the task of bringing wary backbenchers with him on the journey towards X case legislation.

By that Tuesday night, at the Fine Gael parliamentary party meeting, anti-abortion TDs and Senators were up in arms. An abortion train seemed to them to be leaving the station, with Tanaiste Eamon Gilmore, Reilly and Kenny manning the engine. Kenny ruled out postponing dealing with abortion until the end of the Irish Presidency of the European Union the following June: he wanted the issue dealt with 'as quickly as practicable', he said, rather than being 'forced from either end of the spectrum here to deal with it'.

Reports from the Fine Gael meeting said that those queasy about any legislative move on abortion felt they were being side-lined and that the assurances of being consulted were being shown to have been disingenuous. Twelve TDs and Senators spoke, criticizing the pace at which the process was moving and the direction in which the Government seemed to be going. Minister of State Lucinda Creighton is said to have made an 'impassioned' contribution, insisting there was no obligation under the European Court of Human Rights' ruling to legislate. Though the Government had promised hearings on the expert report at the Oireachtas Health Committee in January, by then, she argued, the decision would have been taken. 'Disgruntled Fine Gael backbenchers see yesterday's announcement as a "victory" for the Labour Party, whose Ministers argued strongly that the Government must act speedily,' wrote political reporter Mary Minihan in the *Irish Times* on Wednesday, 28 November.

Meanwhile, confident Labour Party members kept up the pressure. Senator Ivana Bacik told the Seanad, 'I think it's pretty clear now that it is incumbent on the Government to move swiftly to legislation. I think we have to be conscious of how high feelings are running since the tragic death of Savita Halappanavar.'

Pressure for action was inevitable after twenty years of inaction. But the effect of the pressure may have been to drag the process out rather than speed it up. The prospect of action being taken soon heightened anxiety among many Fine Gael TDs, forcing Kenny to allow a longer 'listening' process. This, in turn, gave the more radical elements of the anti-abortion lobby the opportunity to try to wear down the public appetite for anything more than the minimum required by X and the European Court of Human Rights.

By the following weekend, Kenny was facing a revolt within his party. Outside, pressure continued to mount from anti-abortion campaigners, including the Catholic Church, and – in the opposite direction – from human rights bodies at home and abroad as well as from pro-choice campaigners. As pressure to legislate mounted, so did the need to salve and reassure.

Irish Council for Civil Liberties director Mark Kelly

referenced the international bodies bearing down on the Government: 'The Government must now inform the Oireachtas and the Committee of Ministers of the Council of Europe of its precise timeline to enact the necessary reforms,' he said on Wednesday, 28 November.

In Dublin on 6 December, US Secretary of State Hillary Clinton gave a speech on global peace-building at Dublin City University. During the course of an almost hour-long address, she made time to mention that global programmes had been refocused to ensure that the lives of women and girls were saved and their health improved. 'So our starting point must be this: women's lives matter. And promoting the human rights of women begins with saving the lives of women whenever we can.'

Just as Clinton was making her remarks, the Catholic Bishops fired their opening salvo in what the religious affairs correspondent for the *Irish Times*, Patsy McGarry, forecast would be 'the mother of all battles'. The bishops warned that abortion could '*never* be morally justified'. From their winter meeting in Maynooth, they gave their 'initial response' to the Expert Group report.

Of the four options set out in the report, said the bishops, three could never be justified. Guidelines alone – leaving the law which had given rise to the X case untouched – was the only morally acceptable way forward. 'If guidelines can provide greater clarity as to when life-saving treatment may be provided to a pregnant mother or her unborn child within the existing legislative framework, and where the direct and intentional killing of either person continues to be excluded, then such ethically sound guidelines may offer a way forward.' They re-iterated their stance that the legal position was already clear for doctors and nurses in obstetrics: 'This has been an important factor in ensuring that Irish hospitals are among the safest and best in the world in terms of medical care for both a mother and her unborn baby during pregnancy. As a country this is something we should cherish, promote and protect.'

A few days later, the UN Rapporteur on the Right to Health, Anand Grover, was in Dublin to address an event organized months earlier by the National Women's Council. He declared that abortion must be decriminalized and made safely available to women where continuing the pregnancy would put their health at risk. He said the mother's right to life was 'more important than the right to life of an unborn whose life is conditional on a safe delivery', adding that he was 'particularly concerned about [the situation of women in] Ireland . . . You cannot afford to lose people's lives like this. It would not have happened in India. There is a lot of distress and discussion in India about [Ms Halappanavar's death]. Maybe out of this tragedy something good will come.'

The same week, the Council of Europe – where Europe's human rights ministers had been discussing the Expert Group's report – said that the Government must 'expedite' its plans to provide legal clarity: 'Ireland is under legal obligation to put in place and implement a legislative or regulatory regime providing effective and accessible procedures whereby pregnant women can establish whether or not they are entitled to a lawful abortion.' It reiterated the view of the European Court of Human Rights that the 'general prohibition on abortion in criminal law' was a 'significant chilling factor for women and doctors' when considering whether to seek or carry out an abortion in Ireland.

On Tuesday morning, 18 December, Minister Reilly brought a memorandum to Cabinet setting out the Government's intention to go with the fourth option: legislation plus guidelines. The Government promised also to listen to all sides: three days of hearings at the Oireachtas Health Committee in early January would provide an opportunity for all views to be heard. The committee would then write a report, without recommendations, and this would feed into the legislation.

The next day, Minister Reilly went to meet Praveen. He had

promised Praveen in November that he would get a preliminary report from the HSE inquiry 'before Christmas'. But having asked Praveen and solicitor Gerard O'Donnell to travel to Athlone to meet him, the Minister had no written report from Professor Arulkumaran to offer. 'We had expected to be perusing a document of some kind. Instead what we got was a sort of verbal report,' said O'Donnell afterwards. 'Praveen indicated he was not at all happy with that and the Minister took that on board. The reality is we were to receive a report and the reality is we received nothing.'

Praveen was under a great deal of strain. He had returned to work at Boston Scientific, his job involving some travel around the country. He went to the gym, he slept and he ate, said friends. 'He doesn't want to go to social gatherings. Savita used to drag him out to all these gatherings and get-togethers at weekends.' He turned his energy hopefully to the opening of her inquest in Galway in the New Year.

Pro-choice and anti-abortion campaigners' energies were being honed too, as they looked forward to Health Committee hearings scheduled to get under way on 8 January, not in the usual committee room, but in the grand environs of the parliament's upper chamber, the Seanad. It was thought that the usual committee room would not be able to cater for the numbers of parliamentarians and media representatives who would want to take part.

TDs and Senators who are not members of committees can attend committee meetings and ask questions. It was envisaged that a substantial number would want to be present at the sessions.

Chairman of the committee Jerry Buttimer, TD, said: 'It was about being inclusive of the Houses of the Oireachtas, to accommodate those of whatever view. Also, the Seanad chamber is a very magnificent room and I think it reflected the sense of the importance of the debate and the occasion and also, I think, it grounded people to be more tolerant and careful because they were in the Upper House.'

Before the hearings began on Tuesday, 8 January they were already being criticized as window-dressing, a talking-shop to give the appearance of consultation. There was a great deal of heard-it-all-before comment from participants – from both anti-abortion and pro-choice advocates and from the Churches. (Some wondered aloud whether the Churches should have been there.) The hearings were valuable, however, for the hard information they brought forward and for what they told about where the national discourse on abortion now was, of how the centre of political gravity had shifted.

For the first time, obstetric experts provided facts about how many terminations were carried out in Irish hospitals (about thirty a year: never recorded as 'abortions' or 'terminations' in annual hospital reports but as miscarriages or perinatal deaths); they enunciated the complex reality of dealing with difficult cases in an uncertain legal environment; they refuted the anti-abortion argument that termination is never needed to save the life of a mother, and they unequivocally dispatched the fear that there could ever be any intention in an Irish maternity ward of killing babies.

It was generally agreed afterwards that the star turn of the proceedings was Rhona Mahony, Master of the National Maternity Hospital. Few outside obstetrics had heard of her before her testimony on the first day. The following day, she was on the front page of many newspapers. It did her no harm that she is attractive, stylish and has a knockout smile, but she also impressed with her succinct, no-nonsense and assertive declaration that the current legal situation simply wasn't good enough: 'The current framework under which medical practitioners operate is not satisfactory and further clarification and guidance is needed,' she said.

'Abortion in Ireland is a criminal offence,' she reminded the committee, 'punishable by penal servitude. That law stands today and I need to know that I will not go to jail if in good faith I believe it is the right thing to terminate a pregnancy in order to save a woman's life. I want to know that I will not go to jail and I want to know, by the way, that she will not go to jail.'

How high did a risk to a mother's life have to be to make termination of a pregnancy legal and allowable? 'Can it be a 10 per cent risk or an 80 per cent risk of death? Or a requirement for intensive care support? Must the risk be immediate or could it be delayed?' It was impossible in medicine to be certain, she said, but doctors needed to know that if they acted in good faith the law would support them.

Later she said that she had found the hearings 'very difficult' and that, if it had been possible, she might have chosen not to attend.

'I had always said as Master that the one topic I would never speak about publicly was abortion. To talk about abortion, as they say, "no good can come from it" and I always felt that no matter what your view on it or how well you explained it, it would be used and twisted.

'But when I got the invitation from Government I felt it was [my] duty. The Government had asked me to come, I had experience in the area and I also felt that we [obstetricians] belonged in this conversation. It's about saving women's lives. I felt it was very important that we spoke up and that we were involved.

'I went in very innocently. I thought I was going in to just give my medical opinion.' She was somewhat taken aback by the experience.

'No one explains to you. You just arrive in, thinking it's going to be a polite friendly meeting, and you find yourself being inter-rogated for two hours. It's quite an intense place and they're asking a lot of questions, and I'm there frantically scribbling and of course I can't read my writing . . . I was exhausted by the end of it, because you're waiting for the trick and the trap. In theory you're there to give your honest medical opinion but it doesn't feel like a very honest forum. You have people with their political agendas deliberately trying to catch you out. You're not really protected and everything you say is then reported. I found it very stressful.

'There were some ridiculous questions. Some of them, because they were based on ideology and not on real life, were very hard for us to understand . . . The questions don't make sense in a medical setting. You find yourself wondering, "What is the person really trying to ask me?" And it's not my business to react to that but you just think it's so disingenuous and so dishonest. And it becomes very difficult then to have the factual debate, because you're not being asked what the situation and reality is. What they are trying to do is set ideas in motion – by asking the question and throwing out the terms they are just trying to get it out there.'

She hadn't anticipated being so prominently reported the next day. 'People say you put yourself out there, but I didn't feel I did. I did what I had to do. I feel really, really strongly about this. I don't understand why this country is having this conversation. There should be no question of women dying . . . If she dies her baby dies too. It defies logic.'

In her conclusion at the hearing, she appealed against 'absolutism' and for flexibility. It would be 'extremely difficult' to draft perfect legislation and regulation to cover every eventuality 'now and into the future'. But 'society must be reassured that clinicians in Ireland will continue to work tirelessly to preserve life in all circumstances.'

Jerry Buttimer, a 'strongly pro-life' former seminarian who chaired the hearings, said the testimony of all the obstetricians was very important. 'What assured me during the hearings was – be it from Rhona Mahony, Sam Coulter-Smith [Master, Rotunda Maternity Hospital, Dublin], Mary McCaffrey [consultant obstetrician, Kerry General Hospital], Gerry Burke [consultant obstetrician, Mid Western Maternity Hospital, Limerick] – was that it was about saving both lives and that is very important to any of us.'

Buttimer was among the anti-abortion Fine Gael TDs who, the previous July, had sought assurances from the Taoiseach and the Minister for Health that they would be consulted on the Expert Group report before there was any move to act on it.

'My life has been coloured by three things. One is the fact that I was born 13 weeks premature myself as a result of my mother having had a crisis in her pregnancy. So I recognize my being here is a gift. Secondly is the fact I spent five years in Maynooth as a seminarian. I have a degree in theology, so life to me is about you're called in and you're called out and you have no control over that. And, thirdly, as a consequence of life experiences and meeting people, and having been the only politician who sat for six days through all the hearings and didn't ask a question but listened and observed and reflected, more than anything I know that life isn't black and white.

'I say that as somebody who would be profoundly pro-life, who would not be in any way for abortion, but who recognizes there are occasions where a doctor has to intervene. And every obstetrician, no matter who they were, made that case. To me it's about preservation of life and of giving life.'

Dr McCaffrey, who described the experience in smaller hospital units, spoke of the difficulties faced by doctors working alone in emergency situations, where they might want a second opinion before intervening. 'At weekends, immediate access to a second obstetrician within smaller hospitals may not always be possible.'

'That struck me very forcefully,' says Buttimer, 'that we do need to give clarity. My view is still very strongly pro-life but over the last six months the nuance of my view has changed.'

He says the inclusion of Church representatives at the January hearings was important: 'The religious leaders are the moral guardians for people of faith and they have a right to espouse their dogma and elucidate their position'.

Politically, it was probably important to invite the Catholic Church, in order to be seen to be listening to and accommodating this constituency, but if the Catholic Church was getting a platform so too must the others. So, on Day 3 the committee heard from the Irish Catholic Bishops' Conference, the Church of Ireland, the Presbyterian Church, the Methodist Church, the Irish Jewish Community, the Islamic Cultural Centre and Atheist Ireland.

The lack of reverence shown to the Catholic Bishops drew comment. 'There was courtesy, but no deference,' observed former *Irish Times* editor Geraldine Kennedy, who attended every day of the hearings. Political commentator Noel Whelan said that while it might still be important, just about, to take the Catholic Church's views seriously, there was too 'an older generation of Catholics less tolerant of Church diktat'. He pointed to the scandals that have hit the Church since 1992. 'In fact in this debate the Church stuff is irrelevant, and yet there's a certain core even among Church followers, who look around instead for conservative Catholic voices of standing that they will defer to. And Enda Kenny is one of those – a country politician who's conservative on these things. If someone like him can live with legislation, that reassures a lot of people.'

Bishop Christopher Jones of Elphin, chair of the Catholic Bishops' Council for Marriage and the Family, told the committee on Thursday, 10 January that legislating for X would 'allow for abortion, for the direct and intentional killing of the baby in the womb'. He added that it was 'not necessary to legislate for the X Case to ensure that women in Ireland receive all the life-saving treatment they need during pregnancy' . . . Buttimer, a passionate believer in the 'preciousness of unborn life', disagreed. 'The testimony given to us indicated otherwise.

We had to give protection to the medical personnel and the Medical Council. As legislators we have to do what is right for the people. There are grey areas and in those grey areas, unfortunately, women can die. If the woman dies the baby dies too. I have prayed about this and I have gone away in contemplation and sought spiritual direction on this. I am genuinely very much at peace with what Government has done.'

Barrister and doctor Simon Mills made the point that there were three sides to the debate: an anti-abortion side, a pro-choice side, and the largest but most silent side – the moderate middle ground where somewhat anti-abortion and somewhat pro-choice elements 'frequently overlap, precisely because of their reasonableness in the face of clean-looking principles that cannot be applied neatly to the rough-hewn surface of real life'.

This middle ground was now adopting views that would have been called 'pro-choice' in 1983 or 1992, or even in 2002. This was the most significant fact to emerge from the January hearings, and Savita contributed to it, says Noel Whelan. 'The Savita story pushed the abortion issue to the top of the media and political agenda in an urgent way that never would have happened on foot simply of the Expert Group report . . . One of the effects is that what had been the pro-choice argument – seeking legislation for the X case – was now being made by the Government, by the medical profession, by the legal profession. That became the common-sense middle ground, and that's different . . . Sane voices are gems in policy-making – people with no bias, no agenda, just expertise in the area, who can go out and make the arguments and people will accept them, take them seriously in a way which they won't in relation to an activist group.'

This, says Breda O'Brien, a writer with anti-abortion views, made the hearings a thoroughly 'frustrating' experience.

'First our submission had to be terribly rushed. Although Jerry Buttimer was extremely fair and efficient as a procedural chair, my strong impression was that the hearings were a box-ticking exercise, and that there was little listening to substantive points.'

O'Brien had also spoken at the abortion hearings at the Oireachtas Committee on the Constitution in 2000 chaired by the late Brian Lenihan.

'Those hearings were much more substantial and there was a real sense of being listened to. Jerry was very good at moving things along, in an overly crowded schedule . . . [but] Brian was acutely interested in the issues, and asked probing but fair questions, as did the other members.'

Speaking in her capacity as patron of the Iona Institute, O'Brien addressed the committee with colleagues from the anti-abortion lobby, all of whom argued against the inclusion of suicide as a reason for permitting abortion. 'Legislating for the provision of abortion on the grounds of suicide would be both unsafe and unjust,' she said.

The suicide issue emerged at this point as the 'drama' that would dominate the debate all the way to legislation in the summer. It had been ruled lawful by the Supreme Court in 1992 and was thus the law of the land. To include suicide as grounds for an abortion, however, would lead inexorably to 'abortion on demand', argued many. It would 'open the floodgates'.

On this, former Supreme Court Justice Catherine McGuinness, addressing the committee, said if people were afraid that the floodgates would open, they were afraid of the Irish people: 'afraid the Irish people are – for themselves – going to open the floodgates. I think we ought to have a bit more trust in them and in Irish doctors rather than suggesting that the moment that this is introduced into law everyone will be galloping to do something that they do not do already.'

Breda O'Brien describes herself and other anti-abortion advocates as voices on the outside battling to be heard. 'There seemed to be an almost wilful desire to ignore dissenting voices,' she told me. Perhaps echoing Whelan's commentary on what the hearings showed, she refers to a 'groupthink' among the 'elite' on abortion.

Her colleague David Quinn, founder of the Iona Institute, told me: 'Public opinion in my mind is definitely moving in a more pro-choice, pro-abortion direction all the time . . . For us, arguing our points is always like playing away from home and more so all the time. The crowd is less and less with us and this debate will have pushed it even more heavily in that direction.'

As the hearings closed on Thursday, 10 January, Jerry Buttimer and his committee began preparing a report for the Government.

In Galway meanwhile, Praveen and his solicitor were preparing for the preliminary hearing for Savita's inquest, set for the following Friday, the 18th.

Coroner Dr McLoughlin recalled: 'We got the [medical] notes quickly but they were very difficult to read. Because they came from a doctor, consultant, midwife, doctor, they were difficult to follow or to tell who was who.'

He decided the best way to proceed would be to get a statement from anyone who had made an entry in the notes. The Gardai, having taken Praveen's statement, then set about creating what Dr McLoughlin described as a 'spreadsheet timeline' using the notes and Praveen's statement.

'We looked at everything that happened to Savita, who was there, and where was Praveen, and cross-checked who we needed to call for a statement.' The Gardai in Galway, he said, had a qualified midwife among them and she was called in to help decipher the notes. 'She knew everything to look out for,' says Dr McLoughlin.

He knew that he was 'in over the top' in the case and that he would need his own expert witnesses. But these had to be paid for, and for that he had to get permission from county manager Martina Moloney.

'Because it had become such a high-profile, such a controversial case, the manager wrote back and said, "No problem". Now, if there hadn't been all the controversy there probably wouldn't have been the expert witnesses.' He said he needed an independent expert in obstetrics and another in microbiology. 'I knew [Dr Peter] Boylan and [Dr Susan] Knowles were the most highly respected people in their fields in the country, and it was important not to take anyone from either the extreme right or the extreme left in terms of the morality of abortion. It had to be experts who would be very objective.'

He wrote to them both in mid-December and both replied in January, accepting his invitations. Dr Boylan recalls the phone conversation in which Dr McLoughlin asked him to participate in the case: 'I was fascinated by it and was happy to do it.'

The Gardai took statements from non-hospital witnesses, while the HSE gathered statements from its employees. Says Dr McLoughlin: 'The HSE told me they would have all the witness statements in December, then it was January, then it got pushed out almost until April. Some were on holidays and then we didn't estimate the huge amount of work involved in getting the statements made, giving them then to the HSE and then I presume they were legally vetted by RDJ Glynn solicitors [acting for the hospital].'

The preliminary hearing opened in court number one at Galway courthouse, on Friday, 18 January. Praveen sat quietly and alone at the back as Dr McLoughlin opened proceedings by extending his 'sincere sympathies and condolences' to him and undertook to 'conduct this inquiry with solemn respect, dignity and courtesy to you and the memory of the deceased, your beloved Savita'.

There were ten items on Dr McLoughlin's list to work through, including the verification of documents furnished by the Health Service Executive, the question of expert witnesses that might be called by both parties as well as by himself, photographs to be used and the identification of witnesses to give evidence.

Declan Buckley, SC for the Galway Hospital Group, told the court at that point that there were two witnesses who had made entries in Savita's notes who were in 'a difficult position' with regard to giving evidence: they had certificates from doctors to this effect. Gerry O'Donnell raised his eyebrows as he looked over to his junior counsel, John O'Donnell, who in turn got to his feet and said he would want to know what evidence the two absent witnesses would give if they were to attend.

Dr McLoughlin recalls getting the two medical certificates from these witnesses and says he contacted the doctors who had written those certificates: one was a GP and the other a psychiatrist. One did provide a statement to the inquest, though it was not read out.

As to the other, she never did give a statement, or evidence at the inquest. She was the midwife who recorded Savita's collapse into sepsis over the night from Tuesday 23 October to Wednesday the 24th. Her evidence could have been crucial. But it has never been heard.

Speaking outside the courthouse after the opening session, Praveen said he was relieved the process was at last under way. He described the past few months as a 'tough journey', saying people kept recognizing him but that they had been supportive. 'Basically, everyone knows me now. There has been huge support from my friends and my colleagues in work, so that has been some kind of boost. That has given me strength. I believe I am getting the strength from someone, from Savita. That's the kind of person she was. She was always there for me.'

9

You 'lose your rights basically when you are pregnant' in Ireland.

It is 19 April, 2013, and the final day of the inquest into the death of Savita Halappanavar. Praveen was in no doubt about his verdict. Standing outside Galway county hall, addressing a phalanx of media from across the world, he said the way Savita had been treated during her last week in Galway was horrendous, barbaric and inhumane.

Minutes earlier, the eleven-member jury at her inquest had returned a verdict of medical misadventure in relation to her death at UCHG. It had endorsed nine recommendations put by the coroner, Dr Ciaran McLoughlin – seven relating to administration and management of care in hospitals, one that additions should not be made to medical notes after a patient's death, and one that the Medical Council lay out in its guidelines exactly when a doctor can and should intervene to save a mother's life.

It was the culmination of seven days of evidence, heard over two weeks, in two different venues, from over thirty witnesses. Though the jury had not been able to make any recommendations as to the laws on abortion, Dr McLoughlin in his summing up had said the Oireachtas could 'take cognizance' of what had been heard at the inquest.

The inquest was to be a story of two halves.

The first five days were spent in the somewhat ramshackle Galway courthouse dating back to 1815, where we heard the litany of failures that marked the first four days of Savita's time in UCHG, characterized by confusion, jobs not being done properly and chaos.

The following week the hearings moved across to the gleaming new county hall offices where we heard of the heroic efforts made once Savita was taken into the hospital's Intensive Care Unit. We also heard from expert witnesses who clarified what could, should and couldn't have been done for her.

And we learnt that Praveen's recollection of events, as he had told it consistently and alone over the previous six months, was substantially true.

Under the careful, thorough stewardship of Dr McLoughlin, the longest inquest in the history of the State had pushed the boundaries of the coronial system as far as anyone might have hoped, elucidating not just the lapses that had occurred but on whose watches.

But, said Praveen, facing the reporters, cameramen and photographers, with their microphones, Dictaphones and cameras, we hadn't heard why she had died. Had individuals failed her? Had hospital 'systems' failures? Had religious dogma? Or had it been a constitutional position that conflated a healthy thirty-one-year-old woman's life and health with the life of her dying and unviable foetus?

'I haven't got my answers yet why Savita died,' he told the *Irish Times* later that evening. 'I will get to the bottom of the truth.'

The main figures at the inquest were Praveen Halappanavar, his solicitor O'Donnell, his senior counsel Eugene Gleeson and junior counsel John O'Donnell. Acting for Galway University Hospital and the HSE was Declan Buckley, SC. Acting on behalf of Dr Katherine Astbury was Eileen Barrington, SC.

Eleven days earlier, on Monday, 8 April, Praveen had read into the court record the statement he had made in Oranmore Garda Station on 20 November. His voice, soft as ever, could not be heard properly by the jury and stenographer and seven minutes into his statement he was asked by Dr McLoughlin to start again and lean into the microphone. A diminutive man, he had to stand now to lean in and read his 22-page statement from the beginning. It took him over an hour. Dr McLoughlin took him through some points in his statement, as then did his SC, Eugene Gleeson. He asked his client how Savita, to his eyes, had been between Sunday 21 and Tuesday, 23 October.

'She looked OK. Once her parents left for India her focus turned to her future pregnancy. She kept talking about a future pregnancy. She wanted to get pregnant before the 30th March [her due date]. She said it's going to be a tough day for her so she wanted to make sure she was pregnant before that . . . She was not in any kind of pain until Tuesday night.'

Gleeson asked him: 'To the best of your recollection, when did Savita first ask for a termination?'

'After the first scan was done, she couldn't take looking at her baby on the monitor and she knew it was not going to survive. It was Monday morning. Basically she said she can't take it. How can a mother wait for her baby to die? She was in tears.'

'To whom did she make the request?'

'The consultant.' Praveen said she had asked twice, a couple of minutes apart, and the second time more insistently. 'Savita was very insisting. Savita is a very strong person. If she was not happy with the treatment she would not let the doctor go that way. Because Savita insisted the consultant said she would check with someone and come back.'

Praveen said he had expected Dr Astbury to return in 'maximum half an hour' and when she did not he was 'asking the midwife nurses', but no doctor came.

'The following day, the 22nd, on the ward round, did this issue of termination arise again?'

'Yes, that's right,' said Praveen. 'Savita raised it to a midwife nurse [on Tuesday morning] and the midwife nurse went and rang Katherine Astbury. She came back and said the same thing, "Sorry, it's a Catholic thing and we won't be able to help you".' He hadn't been there at this point, but Savita's best friend, Mrdula Vaseali, had.

Praveen said there had been three requests for a termination over the Monday and Tuesday, though this would be disputed by Dr Astbury. His counsel, Mr Gleeson, asked him: 'At any stage on Tuesday 23rd did Dr Astbury say, "I have spoken to certain people about your request and this is the situation"?'

'No.'

'And on Wednesday 24th, was there any request for a termination?'

'No, Savita was not in a condition to make any request. Basically Savita got very sick. She turned very pale and she was not breathing, basically. She complained about uncomfortable breathing and she was also sweating and she was in terrible pain as well.' At this point she had an oxygen mask and two drips, he said.

'Did anybody, any of the medical people or any of the nursing people, indicate to you the issue of sepsis had arisen, or infection?' asked Gleeson.

'No.'

'Are you sure about that?'

'Yes. Certain.'

'That didn't occur, notwithstanding the fact Savita was at some stage put on antibiotic therapy?'

'No,' said Praveen.

Declan Buckley, SC for the hospital and the HSE, then rose to his feet.

'Good afternoon,' he said. 'The last thing I want to do obviously is add to the level of distress and grief you are suffering, but there are differences between what you have said and what various people inside the hospital have said. I think you understand that and to a large extent where the differences rest. Unfortunately I am going to have to ask you about those differences. If at any stage you want to take a break . . . perhaps you could indicate that to the coroner.'

Buckley put it to him that on the Sunday, when he and Savita had arrived at the hospital, returned home and then returned to the hospital, they had arrived early afternoon, and not late morning as Praveen had said. 'That is not true,' said Praveen.

They agreed the senior house officer on duty, Dr Andrew Gaolebale, had told them the pregnancy could not be saved but disagreed about whether he had also said the miscarriage would be 'over in a few hours'. The registrar would say in evidence, said Mr Buckley, that the 'conversation didn't run along those lines' and in fact 'he said to you it was not possible to predict timing and you have to wait and see'.

'He will also say he didn't say to you, you would be able to go home immediately afterwards, because again that would not be correct,' said Buckley.

Dr Gaolebale would give evidence to the inquest conflicting with Praveen's on this issue, of whether he had told Savita and Praveen the miscarriage would be over in a matter of hours. It would appear from his statement to Professor Arulkumaran's investigation for the HSE, which would be published in June, that it was certainly his opinion at the time of this conversation with Praveen that it would be a matter of hours before miscarriage. Whether this was discussed with Praveen and Savita or not is unclear.

Buckley went on, putting to Praveen his statement of what happened on the Tuesday night into Wednesday morning, at around 2 a.m. 'You're talking about the events of the early morning of Wednesday,' he said to Praveen. Praveen had described Savita in pain that Tuesday night, 23 October, and he had woken to hear Savita vomiting and rushed to the toilet to find her very sick. Two nurses had come to her aid as Savita was 'leaking fluid and vomiting'.

'Can I suggest to you that the description that you provide there is actually the events that occurred on Sunday night going into Monday morning? All I am suggesting is perhaps you got the nights mixed up.'

'I think also the mix-up by the medical staff could be also possible,' said Praveen, 'because there have been retrospective entries made [in the notes] since the news broke out.'

Buckley and he disagreed about whether Dr Astbury explained to Savita and him the rationale for continuously monitoring the foetal heartbeat – to ensure Savita was not left 'sitting around with a dead foetus' – and also about whether Dr Astbury had seen Savita after Savita had been sent for a scan on the Monday morning. Buckley said Dr Astbury would say she did not see them again on the Monday after Savita went for a scan.

'[Dr Astbury] did come back and we had a discussion,' said Praveen.

'She will say that either that morning or the following morning – she is pretty positive . . . it was the following morning, on only one occasion was there discussion of a termination with your wife and she does not believe it was that particular morning [Monday],' said Buckley.

'No,' said Praveen, 'it was on Monday morning the first request for termination was made.'

'She's going to dispute that,' said Buckley. 'She thinks it was the following morning. I'll go through what she says about the following morning with you, but is it possible that you are mistaken about this?'

'No, I'm not mistaken, no. I was there all the time, so.'

Praveen in his statement had said Dr Astbury told them, following a request on Monday, after the scan, that she would 'have to go away and check' as to whether Savita could have a termination.

'I am very sure she did say that. She went and she never came back,' said Praveen.

'She will say that firstly that didn't happen and secondly there would have been absolutely no reason to go away and check because a termination was not warranted at that time,' said Buckley.

'But there were other witnesses. There were junior doctors, they were always with her so.'

Mr Buckley told Praveen: 'Well the evidence from other witnesses, in particular Dr Astbury, is that particular morning there was no actual risk to the life, to the health of your wife and accordingly no reason to even consider a termination.'

'Maybe.'

'And accordingly even if you had asked for it, which she disputes, there would be absolutely no reason, nor would she have gone off to ask about it because it simply wasn't indicated and wasn't warranted.'

'I don't know,' said Praveen.

Praveen had said he and Savita had been told on Monday by Dr Astbury that a termination was not possible while the foetal heartbeat remained and this was because Ireland was a 'Catholic country'. He also said Savita and her friend Mrdula had been told on the Tuesday, while he was travelling to Dublin airport and back, that a termination was not possible because 'it's a Catholic thing'.

Eileen Barrington, SC for Dr Astbury, said she wanted to go over 'just a few points or details', as Buckley had covered most issues.

'You prepared your statement without having looked at the medical records, isn't that right? And in so far as you give timings in your statement you accept they may not be correct?' For example, she said, he had put the ward rounds at 10.30 each morning when in fact they happened at 8.20 a.m.

She put it to him that he was 'wrong', 'incorrect', 'unaware' or 'a bit out' on a number of points in his statement.

'Can I just clarify that to summarize what you said to Mr Buckley, that conversation that you describe as having taken placc on the Tuesday, and you now say could have happened on the Monday morning and although you state that Mrdula was present that she may not in fact have been. And in so far as you state your friend who worked in the hospital was there on Monday morning you might be wrong about that as well,' she said.

Praveen remained calm throughout, conceding he might be mistaken on some points but sticking consistently to his assertion that he and Savita had first asked for a termination on the Monday and that she had asked again on Tuesday. He told me later that he was certain about this because Savita was 'very determined' to get home to hcr parents in Roscam before they left for India the following morning. 'She wanted to get back to tell them she had lost the baby before they got home and started telling friends at home about the pregnancy. She was very determined.' He said he didn't understand why Astbury disputed this.

Praveen had always said there had been three requests for a termination – one on Monday morning by him and Savita and two on Tuesday morning by Savita alone and later by both her and Mrdula.`

Dr Astbury in her evidence would dispute Praveen's account of the request for the termination, insisting none had been made on Monday and that one had been made on Tuesday the 23rd by Savita. In her statement to Professor Arulkumaran's investigation, however, she would say Praveen was present for the termination request. If Praveen was present, the request would have to have been made on Monday, as he was en route to Dublin airport with Savita's parents on Tuesday.

Praveen's account also appeared to be confirmed in a passing comment by Savita's friend Mrdula Vaseali, in her evidence the next day. Asked by counsel for the hospital how Praveen had reacted when she had told him, on Tuesday evening, that a midwife had told her and Savita that a termination was impossible when there was a foetal heartbeat, Mrdula said he hadn't been shocked.

'He was told the same thing before so he knew that. I think on Monday [he was told no termination possible].' She said Praveen had told her husband, Sunil, this on Monday the 22nd.

It was this episode, when Savita was told a termination would be impossible in Ireland as long as there was a foetal heart and her life was not in danger, because Ireland was a 'Catholic country', that had ignited consternation across the world. It was to emerge as one of the moments of genuine compassion shown to Savita during her week in University College Hospital Galway, and she who said it as one of the inquest's quiet stars.

Senior midwife Ann Maria Burke, who spoke to Savita on the morning of Tuesday the 23rd, had not been due to give evidence at the inquest at all. She had given an unsworn statement which made no reference to the 'chat' she had had with Savita. 'What helped us there,' said Dr McLoughlin, 'was the young Indian woman, Savita's friend.'

Mrdula Vaseali had spent Tuesday morning with Savita while Praveen was taking his parents-in-law to the airport. She said: 'Maybe around 11 or 12, a nurse dressed in dark blue came to check the heartbeat. I stood outside. The heartbeat was still there. The midwife came out. She couldn't continue because of Savita's crying. When the midwife stopped I thought she had finished and I came back inside. We both, Savita and I, asked, "Is there a possibility of saving the baby because there is still a heartbeat after three days?"

'Savita said, "Can you please save it? If you can't do something to stop the foetal heartbeat I can't take this waiting for the baby to die." The midwife said she would check it with the doctor and come back. She came in ten or fifteen minutes. She said she spoke to a doctor about what we can do, give a stitch, but the doctor said, "Her membranes are bulging, there is no way of saving the baby." We both said, "What about doing something to stop the baby's heartbeat?" She said, that is the midwife, "We don't do that here, dear. It's a Catholic thing." The midwife said,

"Anything else I can do for you?" Savita said, "I understand you can't do anything but I can't stay like this."

'Then lunch came. Another nurse said, "If you don't eat you'll not have energy for the next [pregnancy]. I will not be happy." This was said with love. Savita smiled and ate. The nurses were lovely. They took care of her. It's the system that is wrong.'

Mr Buckley cross-examined Ms Vaseali rigorously. 'I just want to say this to you, there is no record in the notes about this conversation having taken place and certainly none of the statements that I have seen recount that conversation taking place or any person having that conversation with you or Mrs Halappanavar.'

He asked her about what she and Praveen had discussed on the way home from the hospital on Tuesday evening. 'You told him about the midwife saying it couldn't be done because it's a Catholic thing?' he asked her.

'I said, "They can't do it, it seems". I never thought saying the Catholic thing is a big deal.'

'Well, are you wrong about it?' asked Buckley.

'No, I am not wrong,' she said.

'Are you wrong that somebody ever said that?'

'No.'

'Well why didn't you tell Mr Halappanavar that's what was said?'

'I don't know. We were talking about many things.'

'Presumably the most important thing you were discussing was what was happening to Mrs Halappanavar?'

'The most important thing at that time was Savita's health.'

'I appreciate that.'

'No. That is the thing we were talking about.'

'OK. But the one thing that happened in the five or six hours that you were there, and it's important because it is highlighted in your statement, is that you asked could something be done about the baby and the midwife said to you, "No, we can't do that. It's a Catholic thing." What I am asking you is why you didn't say that to Mr Halappanavar?'

'I said that they won't do it,' she said.

'But that's different from saying they won't do it because it's a Catholic thing. Ms Vaseali, isn't that probably your assumption? Isn't it possible that that is an assumption you have made?'

Dr McLoughlin intervened at this point. 'Counsel, please.'

She answered: 'When somebody is not well in the hospital, we will be talking about how she is going to get well and how and what will happen to her. Why would we be talking about who said that, who said this? We were discussing about her and her health.'

'But it's important,' said Buckley, 'because that is the explanation given for not terminating . . .'

'For because she died,' interjected Ms Vaseali.

Dr McLoughlin turned to the hospital's counsel. 'I wonder, Mr Buckley, is it possible to identify the midwife who said, "It's a Catholic thing"?'

'Em, I think we looked at that. I can take formal instructions again. I don't think it's possible to identify . . . I'll make an inquiry. If you want to rise for five minutes I can certainly just seek clarity.'

Mr Gleeson, for Praveen, then got to his feet to say Praveen's solicitor had asked for the St Monica's ward roster and this was refused by the hospital.

Mr Buckley was quick. 'That is not correct. The parameters of the inquest were pointed out to Mr O'Donnell, and Mr Gleeson knows precisely [he's] not entitled to that documentation.'

Mr Gleeson said: 'They didn't give us the roster. They made an excuse that "This is an inquest and we're not giving them to you". That's a refusal.'

The inquest rose and about fifteen minutes later Mr Buckley was able to tell the coroner: 'Insofar as this particular incident is concerned it is clear there were a number of nurses and obviously midwives on duty. The best we can possibly make out and going on the description this witness has furnished, of somebody dressed in blue, that would seem to fit with a clinical midwife manager, as opposed to a midwife. The clinical midwife manager on duty that day as far as we can identify is Ann Maria Burke, who has actually furnished a statement to you. As you are aware in the statement she doesn't refer to that comment being made at all.'

Dr McLoughlin said: 'For completeness' sake, we'll add her to the list of witnesses.'

The following day, midwife Burke appeared.

'I know this might be hurtful to you,' said Dr McLoughlin, 'but did you say to Savita that "It can't be done, this is a Catholic thing"?'

'Em, yes,' she said, pausing. 'To be honest, yes. I'm upset about this.'

'I know you are,' said Dr McLoughlin.

'I am very upset about this. I did say, "This is a Catholic country". I didn't mention it in a hurtful context,' she said. 'It was in the context of a conversation that I had.'

In her mid-fifties, with short brown hair and heavy-set features, she seemed, recalled McLoughlin, 'a very maternal woman who would have felt the pain Savita was feeling that morning. I felt sorry for her, because she seems a nice woman. She was distraught that day.'

Savita had talked to her about India. 'She mentioned in that in India, why can't the baby be taken, because in India there's no problem. The Hindu faith was mentioned in conversation. Savita was upset. So it was not a context to offend her and I am sorry if it came across that way. I hope I came across sensitively at the time. It does sound bad now but at the time I didn't mean it that way. It was to give information and to throw light on our culture.'

'I know,' said Dr McLoughlin, nodding. 'But that went around the world. What we can say is that all public hospitals in this country do not follow any religious tenets or dogma of any religious description.'

'I know that, yes,' said Ms Burke. 'It was something I said, I regret. She was puzzled. I was trying to explain. I had told her it was the law. She mentioned the Hindu faith and said in India it would be no problem and I really had to say something. I probably shouldn't have said it. I'm sorry I said it.'

Later, when pressed by counsel for the hospital to state that she had not said this on the instruction of anyone in the hospital, she agreed. 'I was trying to be as broad and explanatory as I could. It was nothing to do with the medical care at all. I was just trying to explain to her. This is Ireland.'

Praveen was grateful to Ms Burke. He said he and Ms Vaseali had not expected her to tell what had happened. 'It is a relief the truth is coming out,' he said. Her parents too, in June 2013, would express their gratitude to Ms Burke. 'This is a very kind, very wonderful woman. She told Savita the truth and she told the truth after, too. We will always be grateful to this woman,' Mr Yalagi told me.

Dr Katherine Astbury took the stand on Tuesday morning, Day 2. She read her statement, confirming how she had first seen Savita in the hospital on Monday 22 October at 8.20 a.m., had sent her for an abdominal scan to confirm foetal-heart presence, 'and I discussed the rationale for this in terms of the risk of sepsis with ruptured membranes and therefore the need to avoid her sitting on the ward undelivered for a protracted period after foetal demise.'

She would be asked by her counsel, Eileen Barrington, whether there had been a 'formal request for a termination at that stage?'

'No,' replied Dr Astbury.

'Mr Halappanavar said at this stage, on the Monday . . . the question of termination was brought up.'

'We discussed the management options in terms of induction

if there was no foetal heart versus awaiting events if there was a foetal heart.'

'There was no request for any [termination]?' asked Dr McLoughlin.

'No.'

She said she saw Savita again the following morning with the team at 8.20.

'She was very upset by the situation and enquired about the possibility of us giving her medication to cause her to miscarry as the outlook for the pregnancy was poor and she did not want to have to await events.'

She told Eugene Gleeson, senior counsel for Praveen, her recollection of the conversation they had had that Tuesday morning.

'We had been discussing again the fact that she had no contractions and the fact it was very hard to predict when delivery might be likely to take place and she basically said that she was finding it very upsetting and difficult to have to sit with a baby in her knowing the ultimate outlook for the pregnancy was that she was unlikely to come out with a live baby, and that she didn't want to have to sit and wait for something to happen. And I said to her that in this country it was not legal to terminate a pregnancy on the grounds of poor prognosis for the foetus. There was no suggestion that she was in any way unwell or that there was any risk to her life. So I couldn't offer her a termination on those grounds.'

Mr Gleeson put it to her that Savita had been very distressed at this point, so distressed that she was asking for a termination.

'She was emotionally distressed. She was not physically unwell,' replied Dr Astbury.

'She has been told by a colleague of yours that the foetus is not viable, that she's going to miscarry, it's inevitable. You on the other hand are holding out for foetal viability,' said Gleeson.

'I am waiting because the law states that in the absence of

risk to the life of the mother there is no reason to intervene.'

'Did you feel in any way constrained or inhibited by Irish law in terms of the treatment you could afford Savita?' asked Gleeson.

'Yes. Because termination of pregnancy, which is what she was requesting, is not legal in the context in which she requested it.'

'May we infer from that if these events had occurred in a neighbouring country such as England that Savita would have had her termination on the Monday or perhaps on the Tuesday, upon request?'

'Yes,' said Dr Astbury, 'patients are usually offered, as I under-stand it, if it's under 20 weeks termination is permitted, patients are offered either the option of termination or continuing with the pregnancy.'

She added: 'The law in Ireland does not permit termination even if there is *no* prospect of viability. That would be my under-standing of the legal position based on the judgment in the X case and on the basis of the Medical Council guidelines.'

He put it to her that she had in fact said to Savita, 'Unfortunately I can't. I am bound by the law. This is a Catholic country. We cannot terminate because the foetus is still alive.'

'I did not say that.'

'Would you agree with me that to use those words to Savita in those circumstances would be insensitive, uncivilized and wrong?'

'It would certainly be insensitive, yes,' she said.

Gleeson asked Dr Astbury to identify where in Savita's medical notes she had recorded this conversation. She hadn't. 'I don't record all conversations which I have with patients.'

'I appreciate you don't record all conversations,' said Gleeson. 'But this is not a how's-your-father conversation. This is a very important conversation. This is, "Please, I can't bear it. Please, I'm going to lose my baby. Please" . . . You say, "I can't because of the state of Irish law." Would you not put that in the record?'

'Well on the day we had that discussion, on the Tuesday, I didn't record a note of it,' she said.

The clear threads in Dr Astbury's evidence were that there was, she said, only one request for a termination and that this had been made on Tuesday morning, 23 October; that her decision as to whether or not to intervene relied on her understanding of the law on abortion and also that she had been basing that decision on whether Savita's life was at risk. To make this assessment, she was reliant on good-quality clinical information about Savita's declining health.

The inquest demonstrated beyond doubt that from almost the moment she and Praveen entered St Monica's ward at 9.30 a.m. on Sunday 21 October until Wednesday afternoon, the clinical care taken with Savita's case was woeful.

A key tool which would have improved monitoring of Savita is the Modified Early Obstetric Warning System. The Early Warning System is a basic tool: a person's vital signs (pulse, blood pressure, temperature) are recorded regularly and entered on a colour-coded chart. If a number of vital signs are abnormal together, their recording together on the chart will visually trigger early alarm bells to alert staff to possible sepsis. It was in place in two of the three obstetric wards in the hospital in late October 2012, but not in St Monica's ward.

Dr Geraldine Gaffney, women and children's director at the hospital, was asked to explain this, by John O'Donnell, junior counsel for Praveen.

'My understanding was that the Modified Early Obstetric Warning score was introduced to the ante-natal and post-natal wards as early as 2009 but for reasons that I am not sure about . . . it wasn't present on that ward. The plan was for the hospital [to have in place] the national Early Warning System, hospital-wide from November 2012, which would include St Monica's ward and those patients that were on that ward and were pregnant would have the MEOWS,' said Dr Gaffney.

Asked when the hospital-wide plan was decided on, she said she wasn't sure.

'It was certainly discussed by all hospital directorates . . . several months previously as far as I am aware.'

John O'Donnell asked why the system was being used for some patients and not for others.

'I'm not sure. There was only one ward where it wasn't being used.' She said it was being used in the ante- and post-natal wards. 'But why it wasn't being used in St Monica's ward, I don't know.'

'Whose decision was it not to use it in St Monica's?'

'I don't know.'

'What is the purpose [of MEOWS]?'

'To identify, to alert people to early warning, so people are alerted early on to changes in the vital signs.'

'Is it not an essential process to be had in . . . a university hospital?'

'Indeed, no doubt. It was desirable certainly, yes,' said the women and children's director.

The MEOWS was introduced hospital-wide within a fortnight of Savita's death.

The first doctor to see Savita and Praveen that morning of Sunday the 21st was Dr Olufoyeke Olatunbosun, an obstetrics and gynaecology senior health officer who was on call that weekend. Following their return to the hospital on Sunday afternoon, after Savita had 'felt something coming down', Savita was admitted and Dr Olatunbosun was instructed by Dr Gaolebale to order a full blood count as a baseline, in case Savita was to need bloods later. The blood count showed Savita had an elevated white cell count of 16.9 (a normal range for pregnant women is 6 to 15) indicating that she might have been fighting an infection. This was not communicated to Dr Astbury on Monday morning.

Dr Olatunbosun told the inquest she was not attached to any particular team in the hospital when on call and would not have seen Savita again after admission, as she would have reverted to her team the following day. She said the blood results would have been available on the ward 'in a few hours' or 'a bit longer at weekends'. No one on Savita's team looked at them until 8.21 a.m. on the following Wednesday.

Asked whether it was anyone's responsibility to look at the blood counts once they get back to the ward, Dr Olatunbosun said, 'Yes, the team.' Dr McLoughlin said the team the following morning might not know that a blood had been taken. 'Yes,' she agreed, but said the bloods had been taken as a baseline and not because clinically indicated. 'I wasn't concerned about the test results,' she said.

'The baseline was actually not base. It was off the base [i.e. high],' said Dr McLoughlin.

'Yes, I am aware of that.'

'And nobody contacted you about it being abnormal?'

She said to her knowledge there had been a raised white cell count but this was not unusual in pregnancy and as Savita was well it wouldn't have changed her management of Savita in any way.

Dr Astbury would say in her evidence that she hadn't known about the raised count on Sunday the 21st, until Wednesday the 24th and had she known, she would have repeated the count earlier. It was neither conveyed to her verbally nor was it in Savita's notes.

'Yes, I wasn't aware the white cell count was 16.9. If I had known that, yes, I would have rechecked it.'

'Is it not up to your junior staff to tell you that?' Dr McLoughlin asked her.

'Well I would have anticipated it would have been checked by the staff on the Sunday.'

'Is that a system failure?'

'I suppose each team should also check their own results,' said Dr Astbury.

At 12.30 a.m. on the night of Sunday, 21 October, Savita's

waters broke, a normal event, and she was prescribed an antibiotic the following morning at the 8.20 ward round. She was seen by the team on Monday the 22nd at 8.20 a.m. and again on Tuesday at 8.20 a.m. when the first or second discussion – depending on which account is accepted – about a termination ensued.

During Tuesday 23rd, we heard in evidence how things began to go badly wrong for Savita. By Tuesday evening she was showing the early signs of sepsis.

Savita's pulse, which had been 82 beats per minute on admission on Sunday, fluctuated on Tuesday from 100 bpm at 2.45 p. m., to 114 bpm at 7 p.m. to 106 bpm at 9 p.m. A persistent tachycardia, or raised heart rate, over 100 bpm 'is an important sign which may indicate serious underlying disease and should be fully investigated', according to the UK Confidential Enquiry into Maternal Deaths (CEMD) 2006–2008, *Saving Mothers' Lives*.

The CEMD, regarded as the 'gold standard' internationally in gathering information on maternal deaths, is required reading for anyone working in obstetrics and gynaecology in Britain or Ireland. It warns that a woman may be moving towards sepsis if two or more of the following are present: a body temperature below 36 degrees Celsius or above 38 degrees; a heart rate above 90 bpm; a respiratory rate higher than 20 breaths per minute; and/or a white blood cell count below four or above 12 in non-pregnant patients.

Student midwife Elaine Finucane, who was being supervised by midwife manager Ann Maria Burke on Tuesday the 23rd, told the inquest she took Savita's vital signs at 7 p.m. 'I recorded her pulse at 114 beats per minute and 114 beats per minute on recheck. I noted this was abnormal. She was lying on her side in the bed. I asked Ms Halappanavar how she felt at this stage. She didn't verbally respond, just moved her head from side to side. I notified the event to midwife Burke immediately.'

Senior midwife Burke said she got the report from student Finucane at 7.15 p.m. 'I asked her to recheck it and it [Savita's pulse] was 110 on recheck. Then I advised Elaine Finucane that I would discuss it with the senior house officer.'

Midwife Burke told the inquest she bleeped the senior house officer on duty, Dr Ikechukwu Uzockwu, at 7.35 p.m. and told him about the elevated pulse.

Dr Uzockwu told the inquest he did not get this call at 7.35 p.m. He said he got a call 'between 9 p.m. and 11 p.m.' that night from, he thought, 'midwife Gallagher.'

'I was notified that her blood pressure, respiratory rate, pulse rate and temperature were within normal range.' He could not remember 'vividly' who had called him. 'I think it was the midwife [Cathy] Gallagher'.

He insisted: 'I was told the vital signs were stable. I wasn't told there was an elevated pulse. That was my recollection of the events.'

His recollection of a phone call between 9 p.m. and 11 p.m. appears to be accurate when the testimony of midwife Miriam Dunleavy, who was also on duty in the ward that Tuesday night, is examined. The night shift runs from 8 p.m. to 8 a.m. and the day shift from 8 a.m. to 8 p.m.

Midwife Dunleavy said her colleague on the night shift had recorded Savita's vital signs as stable at 9 p.m., though her pulse was 106 bpm. Her temperature was 36.9 degrees Celsius, within normal range. Midwife Gallagher was one of the two witnesses who had medical certificates excusing them from giving evidence. She did provide a statement, though this was not read to the inquest.

Dr Uzockwu and midwife Burke were recalled to try and resolve the differences and both stuck to their accounts. The evidence, however, suggests that midwife Gallagher may have called Dr Uzockwu between 9 and 11 p.m. and may in fact have told him Savita's vital signs were stable. As midwife Gallagher could not be called, this could not be explored. The HSE report appears to support this scenario and makes no mention of a call between midwife Burke and Dr Uzockwu at 7.35 p.m.

What is unclear is whether senior midwife Burke did call Dr Uzockwu at 7.35 p.m. There is her sworn evidence that she did. Dr Uzockwu's sworn evidence was that if he had been told about an elevated pulse at any stage that night he would have come to Savita immediately (and he did at 6.30 a.m.).

'This lady had ruptured membranes and so there was a risk of infection. I would be concerned but I was not told the heart rate was elevated.'

'You should have been told?' asked Mr Gleeson.

'I suppose I should have.'

'There's no supposing about it. Surely Ms Halappanavar deserves accurate communication between the midwifery side of the house and the doctor's side. Is it not too much to ask?'

'I suppose so, yes . . . Yes.'

Savita's elevated pulse at 7 p.m. was the first sign of sepsis and it remained elevated at 9 p.m.

The pulse was not rechecked until 6.30 a.m., over nine hours later, by which time it was 160 bpm, double her pulse (82 bpm) on admission. It was hospital policy that when a woman's membranes ruptured, her vital signs should be monitored every four hours. This was not done. It was, agreed Dr Astbury, a 'system failure'.

Midwife Miriam Dunleavy who had come on duty at 8 p.m. that Tuesday night agreed with Gleeson that she had been aware from the handover that Savita had had a significantly elevated pulse earlier that evening.

'Was that not important?' he asked her.

'Of course it was important.'

He asked her if this was not something that should be addressed by a doctor. 'I suppose.'

'You suppose? We're talking about real people,' said Gleeson.

'Yes.'

'There's no supposing about it. It is essential a doctor comes and looks at this patient?'

'It is, yes.'

She said however that Savita had been 'one of the healthiest patients' on the ward at that point. Her first interaction with Savita on that shift was at 4.15 a.m. 'I answered a call-bell to Ms Halappanavar's room. When I entered the room both Ms Halappanavar and her husband were awake. Ms Halappanavar informed me she and her husband felt cold and requested extra blankets. Mr Halappanavar stated that the radiator was cold. He was lying on a mattress on the floor and the room was cold. On my return with the blankets I observed that Ms Halappanavar was shivering and her teeth were chattering with cold. I recorded her temperature, which was 37.7 degrees. She was alert . . . no complaints of pain. I administered one gram of paracetamol.'

This period in Savita's care was becoming increasingly critical. During the course of Tuesday night and into Wednesday Savita developed chorioamnionitis and sepsis as her health ebbed gravely to a point where her life would be at risk.

Mr Gleeson asked midwife Dunleavy if she was 'seriously suggesting' that when Savita was cold at 4.15 a.m. it was due to the 'lack of heating'.

'No, I'm certainly not. Excuse me. I am a serious midwife. When I pulled the blanket up over Ms Halappanavar I saw her shivering. Why do you think I took her temperature? Of course I took it knowing maybe she had an infection. I felt in my clinical experience I'd give her two paracetamol – the normal, and see did it work and I'd come back in 45 minutes and re-examine.'

'Did you take her pulse?' asked Gleeson.

'No I didn't.'

'Why not?'

'When I had taken her temperature . . . I wanted to see would the paracetamol work first. If there was an elevated temperature still I probably would have taken it at five o'clock.'

'What was to stop you taking her pulse?'

'My clinical decision there and then I decided not to do it. Her overall wellness I felt, a temperature of 37.7, [I gave her] paracetamol to take it down.' She said as far as she was aware, Savita's vital signs had settled down and her pulse was not of concern.

She should have taken her pulse. This was the view stated by both Dr Peter Boylan, who would later give expert testimony, and the coroner Dr McLoughlin, to me in conversation for this book.

'I asked her if she was OK, was she comfortable. She said she was fine and she indicated to me she just wanted to snuggle up and get some sleep.'

By 6.30 a.m., agreed midwife Dunleavy, there were 'dramatic changes'. Savita's temperature was now 39.6, heart rate 160 bpm and her blood pressure had dropped.

She called Dr Uzockwu. He was on the ward again seeing another patient and when told that Savita had developed a fever and a fast heart rate he went to examine her immediately. He was the first member of staff to suspect Savita had sepsis.

'This lady had a pulse rate of 160 beats per minute. She also had a temperature of 39.6 degrees. I noted that she had a foul-smelling discharge. I was concerned. I did feel she had sepsis.' He agreed with Mr Gleeson her condition was 'alarming' at this stage, that it was an 'emergency' and needed to be dealt with 'as quickly as possible'.

'I made a diagnosis of probable chorioamnionitis.' He recorded this in Savita's notes.

Chorioamnionitis is an infection of the foetal membranes and the only treatment for it is removal of the membranes and thus also the foetus, alongside antibiotic therapy.

Dr Uzockwu told the inquest he took bloods for a full blood count to test for renal and liver function, blood cultures and serum lactate test but agreed he did not mark the blood samples as urgent. The samples arrived at the lab at 8.29 a.m.

A problem with blood samples being taken in incorrect bottles emerged, when Dr McLoughlin asked Dr Uzockwu what type of bottles he used. 'For the full blood count I used a haematology bottle. For the liver function, kidney function and serum lactate test I used a biochemistry bottle,' said Dr Uzockwu.

'They don't use a biochemistry bottle to do a serum lactate test in UCHG,' said Dr McLoughlin.

'At the time I did not have that knowledge,' replied the doctor. 'I was working in a previous hospital before where I had taken a serum lactate in a biochemistry bottle for suspected sepsis and the blood test was done.'

'Do you know what the result of that serum lactate was?'

'Well I'll tell you, it was discarded. It wasn't taken at all,' said Dr McLoughlin. It emerged that the serum lactate test should have been carried out on the ward at a point-of-care centre and not sent to the lab at all. A serum lactate test is vital in cases of suspected sepsis, as any reading over 1.5 indicates the body is overproducing lactic acid in response to an inadequate supply of oxygen.

Shortly before the 8.20 a.m. ward round, Dr Uzockwu spoke to Dr Astbury's registrar, Dr Ann Helps, in the corridor.

Dr Helps told the inquest: 'I had been informed by Dr Ike of Ms Halappanavar's critical condition.' He had told her about the foul-smelling discharge and his diagnosis of probable chorioamnionitis.

John O'Donnell, junior counsel for Praveen, asked Dr Helps if the midwife had told her that Savita had been shivering and that her teeth had been chattering during the night. 'I don't recall,' said Dr Helps. She recalled Savita saying she was feeling unwell, that she was cold with aches and back pain. Dr Helps had been carrying Savita's chart during the 8.20 ward round with Dr Astbury.

Dr Astbury had said in her evidence that she had not read the chart before the round. It was usual for the team to read the notes during the ward round, while the doctor was examining the patients. She said she was not told about Dr Uzockwu's concerns about the foul-smelling discharge. 'That's a very significant finding, the foul-smelling discharge?' Mr Gleeson asked her. 'And it's recorded in the notes. Is that acceptable?'

'I should have been told,' she said.

She read from Dr Helps's entry in Savita's notes that morning which said: 'All well this morning.' Dr Helps described the fact that Savita was complaining of aches and feeling cold, that she had spiked a temperature of 39.6 degrees at 6.30 a.m. and that the probable diagnosis was chorioamnionitis.

Had Dr Astbury known at 8.20 a.m. of the foul-smelling discharge, she said, she would not have been querying whether Savita at this stage had chorioamnionitis, she would have diagnosed it and moves to terminate would have been started. Savita had met the legal criteria to have an abortion by that point, she said, and in fact she had 'presumably' met them earlier, at 6.30 a.m. Despite suspecting chorioamnionitis she made no note in Savita's medical notes of considering termination if chorioamnionitis was indeed confirmed. Nor did she move to get a second opinion there and then about termination, to speed up the process if chorioamnionitis was later confirmed.

Midwife manager Patricia Gilligan, who had come on duty at 8 a.m. on Wednesday, was extremely worried about Savita. As soon as she had received the handover from the night staff she went to see Savita.

'I was very concerned for her. I thought she was a septic abortion. When I heard at ten past eight that morning what her temperature was at half past six I thought she was very sick. Her pulse rate was 160 bpm. I thought I really don't hear that too often.' She moved Savita from Room 2 near the exit to Room 9 next to the nurses' station, where there was also immediate access to oxygen.

'Her consultant was coming on duty then. The rounds were

started. Her own consultant saw her. I just made sure Dr Astbury saw her.' She didn't get a chance to talk to Dr Astbury at this time. 'The doctor would have had her chart. The doctor would see what I was seeing,' she told Mr O'Donnell.

However, Dr Astbury neither saw the chart nor was told of the foul-smelling discharge. Nor was Dr Astbury made aware during her ward round of the blood results, ordered by Dr Uzockwu two hours earlier, which were accessed from the ward at about 8.30 a.m. Dr McLoughlin asked her when the ward was told of Savita's blood results, and the fact that her white cell count had collapsed from 16 on Sunday morning, to 1.7 that morning (healthy range in pregnancy: 6 to 15).

'I'm not aware that anybody notified the ward,' said Dr Astbury.

'That would be indicative something very serious had happened,' said Dr McLoughlin. 'If that had been known at eight o'clock would you have changed your mind?'

'I suppose it can be indicative of severe sepsis so, it's one of the criteria of severe sepsis, yes.'

'So you probably wouldn't have gone off and come back at one o'clock.'

'Well I suppose I would have seen her sooner than that . . . At the time we saw her we didn't have any blood results available and we were working on the basis of the clinical signs, and clinically her systolic blood pressure was above 90, so we had no evidence to suggest that she had severe sepsis. Her temperature had settled a bit and her pulse rate had settled a bit. But obviously if we had the blood results back at that stage we might have been considering intervening sooner,' she said.

She did however access Savita's blood results from another part of the hospital, at 11.25 a.m. They showed Savita had a reduced white cell count of 1.7 (normal range: 6–15) and an elevated C-reactive protein of 38.9, indicating sepsis. Dr Astbury did not return to see Savita at this point.

A key witness from this period was the midwife-nurse allocated to care for Savita on Wednesday morning. This midwife submitted a medical certificate to the coroner excusing her from providing a statement and from giving evidence. In his summing up at the end of the inquest, Dr McLoughlin referred to the blood pressure recordings taken by her. At 07.50 Savita's blood pressure was 100/55; at 08.25 98/54; at 10.00 88/50; at 10.30 84/50; 12.00 76/46, and at 13.00 78/42.

'None of the medical staff was apprised of her rapid decline,' said Dr McLoughlin.

At 1.10 p.m. midwife manager Gilligan was informed that Savita's blood pressure had dropped to 78/42. She immediately contacted Dr Astbury, who arrived on the ward 'promptly'. Savita's life was now in peril.

Dr Astbury said: 'I received a phone call from the ward shortly after 13.00 to state Ms Halappanavar's condition had deteriorated in the preceding hour. At the time I was with Dr Susmita Sarma, consultant obstetrician and gynaecologist. I discussed the case with her including the fact that I was of the opinion I would have no option but to deliver the foetus regardless of whether the foetal heart was present. Dr Sarma suggested I speak to Dr Geraldine Gaffney, consultant obstetrician and gynaecologist, and also the clinical director, to obtain a second opinion.'

She collected a portable scanner on her way to the ward where Savita was sweaty and having problems breathing. Her temperature was 37.3, her pulse 150 and her blood pressure critically low at 60/30. Her fluids were increased in an effort to get her blood pressure up and an intern was called to repeat blood tests and to insert a catheter. Dr Astbury left again to talk to Dr Gaffney, to outline the situation and seek her opinion as to whether to terminate. Dr Gaffney agreed it was necessary.

'I collected the portable obstetric ultrasound scanner from the clinic and returned to the ward where a scan confirmed foetal demise.' She carried out a vaginal examination. Savita's cervix was 2 cm dilated and thick.

'My impression at this stage was that Ms Halappanavar was suffering from septic shock secondary to chorioamnionitis.'

She rang the microbiology department for antibiotic advice at about 2 p.m., an hour after the initial call from the ward. Consultant microbiologist Dr Deirbhile Keady advised administering Tazocin and gentamicin and to continue on metronidazole.

She then went to the gynaecology theatre where transfer to the High Dependency Unit was discussed, and a call was made to the consultant anaesthetist, Dr John Bates, who agreed to send someone to assess Savita with a view to transferring her to the HDU.

There was no bed immediately available in HDU, however, and the anaesthetists felt she would benefit from the insertion of central and arterial lines to administer drugs and fluids.

Savita was brought to theatre for insertion of the lines at 3.15 p.m.

'On insertion of the central line she spontaneously delivered a female foetus. Shortly after, she delivered the placenta while the arterial line was being inserted,' said Dr Astbury. Savita was transferred to the HDU at about 4.45 p.m. on Wednesday, 24 October, where she was to have her final conversation with Praveen.

Inevitably Ireland's abortion laws had featured prominently in this first half of the inquest. What came through too in testimony about these first four days were four issues relating to this phase of Savita's care. And then there was the reference to the role Catholic teaching had had in how the events of these four days had unfolded.

The breakdown in basic care, during Savita's first three and a half days in hospital, was appalling as was the sub-standard manner with which some clinical staff performed during that time. Some showed a lack of knowledge of hospital protocols while others, for whatever reasons, appeared to ignore other protocols, particularly the one which demanded four-hourly monitoring of the vital signs of women whose membranes had ruptured. There were failures to recognize persistent indicators not only of sepsis but of fever; there were breakdowns in communication between key staff, at shift handovers, during ward rounds and particularly regarding blood tests and results; inexplicably the Early Warning Score system, that was in place throughout the rest of the obstetrics and gynaecology wards in the hospital and which could have triggered alarm bells sooner if used in Savita's case, was not used then in St Monica's ward. In sum, the high-quality work of some involved in Savita's care in those first four days was effectively brought to naught by the inexcusable breakdown in standards among others.

The second issue was the difficulty of assessing when a threat to Savita's life was 'real and substantial' enough to allow delivery of her foetus. The level of care was an aspect of this. Without rigorous monitoring of what was happening with Savita no clinician would have the information necessary to get this judgement right.

The third aspect was the law.

Listening to Dr Astbury's evidence it was clear that throughout the two or three days from when the question of a termination was first mooted, she was striving not only to provide treatment for Savita but to interpret and apply the law. Under the 1861 Offences Against the Person Act which was the primary piece of legislation governing abortion in October 2012, abortion was illegal. Though qualified by a series of court judgments and referendums since 1992, and nuanced in Medical Council guidelines, the law as it stood was that abortion was illegal.

Explaining the reason she felt she could not consider terminating Savita's pregnancy on the Tuesday morning, Dr Astbury said: 'There was no suggestion that she was in any way unwell or that there was any risk to her life. So I couldn't offer her a termination on those grounds . . . She was emotionally distressed. She was not physically unwell.'

As she proceeded through her evidence she referred variously to Irish law, to the Supreme Court ruling in the 1992 X case, to the legal situation in Britain and to the Irish Medical Council guidelines.

She had felt constrained by Irish law as she understood it. Savita would have been offered an abortion in England on Monday morning as far as she understood the law there. She referred to her understanding of the law based on the X case judgment and the Irish Medical Council guidelines.

Dr McLoughlin read the relevant paragraph from the IMC guidelines to the court.

'In current obstetrical practice rare complications can arise where therapeutic intervention including termination of pregnancy may be required at a stage when due to the extreme immaturity of the baby there may be little or no hope of the baby surviving. In these exceptional circumstances it may be necessary to intervene to terminate the pregnancy to save the life of the mother, while making every effort to preserve the life of the baby.'

'Did you have scope to intervene under that [before Wednesday]?' he asked Dr Astbury.

'I would not believe so. My understanding of that guideline is that it relates to conditions such as cancer. It mentions specifically therapeutic interventions "including termination" so it suggests other treatments which I would understand to be things like radiotherapy, or hysterectomy for cervical cancer which would inevitably result in the baby having to be delivered at the same time.'

Her understanding, she said, was that the guideline referred to situations where the woman was diagnosed with a life-threatening illness that required treatment that would result in the death of the foetus, and that it did not refer to a health- or life-threatening situation which required a direct termination. Asked then if this meant there was difficulty interpreting the guidelines in an emergency situation she said: 'Well that is the Medical Council guideline. It's just that there is no law.'

'So you think it might be a question of law?' asked Dr McLoughlin.

'Yes.'

At one point during the inquest, as she was being grilled by Mr Gleeson about whether she consulted with other doctors in her interpretation of the law on abortion, he asked her: 'Are you a lawyer?' One might infer that doctors in such a situation would benefit from a law degree.

The lack of clarity in the law further 'chilled' – as the ECHR in 2010 had described the impact of the law on Irish doctors – Dr Astbury's course even when she decided Savita was on the point of being legally entitled to an emergency termination. She further hesitated, delaying for up to an hour as she consulted with two colleagues. Between 1.10 p.m. on Wednesday when she was called by midwife manager Gilligan, and 2 p.m., by which time she had consulted with Dr Gaffney, Savita's blood pressure fell from 74/38 to 60/30.

Dr Astbury was, however, clear that a termination is a termination, whatever the reason for it or legal context in which it's carried out. Dr McLoughlin at one point urged her not to use the word 'termination'.

'The mention of a termination is a very emotive term,' he said. 'The term "termination" often evokes the intention of killing the developing baby or foetus. And under no circumstances here was that the intention of the Halappanavars. They wanted this baby.'

'Absolutely. This was very wanted,' said Dr Astbury.

'So can we get away from the emotive term abortion, the

emotive term termination? That doesn't exist in this case. Isn't that correct?'

'Well, if you mean to give somebody medication to cause the baby to deliver and there is a foetal heart my understanding is that legally that is considered to be termination,' she said.

'Oh well, yes, right. That's legally, but we're not talking about the wilful intention of killing the child from the beginning. Something has happened. That's correct?'

'Yes,' she said.

The role of Catholicism in defining Savita's care was named, by midwife Burke, and as quickly rejected by Dr McLoughlin – and others beyond the inquest. There can be no doubt however that the legal parameters which had denied Savita an abortion had been set by a Catholic-inspired amendment to the Constitution twenty-nine years before she died. The ongoing influence of Catholicism in Irish obstetrics would be alluded to by Dr Boylan in his expert testimony later in the inquest.

The fourth clear issue was that Savita had no input into the decisions about what would happen to her. This was taken as given at the inquest and not questioned by anyone outside Praveen's legal team. It would be remarked upon by expert witness Dr Boylan.

As an important aside, a threat to Savita's health, either physical or emotional, was not a consideration at any time.

10

To his dying day Praveen would be grateful for the 'valiant efforts' made by the staff in the high dependency and intensive care units to save Savita, his counsel Eugene Gleeson told Day 5 of the inquest.

It would be evident why. What was to emerge was a picture of highly skilled, co-ordinated care characterized by teamwork, altruism and the utmost in professional care.

Expert witnesses – Dr Peter Boylan, former Master of the National Maternity Hospital and its current clinical director, and Dr Susan Knowles, consultant microbiologist and one of the foremost experts in infection in pregnant women, new mothers and babies in the State – would give their expert opinions on Savita's treatment, opinions that would be variously welcomed and attacked by anti-abortion campaigners.

Dr Knowles commented that as soon as the high dependency and intensive care units became involved from 2 p.m. on Wednesday 24 October, Savita received 'a high standard of care thereafter, with regard to multi-disciplinary management of infection, antibiotic choice and investigation of possible focus of infection while in intensive care'.

The first person down to see Savita from the intensive care and high dependency units was senior house officer Dr Aidan Magee.

He had been sent by Dr John Bates, consultant anaesthetist covering the IC and HD units, following contact from Dr Astbury. She had been in touch with Dr Bates at about 2 p.m. following her review of Savita at 1.20 p.m. Dr Magee told the inquest he had arrived on the ward at 2.30 p.m. Dr Michael Scully, another ICU consultant, arrived on the ward shortly after him. They were to assess which unit Savita should be transferred to.

'Ms Halappanavar appeared to be in septic shock with blood pressure of approximately 60/30, signs of tachycardia of approximately 150 beats per minute and was pyrexic with a temperature of 39.03,' he said. 'We were informed she had chorioamnionitis and she had been commenced on Tazocin, metronidazole and gentamycin and this treatment had been discussed with microbiology.'

Dr Magee said he stayed by Savita, monitoring her blood pressure, while space was being made for her in theatre for the insertion of a central line. He also explained to Praveen what was happening. 'At approximately 15.15 Ms Halappanavar was brought into theatre.' He inserted a central line and while this was happening it became apparent, given the actions of theatre nurses, that she had spontaneously delivered a female foetus.

Dr John Bates told the inquest that on the basis of his conversation with Dr Astbury it was his view Savita was in septic shock at 2 p.m. Her lactate level was 8.8. Had he known early that morning that she had an elevated lactate level, would he have known Savita was 'headed for difficulty'? asked Dr McLoughlin.

'I would [have made] the diagnosis of severe sepsis, yes.'

Vital hours had been lost. Witness after witness from the HDU and ICU told the inquest that time was 'of the essence' with a diagnosis of sepsis. The inquest heard that for every hour that passed Savita's risk of dying increased by 6 per cent. Some nine hours had elapsed between Dr Uzockwu's diagnosis of probable sepsis and decisive action being taken.

In theatre by 3.15 p.m., Savita was given a low dose of noradrenalin which stabilized her low blood pressure.

Dr Brian Kinirons was the on-call consultant anaesthetist in intensive care working 5 p.m. Wednesday until 9 a.m. on Thursday, 25 October. During the handover at 4.30 p.m. on Wednesday afternoon he was made aware that the critical care team had admitted Savita to the high dependency unit that afternoon. On admission, he said, she had had a temperature of 37.4 degrees, a heart rate of 153 beats per minute, blood pressure of 143/99, a high lactate of 6.8, a white cell count of 1.4, in keeping with infection. She was drowsy. Her outlook at this stage was 'pretty poor', he agreed.

'What was clear was she was in severe sepsis, the worst end of that spectrum. What was clear to me over the course of the evening was that despite oxygen therapy her oxygenation levels got worse [and] despite vasopressor support her requirements increased rather than reduced.' Vasopressor support involves the administration of hormones or drugs to try to increase blood pressure.

Dr Kinirons had a discussion with Dr McGee some time after 6 p.m. 'My concern was that we had full input from the microbiologists in selecting the appropriate antibiotics and I was informed microbiology was already involved.'

During the course of Wednesday evening Savita's condition deteriorated. And after 2 a.m. she was intubated, before being transferred to intensive care at about 3 a.m. on Thursday.

'I spoke to Dr Kinirons several times during the night and he was aware of the patient's medical course. I next saw Ms Halappanavar at approximately 06.00 hours. I made some alterations to her ventilation settings in an effort to improve her blood gas parameters,' said Dr Magee.

Dr Bates was in charge of ICU on Thursday and he took over her care at 9 a.m. She had deteriorated overnight and had severe acute respiratory distress syndrome, with severe lung dysfunction due to severe sepsis, he said. 'May we take it that is a very, very serious condition?' asked Mr Gleeson.

'Yes, it's a very serious condition.'

'It's life-threatening?'

'Yes.'

'The prognosis at that stage, on Thursday at 9 a.m., for Savita was very poor?'

'Yes. The ballpark mortality rate for severe sepsis, septic shock is 35, 45 rising to 60 per cent. The more organs that require support the more poor the prognosis is,' Dr Bates told the inquest.

She was now on a larger dose of noradrenalin. 'The blood pressure would have normalized but it only normalized because she was on that drug. In terms of looking for improvement in condition what we generally like to see is a reduction in the requirement for that drug,' said Dr Bates.

He said her lactate levels were elevated and her clotting was 'abnormal'. 'Her oxygen saturation had fallen from 80 per cent to 65 per cent and she had cool hands and feet.'

Dr Paul Naughton, consultant anaesthetist in the intensive care unit, took over Savita's care at 9 a.m. on Friday.

'She was in profound septic shock, the mortality rate for which is 40 to 60 per cent,' said Dr Naughton. 'She was sedated, intubated and ventilated since the day before.' Her body was swollen due to an accumulation of fluids.

'She had a tachycardia of 140 bpm, pyrexia [fever] with a temperature of 40 degrees. She had a normal blood pressure but supported with infusions of noradrenalin. She had a white cell count of 23.5 and a C-reactive protein level of 37.2. She had multi-organ failure.'

Mr Gleeson asked him, given that she had respiratory, cardiovascular and haematological systems organ failure, was death inevitable at this stage?

'No, I didn't think death was inevitable at that stage. A

patient's prognosis worsens depending on how many organ dysfunctions there are. There is no doubt she had respiratory, cardiovascular and haematological dysfunction but given her age I was still hopeful, though her prognosis was poor. The clinical plan for that day was continuous supported care. A CT scan was ordered and she was reviewed by microbiology.

'During the remainder of Friday Ms Halappanavar remained very unwell. We were unable to make any reduction to her inotropic [cardiac] and ventilation support.'

He said that Savita was sent for a CT scan that afternoon to rule out interabdominal infection or retained products of conception. 'She returned from radiology at approximately 17.00 hours after a CT scan of thorax, abdomen and pelvis. The results of the scan showed there was no evidence of interabdominal pathology.' She had signs in keeping with profound sepsis. During Friday evening Ms Halappanavar became more unwell and she was commenced on further therapeutic interventions, he continued.

Dr McLoughlin asked Dr Naughton why, despite the range of antibiotics Savita was on which appeared to have cleared the infection from her body, the sepsis continued to engulf Savita.

'By this time she was in septic shock. The sepsis had set off a cascade of events that leads to an inflammatory reaction that just doesn't stop because you're getting at the bacteria. In Savita's case it was florid and it was progressive. So the inflammatory process was in train and continued after the bacteria were killed.'

'So when someone is in septic shock reversal of that shock is very difficult?' asked Dr McLoughlin.

'It can be very difficult.'

'In this case it proved impossible, despite all of the best treatment available to you?'

'Yes.'

Dr Naughton said Savita remained 'relatively stable' over Friday night.

'When reviewed by myself at two o'clock on Saturday [morning] her condition had not changed significantly since earlier in the evening.'

She was reviewed again at 10 a.m. 'She remained critically unwell with no change in the clinical, haematological or metabolic parameters seen the day before. In addition she continued to require intensive care supports previously commenced. Her blood lactate level continued to trend in an upward direction and I decided to commence dialysis in an attempt to correct her metabolic acidosis.' This is a condition where the body produces too much acid and/or the kidneys are not functioning sufficiently well to remove acid. It can be fatal. Dialysis began, said Dr Naughton, at 1 p.m.

'At approximately 4 p.m. on Saturday Ms Halappanavar's condition deteriorated acutely. She became highly contusive and hypoxic [bruised in appearance due to her body being deprived of oxygen]. She was cool peripherally and her cardiac output fell from 6 litres per minute to less than 2 litres per minute.' In addition her blood lactate had doubled. Dr Naughton performed a cardiogram of the patient and found signs of acute pulmonary embolism, where the pulmonary artery becomes blocked.

At 5.30 p.m., he said, he called a colleague, Dr Kevin Clarkson, consultant anaesthetist, who was at home. 'We discussed the possible sources of sepsis and general organ support measures,' Dr Clarkson told the inquest. 'She was gravely ill. [Dr Naughton] was of the view she had stabilized somewhat after her initial admission but had since deteriorated rapidly. It was apparent Ms Halappanavar was now *in extremis*. I offered to come in and help. However at this stage we were of the opinion that all therapeutic and supportive intensive care measures had been taken.'

Savita continued to deteriorate, Dr Naughton told the inquest.

'After 22.30 her electrocardiogram began to show broadening of complexes and at that stage she was requiring boluses of adrenalin to maintain her heart rate and blood pressure. At approximately quarter to one in the morning on the 28th October the patient had pulseless electrical activity cardiac arrest and despite attempts at resuscitation she passed away.'

Professor of Pathology at the National University of Ireland, Galway, Grace Callagy carried out the post-mortem on Savita. She found Savita to have been a strong and healthy thirty-one-year-old, the only abnormal findings the impact of the septic shock and the efforts that had been made to save her. She outlined how utterly the sepsis had ravaged her. She had acute injuries to both her lungs. Her kidneys bore the evidence of having failed and clots and haemorrhages in various organs resulting from Disseminated Intravascular Coagulation (DIC). DIC is where clots form in vessels throughout the body. They consume coagulation platelets and proteins, disrupting normal coagulation, leading to abnormal bleeding throughout the body. The clots also block blood flow to vital organs, causing them to fail.

The final cause of death had three factors: septic shock, E. coli (extended spectrum beta lactamase) causing bloodstream infection, and the miscarriage at 17 weeks' gestation with severe chorioamnionitis.

The E. coli ESBL was explained as an extremely rare and particularly virulent form of E. coli, resistant to almost all antibiotics. Dr Knowles told the inquest there were enzymes that some bacteria, including E. coli, produced which broke down beta–lactum antibiotics. 'Then there are extended spectrum enzymes which break down a lot of these antibiotics. So ESBL can break down the vast majority of antibiotics, making the antibiotics ineffective.'

The E. coli had almost certainly been present in Savita's bowel and had migrated into the genital tract. When Savita's waters broke, it became an ascending infection moving up into the sterile environment of the uterus and the foetal membranes, where it grew rapidly, causing acute chorioamnionitis. Savita could have been carrying the microbe for months.

Dr Peter Kelehan, recently retired consultant pathologist from the National Maternity Hospital, said he had never seen as severe a case of sepsis in a mother in his thirty-year career. He had been asked by Dr McLoughlin to review the histology slides and post-mortem findings. He did this on 17 January 2013 and again on 21 March, and discussed his findings with Professor Callagy.

Examination of the placenta found severe sepsis and the 'classic appearance of a septic abortion' in the second trimester of pregnancy. This is rarely seen by pathologists,' he said. He had seen fewer than five cases of septic abortion in his career and in all cases the mother had survived though not the foetus. He had never seen a placenta as inflamed as Savita's.

Dr Knowles was critical both of the choice of antibiotics administered to Savita, saying they were not strong enough, and the fact that signs of sepsis taking hold were not acted on.

From the moment Savita came into hospital there was a lack of care, said Dr Knowles. She too criticized the lack of follow-through on the full blood count taken on Sunday the 21st, which had revealed Savita's raised white cell count.

'There was no mention of this laboratory result in the clinical notes and the full blood count does not appear to have been repeated until the morning of the 24th. It would have been prudent to repeat the full blood count on Monday and/or to consider some microbiological investigations such as obtaining a vaginal swab and a urine sample.

'If a sample is taken it is important that the results are followed up,' she told Mr Gleeson. 'I think the result that was found was unexpected in a clinical context. The team that was looking after her should have been aware of that result sooner and if a test result is unexpected and doesn't fit with the clinical findings, they would repeat it and investigate more.'

After the membranes had ruptured early on Monday morning,

Dr Astbury had commenced Savita on a low dose of the anti-biotic erythromycin, as a prophylactic, which though ordered at 8.25 a.m. was not administered until 10 p.m.

'For Savita this was unlikely to be of any benefit with an impending pregnancy loss,' said Dr Knowles . . . 'Nonetheless many other obstetric units routinely administer oral erythromycin if there are ruptured membranes.' Dr Knowles noted also that the chapter on sepsis in the most recent CEMD *Saving Mothers' Lives* report did recommend routine antenatal prophylactic antibiotic with erythromycin, 250 mg orally, six-hourly, though she said at the National Maternity Hospital, where she works, it would not be considered adequate. She also said that one of its side effects could be to delay labour, 'which may not be beneficial [in miscarriage]'.

On the Tuesday evening, she said there shouldn't have been a delay in the arrival of a doctor to review Savita. This refers back to the disputed bleep that midwife Burke said she had made to Dr Uzockwu but which he said he had not received.

'During the evening of 23rd October Savita Halappanavar had a tachycardia of up to 114. A tachycardia was persistently above 100 on three examinations between 19.00 and 21.00 hours. Savita Halappanavar complained of weakness. All of her other vital signs including temperature, blood pressure and oxygen saturation were normal. A medical review was requested and there was a delay in the medical review.

'She complained of being cold and shivery at 4.15 a.m. on Wednesday . . . She should have had all her vital signs recorded. A septic workup is not clinically indicated if temperature is less than 38 degrees although it might be indicated if there were other findings of concern. None was recorded.'

By 6.30 a.m. on Wednesday, it was apparent Savita was clinically unwell, said Dr Knowles. 'When Savita Halappanavar was noted to be obviously clinically septic at 6.30 a.m. with high-grade pyrexia and a marked tachycardia she was examined promptly, investigated appropriately and prescribed intravenous antibiotics within 30 minutes [by Dr Uzockwu].' However, the antibiotic prescribed was co-amoxiclav. Dr Knowles said many E. coli bacteria which do not have an ESBL resistance mechanism will nonetheless be resistant to co-amoxiclav. 'I believe that antibiotics with a broad range of cover for gram negative bacteria E. coli should have been administered at that time of suspected sepsis and chorioamnionitis.'

She also took issue then with aspects of the treatment Savita got at 8.25 a.m., when the team came to review Savita.

'At that time metronidazole was added to increase antibiotic cover for anaerobes which are well-recognized infectious pathogens in chorioamnionitis subsequent to miscarriage. A urine sample was also requested as part of the septic workup, which is good practice.' Asked by Mr Gleeson whether the antibiotic cover at this point was adequate, she said it was lacking.

'For sepsis many centres in Ireland would use an additional antibiotic, for example adding gentamycin, or use an alternative broader-spectrum choice of antibiotics. I have reviewed UCH Galway's antibiotic guidelines that were in place during October 2012. There was no specific recommendation for chorioamnionitis or for sepsis secondary to a genital tract source.' She looked at the antibiotic guidelines in the three Dublin maternity hospitals. 'All three hospitals recommend different antibiotic regimens for chorioamnionitis. However gentamycin is included in all regimens as it is a broad-spectrum antibiotic for bacteria such as E. coli.'

Would she have used these antibiotics [those prescribed by Dr Astbury and Dr Uzockwu] for Savita at this point?

'I wouldn't have used those choices,' she said. 'Although I personally believe that co-amoxiclav and metronidazole do not provide sufficient antibiotic cover for chorioamnionitis in sepsis this choice is recommended in a major UK report on maternal sepsis which was published in 2011. Staff working in obstetrics in Ireland would be aware of these UK reports.'

Asked about the hospital's own flow chart on dealing with sepsis, she agreed it hadn't been followed. 'That's right. The antibiotics recommended in that protocol were administered during the early afternoon of Wednesday [once microbiology got involved].'

'But up to that time the protocol had not been adhered to?' asked the coroner.

'That's correct.'

'So the treatment she was on from seven o'clock in the morning until one o'clock wasn't effective?'

'Exactly.'

Again, vital hours had been lost.

Intravenous antibiotics were only one part of the management of chorioamnionitis, Dr Knowles continued. 'Delivery is essential to cure,' she said.

However, there was no note made in Savita's chart that this course of action may become necessary. Nor was there a plan to seek an early second opinion about a delivery, so as to avoid delay in such an event. This passive approach to Savita's treatment betrayed a lack of urgency, suggested Dr Knowles.

'There is no mention in the note written after the ward round of a plan regarding delivery. One may infer that the position was to await spontaneous events. After the ward round on the morning of the 24th October there was a delay in recognizing that Savita Halappanavar was deteriorating further. The medical staff should have been called earlier when the systolic blood pressure was dropping. It is not clear when the clinical team became aware of the blood results, especially the full blood count and lactate results. The team should have been actively managing Savita Halappanavar at that time [Wednesday morning after the ward round] including seeking an earlier second opinion regarding the need to deliver, especially when the systolic blood pressure dropped below 80 to 90 mg of mercury.'

During the hours that followed the ward round Savita's blood pressure was falling. No one was alerted until 1 p.m. 'At 10 a.m. the systolic blood pressure fell below 90 mg of mercury and at midday it was below 80 mg. Savita had had marked tachycardia consistently since 6.30 a.m. of 140 to 168 beats per minute. Hypotension in a young woman is usually a late sign of deterioration. This should have been brought to medical attention sooner,' said Dr Knowles.

'It is not clear when the team became aware of the blood results, especially the full blood count and lactate results. It is not clear from reading the notes when a high serum lactate was known. Again this was an indicator of severe sepsis.

'The full blood count received in the lab at 8.29 a.m. revealed a low white cell count. A low white cell count in sepsis is usually of more concern than a higher count. This result should have been available within a short period of time of the septic workup being performed. All of these factors should have alerted those caring for Savita that she was deteriorating and had more severe sepsis than was initially apparent.'

'Between 8.25 and 13.00 there was poor documentation in the medical records, especially recognition that her blood pressure was falling. Between [the] time of the ward round and admission to HDU most of the notes were retrospective.'

Anti-abortion campaigners were swift to seize on Dr Knowles's evidence. Youth Defence said her evidence showed that ineffective antibiotic treatment had allowed the sepsis to progress to septic shock – which indeed it had – and this was the cause of death, asserting that this disproved the argument put forward by Praveen that what Savita should have had was the abortion she requested on Monday or Tuesday.

Of course the chorioamnionitis would arguably not have developed at all and probably would not have killed Savita had the pregnancy been terminated on Monday or Tuesday.

Youth Defence also argued during the inquest that it was 'now also evident that the obstetrician treating Ms Halappanavar in Galway University Hospital was prepared to deliver Savita's baby and end the pregnancy once septicaemia had been diagnosed. This is a crucial point as it clearly shows that obstetricians in Ireland can, and do, intervene to end a pregnancy if there is a life-threatening complication.'

They do, if they are confident in good time that the mother's life is threatened. The breakdown in care clearly was a major factor in delaying Savita's access to an abortion. However, so too was the lack of legal clarity, which saw Dr Astbury apparently believing she must wait until Savita was definitely at risk of dying unless she intervened (and perhaps she was correct to believe this) and then delaying further while she sought a second opinion. The 'chilling' effect of the law in Savita's case is indisputable.

Dr Peter Boylan, who took the stand on Wednesday, 17 April, said it was 'highly likely' Savita would have lived if her requests for a termination had been acceded to. In the most controversial contribution to the inquest, the respected obstetrician went methodically through what happened to Savita at the hospital, weighing when the threat to her life emerged and when she would have been legally entitled to an abortion. He had been asked in December 2012 to write a report by the coroner. He was chosen, said Dr McLoughlin, because of the national respect for his opinion and because 'it was important not to take anyone from either the extreme right or the extreme left in terms of the morality of abortion. It had to be someone very objective.'

His report takes the reader day-by-day through what was happening with Savita, noting her state of health, with commentary. On Monday the 22nd, he says none of Savita's readings 'gave a cause for concern. There was nothing to indicate that Ms Halappanavar's life was in danger at this time.'

Of Tuesday the 23rd he comments: 'At this time Ms

Halappanavar was stable and her life was not at risk. Termination of pregnancy was therefore not a practical, legal proposition on the 23rd.'

Dr Boylan was critical of many aspects of Savita's care, particularly singling out six: the failure to note her elevated white cell count on admission and subsequent failure to repeat the test for three days; the confused lack of communication between the ward and the senior health officer on Tuesday evening about Savita's elevated pulse; the failure by midwife Dunleavy to take Savita's vital signs at 4.15 a.m. on Wednesday when she was having a rigor; the fact that the antibiotics prescribed for Savita at 6.30 a.m. were not the ones recommended in the hospital's own guidelines on sepsis; confusion over the lactate measurement on Wednesday morning, and the 'serious deficit' in note-keeping through Wednesday morning and early afternoon.

Had moves been made to begin termination after the morning ward round on the 24th, he said, it was likely Savita would have been transferred to the delivery ward for an oxytocin infusion in an attempt to achieve vaginal delivery. From experience he knew, however, there could be further delay there if midwives in the unit had a conscientious objection to termination, even in an emergency. Transfer and termination, he said, would be 'dependent on the midwives in the delivery unit accepting care of Ms Halappanavar when it was known that the foetal heartbeat was present'.

He was critical of individuals, without naming names.

'The lack of a statement from the nurse caring for Ms Halappanavar on the morning of 24th October gives rise to serious deficit in reaching an understanding of the sequence of events on that morning.'

Later he notes that until blood test results on Wednesday the 24th, ordered at 6.30 a.m., were accessed at about 11.30 a.m. 'the doctors were effectively in the dark as to the condition of Ms Halappanavar.

'However I find it difficult to understand how the white cell count of 1.7 did not stimulate a reaction [by Dr Astbury] to review Ms Halappanavar in person. Had she been reviewed however I think it is highly unlikely that any intervention at that time would have made a difference to the eventual outcome, although the initiation of appropriate therapy might well have commenced an hour or two earlier than it did.'

His commentary concludes: 'Had Ms Halappanavar's pregnancy been terminated on Monday 22nd October or Tuesday 23rd October it is highly likely, on the balance of probabilities, that she would not have died. Termination of pregnancy at that time was not a practical proposition because of the law.

'There are a number of deficiencies in her care which I have outlined above, none of which on their own is likely to have resulted in Ms Halappanavar's death. Cumulatively however they resulted in a delay in appropriate treatment of several hours and it is well known that each hour delay in appropriate treatment increases the mortality rate by six per cent. Nevertheless I think there is a strong argument that even if appropriate intervention had commenced in the early hours of October 24th that the outcome would not have been any different.

'The real problem,' he said, 'was the inability to terminate the pregnancy prior to Ms Halappanavar developing a real and substantial risk of death. By that time it was, effectively, too late to save her life.'

The reaction in court was immediate as people took in what Dr Boylan had said. Journalists left the room at once to call their news desks as others typed furiously on laptops to file the line to their organizations' websites and newsrooms.

Within hours the Life Institute had a new page on its site, titled, 'Who Is Peter Boylan?' 'The inquest into Savita Halappanavar's death has heard that she died from the worst case of E. coli infection that experts have ever seen – and that doctors missed signs of the infection. Yet Dr Peter Boylan has tried to blame Ireland's ban on abortion for Savita's tragic death.'

It goes on to attack his professional integrity, making such claims as that he had previously publicly stated that he wanted 'abortion legalized in Ireland'; that he was contradicting himself; that other doctors disagreed with him and that 'he is not representing a body of doctors in making this claim'.

In his report Dr Boylan in fact devoted more attention to the deficits in Savita's care which led to her sepsis being missed than he did to a discussion of abortion law, though in his concluding remarks he came squarely down on the law as the most important factor. His remarks on the abortion law inevitably attracted more attention and it would be naïve to have expected otherwise. The evidence presented does seem to indicate that if Savita's life were to be saved, a termination should have been carried out on Tuesday evening at the latest. Whether such a course would have been legal is unclear. If it were legal, it would have only just been, and legality could have been disputed.

The ongoing, raging debate about Ireland's abortion laws swirling around this inquest was of little concern to Praveen, who had spent most of the eight days sitting alone at the back of whichever chamber the inquest was being held in. Friends had asked to come and keep him company but he had turned down their offers. Through some of the testimony, particularly that from intensive care nurses who had described Savita's last hours, he bowed his head, rubbing his forehead gently, his eyes closed. During breaks he would go for walks; at other times he would sit in quiet meditation.

On the final morning, Friday, 19 April, his senior counsel, Eugene Gleeson, rose to his feet to make an unexpected submission, in the absence of the jury, before Dr McLoughlin began his summing up. While the primary function of the inquest was to find out how Savita had died and although Dr McLoughlin had interpreted this function with 'admirable clarity, patience, compassion and fairness throughout', Praveen's situation remained. Gleeson continued:

'When this inquest ends Praveen obviously will have to go home and he will be going home, not to a place full of the beautiful and unique atmosphere created by a young man and woman in love. He will be going home to a very cold and lonely place . . . Praveen's large and deeply intelligent eyes have seen enormous sadness, unbearable sadness, particularly in the week commencing the 21st October last and then that awful and solitary journey home with his wife's body to southern India for her funeral ceremony.

'It was only during this inquest, because of the exhaustive and comprehensive analysis of the facts that you, Coroner, have made, that Savita's position during that fateful week has become much clearer than before. We now know Savita had no input into her own care while at University College Hospital. That was not unique in Irish law. There are two other categories of Irish patients who do not have any input into their care. The first category is minors . . . and the other cohort is the mentally ill.'

During the time Savita and Praveen were together Praveen was devoted to her, he said.

'Praveen is most anxious and determined that some person or persons are held accountable for what happened to Savita. He does appreciate that this is an inquest and that certain constraints are imposed by law, but he is most determined that someone or people are held accountable for the events that happened on the Monday, Tuesday and to the point on Wednesday 24th October when the ICU facilities took over her care.

'So,' Gleeson urged Dr McLoughlin, 'if you or the jury are considering making any recommendations after the verdict is reached, Praveen would urge you, Coroner, that it be done as strongly and as clearly as the English language will allow and as close to accountability as Irish law permits.'

Declan Buckley, SC for the hospital, countered at length that it would be 'entirely imbalanced and unjustified' to lay blame or censure staff for what had happened, while Eileen Barrington, SC, for Dr Astbury, said there was no basis in law or in the facts presented at the inquest for Mr Gleeson's application for the jury to make recommendations 'touching on accountability'.

Dr McLoughlin said he was prohibited from seeking accountability that implied civil liability. In his summing up, however, he pushed the boundaries probably as far as a coroner could in a thinly veiled attack on two decades of legislative torpor.

'The coroner's court is a creature of Statute. It is not for the Court to advise the Oireachtas on the law or amendments to the law. The Oireachtas may take cognizance of these proceedings.

'The Medical Council is a statutory body whose function is to regulate the medical profession, maintain a register of doctors, give ethical guidelines, initiate disciplinary enquiries and impose sanction in breach of the code.

'The guidelines on abortion are very brief,' he continued. 'Yet a practitioner found in breach of the guidelines may be subject to a criminal sanction and have the most severe sanction imposed on him or her – erasure from the Medical Register for infamous misconduct – a path of ignominy and shame. Doctors who practise medicine with the utmost good faith and to the highest professional standards and in the service of patients should not have to labour under the threat of these sanctions.' Given that the Medical Council must stay within the law when framing its guidelines, Dr McLoughlin had come as close to pleading for legislative clarity on abortion as a coroner could.

He then made nine recommendations to the jury:

1. that the Irish Medical Council lay out exactly when a doctor could and should intervene to save the life of a mother in similar circumstances; that An Bord Altranais, which regulates nurses, should do likewise;

2. that blood samples are always properly followed up and proper procedures be put in place to ensure that errors don't occur – to be applied nationally;

3. that protocols on the management of sepsis are followed and that proper training and guidelines for all medical and nursing personnel be put in place – to be applied nationally;

4. that proper and effective communication occur between staff on call and the oncoming team, and that there be a dedicated handover time – to be applied nationally;

5. that a protocol for sepsis be written by the microbiology department in each hospital, for each directorate in the hospital – to be applied nationally;

6. that a Modified Early Warning score chart be adopted by every hospital in the State;

7. that there be early and effective communication with patients and relatives to ensure the treatment plan is readily understood – to be applied nationally;

8. that medical notes and nursing notes be separate documents and kept separately – to be applied nationally;

9. that no post-mortem additions are made to the medical notes of deceased persons whose death is the subject of a coroner's inquiry, as these may inhibit the inquiry – to be applied nationally.

The jury deliberated for about three hours, breaking for lunch, before returning a verdict.

'We the jury have arrived at a unanimous verdict of medical misadventure. With regard to the coroner's recommendations numbers one to nine we strongly endorse each of them after much consideration,' said the foreman.

Dr McLoughlin then delivered his closing statement, saying the jury had identified the deceased as Savita Halappanavar who had died at University Hospital Galway on 28 October 2012. The cause of death was fulminate septic shock from E. coli bacteraemia, ascending genital tract sepsis, a miscarriage at 17 weeks' gestation and no comorbidities. Having reiterated the nine recommendations, he turned to Praveen.

'I want to offer you my sincerest and deepest condolences on the death of Savita. You showed tremendous loyalty and love to her during her last moments. All of Ireland has followed your story and on their behalf I offer you our deepest sympathics. You will always be watched over and protected by the shadow of your beloved Savita. You are in our thoughts during this painful and difficult time.'

Several minutes later, Tony Canavan, chief operating officer of the Galway Roscommon Hospital Group, was the first to make a statement to journalists and photographers waiting outside the county hall. He said that Savita's death had caused 'deep upset among hospital staff'.

'Sadly there were lapses in the standards of care but I am sure people appreciate we always try to do the best for our patients. We will take on board the coroner's recommendations to ensure deficiencies will be rectified by the hospital. We owe this to all of our patients and to our staff, to ensure they are in an environment that operates to the highest standards.' He said the hospital had already introduced a range of improvements, including: the implementation of early warning scoring systems; the education of all staff in the recognition and management of sepsis; the introduction of a new multidisciplinary training programme in the management of obstetric emergencies, including sepsis; and that it would be introducing a system for doctors' handovers.

He then read the statement in Irish and didn't take any questions from the press.

Praveen emerged with his solicitor, Gerry O'Donnell, and

several friends who had come to support him on the last day. O'Donnell said Praveen had been vindicated, his account of what had happened proven to be correct. Praveen had, since the death of Savita, been in pursuit of the truth, he said, and would continue to be. Choosing his language carefully he said we now knew there was a significant number of failures and shortcomings in the care of Savita; we knew about the poor communication that took place between staff; we knew there were very poor records and in some instances no records at all were kept; we knew tests were not followed up and some weren't conducted at all; we knew documents were not read; we knew files and charts were not looked at, all of which were, in his opinion, hugely significant factors in the poor treatment Savita received. We knew too there had been inappropriate antibiotic treatment.

'All of these individually did not contribute to her death. But, in our opinion all of them taken together had a significant impact. They delayed her treatment, and delayed treatment ultimately resulted in her death . . . Time was of the essence. Savita Halappanavar, in my opinion, was deprived of medical treatment when it was urgent. Savita Halappanavar had requested on . . . Monday and Tuesday that she should be granted a termination, [a request] that was not documented but [an act that]would have been life-saving. She was not granted this request and as a result, sadly, she is not here today. It is an extremely worrying situation for women in Ireland that [they] go to a hospital suffering from a miscarriage and [are] told that they must wait until they are gravely ill or until the baby is delivered before there is medical intervention, should they be suffering from sepsis. I would . . . be of the opinion that the legislature should look at this, that Government should look at this and ensure that if legislation is required to ensure that something like this should never happen again . . . it be done with extreme urgency.

'In my opinion, Savita Halappanavar has been denied her constitutional right to life.'

Praveen then gave his reaction. 'Savita was not benefited in any way going to the hospital until the 24th afternoon. The care she received was in no way different to staying home. Medicine is all about preventing the natural history of the disease and look what they did. She was just left there to die. We were always kept in the dark. If Savita had known her life was at risk she would have jumped off the bed to go straight to a different hospital. We were never told, and it's horrendous, it's barbaric and inhuman the way Savita was treated in that hospital.'

He said there were still questions. 'I haven't got my answers yet, why Savita died.' He said he owed it to Savita, and to her parents, 'to know the truth'. Someone had to 'take ownership of the patient when they walk in to the hospital'.

He told me later he hoped no woman in Ireland would ever have to go through what Savita had. 'You lose your rights basically when you are pregnant here, I think. You lose your rights to get necessary healthcare. Savita and me, we knew that abortion was illegal in Ireland but not termination when it's a planned pregnancy, when you can't save the baby and the mother may die if you don't do something like terminate. That was a big shock for us.'

It was a 'small bit of comfort that the truth' had emerged at the inquest, he said. Within hours, however, the anti-abortion lobby were denying his truth.

Dr Berry Kiely of the Pro-Life Campaign, while claiming to acknowledge 'how difficult and upsetting the experience of the inquest must have been for Savita's husband', went on to rebuff him, saying 'it is now clear from the facts presented at the inquest that a number of . . . systems failures and communication short-comings . . . delayed the moment at which the medical team recognized the seriousness of her condition'. She said she hoped the inquest had 'brought clarity to the events which led to the tragic death of his [Praveen's] wife'.

The nine recommendations were seized on as 'proof' that the

case had nothing to do with abortion. Dr Patricia Casey of the Iona Institute said that if they were all implemented it would ensure 'this situation of multiple systems failures doesn't happen again'. Indeed, but it might not ensure that a case such as Savita's wouldn't. She said she had 'no difficulty' with the call on the Medical Council to clarify when intervention should take place.

'It is the Medical Council that should be doing this and not the law,' she said ignoring the fact that the Medical Council is bound by the law. For its part, the Medical Council said it would study the inquest's findings and review its guidelines in light of any legislative change on abortion.

The Life Institute too stepped in to reject Praveen's views. Displaying perhaps a lack of knowledge about the limitations of the inquest system, the organization's website reported: 'Savita inquest: E. coli cause of death; change in law not put to jury.'

Praveen has probably never heard of the Life Institute. He told me he hoped something good would come out of the inquest and in particular said he hoped it would bring legislation to clarify when Irish women were entitled to abortion. 'Fingers crossed. I am optimistic about it. I hope something good comes of it. I do hope it for Irish women and I owe it to Savita. I know her parents want that too.'

Anti-abortion campaigners who spoke to me articulated their frustration that the 'Boylan narrative' had dominated. Breda O'Brien diplomatically described as 'a pity' the fact that there was not more focus on the sepsis in the post-inquest discourse.

'To me there are two narratives running in parallel from the inquest. One is the Peter Boylan line, that the doctor couldn't have done anything, it's the law. And the other is the Susan Knowles line, the microbiologist who looked at the sepsis, the inappropriate response. And the Peter Boylan line is the one that has become dominant . . . I do think that's a pity. The whole question of sepsis is massive. I would have loved to have seen, when the story of Savita's death broke, an emergency Cabinet meeting to deal with that, and an expert report and Oireachtas Health Committee hearings on sepsis. I think the coroner's court worked very well, and it can make recommendations that are to save people's lives. But the real life-saving stuff to come out of Savita's death is being lost.'

A co-ordinated attack on Dr Boylan came in the form of a letter, published on the *Irish Times* 'Letters to the Editor' page, on 1 May. It was signed by eight consultant obstetricians, a consultant microbiologist, a consultant anaesthetist and a consultant in emergency medicine, all of whom have either spoken at anti-abortion events or are known to have anti-abortion views. In the letter they 'suggest' that Dr Boylan's expert opinion had been 'a personal view, not an expert one'.

They wrote: 'The facts as produced at the inquest show this tragic case to be primarily about the management of sepsis, and Dr Boylan's opinion on the effect of Irish law did not appear to be shared by the coroner, or the jury, of the inquest.'

'Obstetric sepsis is unfortunately on the increase and is now the leading cause of maternal death reported in the UK Confidential Enquiry into Maternal Deaths. Additionally there are many well-documented fatalities from sepsis in women following termination of pregnancy. To concentrate on the legal position regarding abortion in the light of such a case as that in Galway does not assist our services to pregnant women.'

The letter goes on to highlight the need for a 'back-to-basics' approach in clinical care and the growing problem of antibiotic-resistant organisms, then sets out the argument about Ireland having a very good record on maternal deaths. 'It is important that all obstetrical units in Ireland reflect on the findings of the events in Galway and learn how to improve care for pregnant women. To reduce it to a polemical argument about abortion may lead to more – not fewer – deaths in the future,' they conclude.

Not one of the signatories was at the close of the inquest to hear Dr McLoughlin's summing up.

Interestingly, though published in the *Irish Times* on 1 May, it had appeared on a number of anti-abortion sites the night before and was being retweeted through the night of 30 April.

'So it wasn't just a letter,' Dr Boylan told me. 'The letter was released as a press release on various social media the night before it was published. It was a co-ordinated, planned attack on my professional integrity by so-called pro-life groups.' The letters editor at the *Irish Times* knew nothing of such press releases.

Several weeks after the inquest, Dr Boylan spoke again about Savita's request for a termination on Monday and Tuesday, describing it as 'a very reasonable request' and one which would have been listened to, discussed and acceded to, if that was what she wanted, in any other Western country – 'except perhaps Malta'. But he then spoke at greater length about the lapses in Savita's care that resulted in her sepsis being missed for too long. 'There were deficiencies in her care. There is no doubt about that,' he said.

'Had Savita been in Holles Street there is no doubt a termination would have been carried out on Wednesday morning [rather than afternoon], but she still might well have died. She would have been on stronger antibiotics in Holles Street, but she was so sick and the organism so aggressive that, realistically, even then once you've decided to do a termination, got a second opinion, then gone to the labour ward and discussed it with the nurses, she was so ill and deteriorating so quickly, she might well still have died.'

Boylan also explained the reference in his deposition to the delay that might have taken place had Savita been transferred to the delivery unit on Wednesday morning, as this would be 'dependent on the midwives . . . accepting care of Ms Halappanavar when it was known the foetal heartbeat was still present'. These are the factors that can further delay things, he said, even in an emergency. From his own experience, he recounted an incident that took place in another Dublin maternity hospital in the previous twelve months.

'I know . . . in another hospital a senior colleague, in similar circumstances who was told by the senior midwife on the labour ward, "You're not doing a termination in this hospital." He had to pull rank and say, "Then I'm getting agency nurses in," and it was only when a non-national nurse came forward [that the termination could proceed]. That was in Dublin in the last year or so. It was a Savita-type case where a woman needed an emergency intervention. That is why I said in my report "if the nurses in the labour ward were agreeable".'

Dr Boylan said he himself had never encountered such a fast-acting threat to a mother's life himself. Nor has he ever had to refuse a termination request.

'But I've certainly had circumstances where the woman had had to get quite sick before we've intervened. That's the reality. Yes, I've seen a woman have to seriously deteriorate before intervening. That is the law.'

Whether the Government's proposed legislation on abortion would change that remained to be seen.

11

Savita's inquest concluded on Friday, 19 April, on what would have been her and Praveen's fifth wedding anniversary.

A year earlier to the day, legislation that might have saved her life had been defeated in the Dáil. United Left Alliance TD Clare Daly had introduced the Medical Treatment (Termination of Pregnancy in Case of Risk to Life of Pregnant Woman) Bill on 18 April 2012. It was defeated the following day by 109 votes to 20.

Introducing it, Daly said that although a great deal had changed in Irish society since the 1992 X ruling, the law had stayed the same. Her Bill would simply legislate for X 'to allow safe abortion in Ireland where the life of the woman is at risk'. She acknowledged it did not go far enough to reach out to women who were pregnant as a result of rape or incest or whose unborn foetuses had fatal abnormalities. But this was as much as could be legislated for within the constitutional limits.

Responses to the Daly Bill illuminated some of the attitudes and antagonisms which were to be played out in parliament and across the country over the year ahead, as Savita's death gave a new dimension to the abortion debate.

Within Fine Gael there were indications of the struggles some individuals would have on the issue. Michelle Mulherin, from the Taoiseach's constituency of Mayo, said she was against abortion 'in any form' but reflected that this didn't necessarily mean it should be outlawed.

Some Labour Party members said Daly's Bill was too weak. Anne Ferris, while 'somewhat supportive of it', said: 'I do not feel that this legislation goes far enough ... For example in legislating for the X case, which is what the Bill before us will do, the risk to the life of the mother will be covered but not the risk to the health.' She agreed with Daly's point that the Bill was not enough, but rather than view it as a first step argued that this was a reason to vote against it. In the same vein, party colleagues Ciara Conway and Ann Phelan were of the same view.

Their contributions are worth highlighting, given the restrictive, even punitive, terms of the legislation they were to support the following year.

Labour Party TD Aodhán Ó Ríordáin defended the position taken by his party in voting against Daly's Bill. A process was under way, he told me in June 2013, and parliamentary politics was about moving with the process. A year later the political context had changed completely, and Ó Ríordáin pointed to Savita's death as the defining difference.

The anti-abortion lobby and the Church, however, were operating at full and co-ordinated throttle. By April 2013 they had conceded that legislation was coming and they honed their attention specifically to fight the inclusion of suicide as a ground for abortion: this would be abused by women and doctors, they said, and would open the door eventually to 'abortion on demand'.

The political reality however was that the Government had no choice but to include the suicide clause. It was already the law of the land – even if not set down in legislation. It had been the position since the 1992 Supreme Court ruling in X that when suicide posed a real threat to a pregnant girl's or woman's life and an abortion was deemed necessary to avert that threat, she had the right to an abortion.

Article 34.4.6 of the Constitution states: 'The decision of the Supreme Court shall in all cases be final and definitive.' As former Supreme Court judge Catherine McGuinness had said at the January hearings of the Oireachtas Health Committee: 'The Supreme Court reached its decision in the X case; that is an authoritative interpretation of the wording of the 1983 amendment . . . The X case judgment stands and it is the law of this country.'

The Government failed throughout the debate from January to July 2013 to nail the lie that suicide could be omitted from the legislation. This allowed those against the inclusion of suicide to assert, over and over again, that it could be left out. It enabled them to chip away at public sympathy for the rare woman who might need this provision, by asserting that abortion was not a 'cure' or a 'treatment' for suicide and that no psychiatrist could predict which woman with suicidal thoughts would actually kill herself.

The atmosphere in the weeks leading up to the publication of the heads of the Government's Bill to legislate for X was fractious. On 28 April, two days before publication, two of the biggest-selling Sunday papers led with abortion stories. The *Sunday Independent* published transcripts of secretly taped conversations in which Labour Party TDs Ó Ríordáin and Ferris appeared to express support for liberalization of abortion law beyond the X case. Ó Ríordáin was quoted saying of X case legislation: 'It's a starting point. Once you get that . . . then you can move . . . and of course if I'm on the radio and somebody says to me, "It's a starting point for abortion on demand" I'm going to say, "No of course it isn't. It is what it is."'

Ferris was secretly recorded saying: 'We will legislate certainly for what Europe has told us and then we can go further than that . . . we get the first bit done and then we can go on to the next bit.'

The *Sunday Times* meanwhile led with the headline: 'TDs plot abortion poll revolt'. Its political correspondent Sarah McInerney reported that at least seven rebel Fine Gael TDs were planning to gather a critical mass of up to twenty parliamentary party colleagues to vote against any abortion legislation that included a clause to allow abortion on the grounds of suicide risk.

Reacting to the *Sunday Independent* sting, Minister of State for European Affairs Lucinda Creighton, the most senior Fine Gael opponent of legislation that included a suicide clause, said the tapes were worrying. 'It is a matter of concern, if that is the intent of the Labour Party,' she said. Her party colleague Brian Walsh said it was clear that the X case legislation was 'seen as a stepping stone to abortion on demand' by some in the Labour Party.

Minister Creighton's unhappiness with a law which she saw as softening the line against abortion was to be a recurring source of anxiety for Enda Kenny. He and senior party officials would spend many of the coming weeks engaged in what became known as their 'charm offensive', in an effort to win over wavering TDs and minimize the potential damage, caused by the legislation and anger about it, to his own leadership and even to Government stability.

Speaking in Granada, Spain, on 28 April, where he had been having talks with Spanish Prime Minister Mariano Rajoy, he appealed for calm: 'I think that people should wait until they have the explanatory memorandum and the heads of the Bill before they decide to comment on what's actually in it,' Mr Kenny said.

On Tuesday 30 April, for the first time in the history of the State, draft abortion legislation was published by an Irish Government. This was a crucial moment in the history of the abortion debate in Ireland. A 'moral Rubicon' had been crossed, said David Quinn of the Iona Institute. The working title, 'Protection of Maternal Life Bill' had been changed to 'Protection of Life

During Pregnancy Bill', a significant alteration in the eyes of the many who saw it as an opening appeasement of the anti-abortion lobby.

Described as a 'compromise Bill . . . to give effect to the X case', its 33 pages contained proposals to continue to criminalize anyone who gave 'effect' to an unlawful abortion – whether the pregnant woman or someone else – and to punish them with fourteen years in prison and an unlimited fine. A number of possible defences were then provided: an abortion could be lawful if the pregnant woman's life was at risk in an emergency situation, from an ongoing condition or illness, or from suicide.

The legislation would not allow for abortion in cases of rape, incest or fatal foetal abnormality. Despite popular support for inclusion of these conditions, they fell outside the confines of X. Abortions would have to be carried out in one of nineteen approved public or voluntary maternity hospitals. It would be a matter for the patient to decide if she wished to proceed with a termination following a decision that the procedure was necessary to save her life and therefore came within the ambit of the Act.

The draft Bill said that while individual practitioners could opt out of performing an abortion for reasons of conscience, they must pass the patient on to a colleague who would perform the procedure. If a woman or girl was said to be suicidal, she would have to be assessed by three doctors – two psychiatrists and an obstetrician – who would have to agree unanimously that this was the case. Provision for appeal was made if a woman was refused a termination. This would involve a review by a further three doctors, who must also agree unanimously. According to a 'high-level source' who briefed the *Irish Times*, the language of the test suggested that an abortion would only be allowed *in extremis*.

The hurdles and hoops over and through which a suicidal woman would have to pass will have been intended to reassure those who were concerned about the inclusion of suicide in the

Bill at all. But the main effect of the restrictions would be that any woman or child whose life was threatened and who had the resources would go to England for a termination rather than face a State-sponsored inquisition at home. In practice, the law on suicide and abortion would apply only to women and girls in the care of the State – i.e. minors, those with impaired capacity and possibly asylum seekers.

Despite the restrictions it still represented a hugely significant moment and anti-abortion protestors upped the ante.

On 19 May, the Catholic primate elect, Archbishop Eamon Martin, in the *Sunday Times* said no priest should administer Communion to any politician who supported the Bill, saying that, in effect, they would have 'excommunicated' themselves. The head of the Catholic Church, the Primate of all Ireland, Cardinal Seán Brady, said TDs had a 'solemn duty' to oppose this proposed legislation. The Catholic Bishops as a body released a statement saying the Irish healthcare system must ensure the 'complete respect for the sacredness of the life both of the mother and baby' and that this Bill would make the 'direct and intentional killing of unborn children' lawful in Ireland for the first time.

There appeared to be no effort by the Government or the Department of Health to counter the image of babies being 'targeted' *in utero* with blades and poisons.

Anti-abortion organizations had sections on their websites and leaflets handed out at rallies 'explaining' what would happen to unborn babies if the legislation was passed. One leaflet which was carried by thousands of marchers on 6 July at the seventh and final anti-abortion rally in Dublin before the legislation was passed, said abortion could involve injecting a saline solution into the uterus: 'The unborn baby **dies painfully over a period of time from salt poisoning, dehydration, brain haemorrhage and convulsions.**' (Bold text in the original.) It could also be carried out by dilation and curettage in which a 'sharp looped knife scrapes the wall of the uterus. Then **the baby is cut up** before body parts are removed from the womb.' Or according to the leaflet, which does not give the name of the publisher, dilation and evacuation is used in which '**The baby is dismembered, limb by limb**. The surgeon waits for the baby to bleed to death before proceeding. In some cases he crushes its head to allow it pass through the cervix.'

Several people I spoke to at the Rally for Life on 6 July believed there would be saline abortions and babies being dismembered in the womb once the legislation went through.

These images were gruesome and simply untrue.

Abortion methods are not set out in the Act. Abortion is referred to as 'the medical procedure' and this 'includes the prescribing, by a medical practitioner, of any drug or medical treatment'.

On 19 July, in a statement, the Irish Institute of Obstetricians and Gynaecologists responded to some of the graphic descriptions being circulated about second-trimester abortions, 'to allay the fears of the public'.

'The destructive methods described for second trimester termination of pregnancy are currently not carried out in this jurisdiction, nor will they be in the future. The procedure currently practised in the Republic of Ireland is induction of labour using medication called prostaglandins. This will not change as a result of the enactment of this legislation. If a viable foetus is delivered, all efforts are made to preserve its life where possible,' it said.

In Savita's case the mode of termination planned was delivery of the foetus.

In the weeks leading to the legislation the Pro-Life Campaign distributed thousands of pro forma postcards for posting to Fine Gael TDs and Senators urging them to resist it. Alan Farrell, Fine Gael TD, told the *Irish Times* in May he had received hundreds. 'My staff has been hoarding them. We have an entire drawer full at this stage,' he told political correspondent Harry McGee.

John Smyth of the PLC told McGee: 'Since the Expert Group report last December, [the campaign] has intensified quite a bit. The postcard campaign has been much bigger. It's a very visible aspect of the campaign. We have also been getting our supporters to meet politicians at constituency level.' In his piece, McGee wrote: 'At least a dozen TDs have had regular protests outside their clinics. For some, a small minority of the contacts and messages received have been offensive and even sinister. One was called a Nazi, another a murderer. And one TD felt she had no choice but to refer two pieces of correspondence to the Gardai.'

Some of the pressure, on Fine Gael TDs in particular, came close to outright intimidation. Regina Doherty, TD, speaking on the *Tonight* programme on TV3 on 14 May, described the 'lobbying' she was being subjected to by anti-abortion activists: 'The level of abuse and physical threats that I personally am getting at the moment is off the wall. I have a number of people who at the moment are going to burn my house down with my children in it. They are going to spit at me when I walk inside the church grounds Sunday morning at Mass. I have received an email where I was going to have my throat cut from my neck to my navel and my entrails were going to spill out. There are some very strange people in this country who call themselves Christians.'

Doherty is among conservative members of the party who would describe herself as instinctively anti-abortion. But, she told host Vincent Browne, she had come to change the nuance of her views following the death of Savita: 'A year ago I would have told you I would no way in any circumstances have been able to support this legislation,' she said. 'I have changed my mind. I have gone through a journey of doing probably ten different scenarios of "what if" and I have come out in the end having had my concerns genuinely addressed and I would hope we as a party will be able to do that for some of the people who still have concerns . . . What we are doing is legislating to protect women's lives, and I make no apology for that. None whatsoever.'

Asked whether she would have any concern about being threatened with excommunication she said: 'They don't and won't get rid of me that easily, no. No, my faith is a hell of a lot larger than the Catholic Church as a physical body. So no, I'm not threatened.'

But the publication of the proposed measure hardened the attitudes of other Fine Gael TDs. Brian Walsh was the first to state publicly that he would not vote for any legislation that included the suicide grounds. This he did on 29 April, the day before the draft Bill's publication.

The approach in the Bill was a far cry from the compassionate view of the four Supreme Court judges in 1992 – which, according to legal sources, had since provided the template for in camera hearings of similar cases. The legislation was minimal but vital, said the Taoiseach. Legally, it would merely codify a reality already in place.

'The law on abortion in Ireland is not being changed. Our country will continue to be one of the safest places in the world for childbirth and the regulation and the clarity that will now become evident through the Protection of Life During Pregnancy Bill will continue in law to assert the restrictions on abortion that have applied in Ireland and that will apply for the future,' he said.

Minister for Health James Reilly said he believed women's lives would have been saved if the X case had been legislated over twenty years earlier, in the way now proposed.

The draft Bill would now be given over to the Oireachtas Health Committee for further hearings and debate, from Friday 17 May. The committee would sit for three long days, from 9.30 a.m. until 7.45 p.m., and, significantly, this time it would not hear from any lobby or campaigning group. The hearings would be confined to experts in medicine and law. The committee would, however, hear from numerous individuals whose views were well known.

As the hearings opened, an opinion poll in the *Sunday Independent*, on 19 May, found that 78 per cent were in favour of allowing abortion where there was a medical risk to a woman's life other than suicide; 71 per cent in favour when pregnancy was the result of rape, and a slim majority of 53 per cent in favour where the risk to the woman's life was from suicide: that is, higher support for abortion on the more liberal grounds which are common in other jurisdictions, than on the suicide ground at the centre of controversy in Ireland.

The suicide issue would dominate the Oireachtas hearings. On Day 1, the committee heard from a range of experts, including obstetricians. As Dr Rhona Mahony, Master of the National Maternity Hospital, summed up the debate, 'one could be forgiven for thinking that this Bill is about the risk of suicide in pregnancy.'

Yet the Bill was not just about the risk of suicide: 'It is about saving a woman's life regardless of whether that risk to life is physical or mental. Suicide is death just the same as death from infection [caused by] chorioamnionitis . . . A woman who is intent on suicide is indeed at risk of dying. She needs to be assessed appropriately, she needs to be believed and she needs expert psychiatric care.'

Dr Sam Coulter-Smith, Master of the Rotunda Maternity Hospital, questioned the need for inclusion of suicide. He said that he was bringing to the committee the concerns of his Rotunda colleagues.

'It creates an ethical dilemma for any obstetrician who has [been] requested to perform a termination of pregnancy for the treatment of someone with either suicidal ideation or intent.'

Dr Coulter-Smith appeared to clash with his obstetric

colleagues who gave evidence the same day: Dr Mahony and Dr Peter Boylan, clinical director of the NMH. 'The clear divergence of opinion between the Masters' was widely reported. Dr Coulter-Smith, in an interview for this book, said he became 'something of a pin-up boy for the pro-lifers'.

However, the three Masters were broadly *ad idem*. All three said that suicide in pregnancy was extremely rare. All three said there was no evidence that abortion was a treatment for suicide (and Dr Mahony said it couldn't be and psychiatric experts would say it shouldn't be). All three said they would trust their psychiatric colleagues' expertise. And all three said if they were sent a woman or girl, and her psychiatrist had said she needed a termination to prevent her killing herself, they would perform the termination.

Dr Mahony concurred with her two colleagues about the lack of evidence that abortion was a treatment for suicide risk, and suggested there never could be such evidence. 'If one was to truly examine the issue of suicide, one would have to take a group of women who planned to kill themselves and randomize them to termination of pregnancy to prevent them from killing themselves or to not being allowed to have termination of pregnancy. I suggest that study should never be done. What we do instead is we defer to our psychiatric colleagues.'

Dr Boylan said: 'If a woman is referred to me by a psychiatrist whose opinion I respect – an opinion which is not driven by ideology but by care for the woman – and if that psychiatrist believes the only way she will be prevented from killing herself – it is her life I am talking about – is by terminating that pregnancy and if I trust the psychiatrist's opinion, I will terminate the pregnancy,' he said. 'We cannot allow her to get to a situation where she may kill herself. If she kills herself or she dies, the baby dies too.'

Dr Coulter-Smith said: 'This is really more a question for psychiatrists. If the psychiatrists tell us the only way the woman's life can be saved is through a termination of pregnancy, it will require a number of psychiatrists to agree with that view. If that is the case, following a multidisciplinary meeting about the case, that is what we will do.'

This part of Dr Coulter-Smith's testimony was not included on the websites operated by anti-abortion groups such as the Life Institute, which ran its report from the hearing three days later, under the headline: 'Top doctor opposes suicide clause in abortion legislation at hearings.'

Dr Coulter-Smith has since said he would have preferred that direct reference to suicide had not been included in the legislation, but that instead 'it be left broad, that the reference had been to a threat to life and suicide could come within that'.

The following day of hearings, Monday, 20 May, psychiatrists and perinatal psychiatrists addressed the committee and again suicide was centre-stage. Dr Anthony McCarthy, consultant perinatal psychiatrist at the National Maternity Hospital, echoed some of the points made by his colleague at the NMH, Dr Mahony. Other psychiatrists emphasized different points. Anti-abortion TDs and Senators lined up to ask pointed questions. Senator Fidelma Healy Eames (Fine Gael) suggested that women would feign suicide to get access to an abortion. 'If the Government passed a law tomorrow morning providing a mechanism whereby a person could get a 50-per cent reduction in his or her mortgage once there was a stated, certified risk that he or she was suicidal, a lot of people would surely avail of that. We are talking about changing behavioural norms here. We have seen this happen in other jurisdictions [and it] has led to the opening of the floodgates.'

Asked about this question some months later, Dr McCarthy said: 'I don't know what her experience of people fooling her has been but I know I am very familiar with assessing people who are suicidal. Of course people can pretend. Of course there are rare people who can act "suicidal". We see people in A&E here, who have used all their methadone and come in saying they will kill themselves if they don't get more. But as experts, we have a fairly high index of suspicion. We are trained to do this.'

Suicide is very rare in pregnancy, at about one in 250,000. Dr McCarthy told me, however, he frequently saw pregnant women with suicidal thoughts, obsessions, compulsions or fears. He said that he would expect to see a woman at such a level of distress about once every two or three weeks.

'Most want help with their depression, relief from these thoughts that are haunting them. Many are fearful that they might kill themselves, or some believe they should do so because they feel they must be bad because they have suicidal thoughts. And sometimes I see them after a serious overdose or other attempts at self-harm and yet they may still want the baby. Others are haunted by obsessive images of stabbing themselves or hanging themselves, and have even gone as close as putting a noose around their neck. But they don't want to die; it is just that they cannot get the images or impulsive feelings out of their heads.'

Of the suicidal women living in Ireland who come to a psychiatrist and are supported, some will choose to travel and have a termination. Some will choose not to. Dr McCarthy has no idea how many women with suicidal thoughts travel but he suspects most go without any mental health assessment.

Asked whether he has seen pregnant women who were suicidal and who, he felt, needed a termination to ensure they survived, he says: 'Yes, oh yes. I've seen a woman who has stabbed herself in her stomach. I have seen women who have taken major over-doses in pregnancy to try and kill themselves; women who've taken fifty laxatives a day to try and do something, including kill themselves and/or the baby. I've seen a woman who drove her car at speed into a tree. She didn't die but she was very badly injured. People do awful things. They always have done.

'No, we cannot predict suicide, but we are experts at risk

assessment. There have been many psychiatrists out there saying, "We cannot assess suicide." I mean, I find that amazing. We train our medical students, our junior doctors to assess suicide risk. We do it all the time and get involved and try to reduce that risk. And every psychiatrist who is saying "We cannot predict suicide", those very same psychiatrists are every day assessing patients for their risk of suicide.'

As to why in Ireland there is such opposition to the idea that pregnant women may – if only in rare cases – be genuinely suicidal, he points to entrenched negative attitudes both to women with crisis pregnancies and people with mental illness.

'We have an appalling record on the treatment of women in Ireland who have unwanted pregnancies. Whether we think of Magdalene laundries, industrial schools, sending them to England to have their babies adopted, it's punishing them, seeing their "sin". The attitude to women and women's sexuality in this country has been . . . judgmental, harsh, punishing, controlling. "We must stop them being sexual." "We don't want sexual women and we will punish them if they get themselves pregnant" . . . "It's their fault" . . . If you add to that the double whammy that they also have depression and may be suicidal – well, there's another group of people who are pretty well judged, because depressed people are lazy, need a kick up the arse, and suicidal people are spoilt and looking for attention. Put those together and you have a toxic mix.'

Mara Clarke, founder of the Abortion Support Network in Britain, spoke to me in May 2013 of some of the cases she had seen over the past year where suicide was a real threat. ASN is a volunteer-run charity in London that helps Northern and southern Irish women and girls in financial difficulty access abortion.

'A couple of weeks ago we heard from the mother of an eighteen-year-old girl who was drugged and gang-raped at her own birthday party. Then she found out she was pregnant. She blagged three packets of birth-control pills and took them and when that didn't work she drank a bottle of floor cleaner and when that didn't work she started cutting herself. Thank Christ she told her mother. They saved up all the money they possibly could, which was €135, to get an emergency passport and thank Christ again they found our phone number. What's the alternative? is what I ask the people against abortion. I don't even get into "Are we pro-choice?" The women who contact us are not exercising their solidarity or their feminism or their right to choose. They are desperate women . . .'

The following day, Tuesday, 21 May, the committee heard from legal experts, most of whom rehearsed arguments already made at the January hearings, though former Supreme Court Judge Catherine McGuinness squarely addressed concern that the legislation would 'open the floodgates'. Such concern was illogical, she suggested.

'On the one hand, it is strongly asserted that Irish people in general reject abortion . . . On the other hand, it is argued that, if the door is even slightly opened to the obtaining of a termination of pregnancy, even in the extremely narrow terms of the proposed legislation, there will be a flood of Irish women seeking abortions on false excuses, supported by a flock of doctors willing to collaborate with them. Who are these supposed women if they are not the Irish people, too? Where are these doctors if they are not the caring doctors who have appeared before the committee to date? Is there not an inherent contradiction in this?'

On the night of 12 June, after ten Cabinet meetings on the text, and having been through fifty-one drafts, the long-awaited Protection of Life During Pregnancy Bill was published. Wrote Arthur Beesley, political correspondent of the *Irish Times*, the following day: 'This is highly complex legally, highly sensitive politically and comes with the Government on the receiving end of an onslaught from the Catholic Church and anti-abortion campaigners.'

The Bill incorporated some of the alterations suggested or requested at the hearings and a new power was vested in the Minister for Health to direct a hospital to suspend services under the law if it was felt the hospital was not complying with the Act. It was hoped this would give some comfort to those who feared the legislation would open the abortion 'floodgates'. It clearly did not provide enough for the party's five TDs and two Senators who would vote against it.

The Bill was still about access to abortion only when a woman's life was at risk. It was not about protecting women's health. It still would not cover abortions for reason of rape or incest. Nor would women carrying foetuses with fatal abnormalities be able to have terminations in Ireland. The law would still criminalize women or doctors involved in unlawful abortions, threatening them with up to fourteen years in prison. The number of locations where abortions could be performed was increased to include some non-maternity units.

The inclusion of two Catholic voluntary hospitals – St Vincent's University Hospital and the Mater Misericordiae University Hospital, both in Dublin - would later in the summer lead to controversy about the legislation conflicting with their Catholic ethos.

Father Kevin Doran, administrator of the Sacred Heart parish in Donnybrook, Dublin 4, who also sits on the board of directors of the Mater hospital, told the *Irish Times* in August the hospital 'could not comply' with the legislation. Like St Vincent's (a spokesman for it told the *The Irish Times* it would follow the law), the Mater is governed by a board, independent of the HSE.

Fr Doran told me in June 2013 Catholic hospitals should defy it or the Church should withdraw from them.

'The situation is, there is a partnership between Church and State. The State contributes substantially to the cost of running the service but the property is owned by the original stakeholder which, in the case of the Mater for example, would be the Sisters of Mercy.' If there was an attempt by Government to force Catholic voluntary hospitals to perform abortions, he said, either the hospitals must defy the Government or the Church should withdraw from the hospitals.

'I think that if a Catholic hospital were to decide that they would regretfully have to abide by the law and offer termination of pregnancy in the case of suicide, I would say, "OK, we can't be part of the governance of this hospital." The Church would always say we have an obligation to operate within the law, provided the law is a just law.'

Timed almost to coincide with the Bill's publication (12 June), the HSE published the report from its investigation into Savita's death, on 13 June. It may have been hoped that media coverage of each would drown out the other.

The timing of the HSE report seemed to show no consideration for Praveen. He had just left to spend a few weeks at home, in Haveri. Although he had been promised he would have ample time to prepare Savita's parents, his solicitor was given just two days' notice by email and had to scramble to get in touch with Praveen to warn him. The Irish public could pore over the Bill's contents before he or her parents would be able to take any of it in.

The headline across the front of the *Irish Times* the following day read: 'Tragic. Inadequate Assessment. Treatment Delays. Devastating'.

'More women could die in Irish hospitals in a manner similar to Savita Halappanavar unless legal clarity is provided for doctors on when they can intervene to terminate a pregnancy, the HSE report into her death has warned,' wrote Paul Cullen. The report did not, in Savita's family's view, adequately answer their question of why she had died.

Chair of the investigation, Professor Sir Sabaratnam

Arulkumaran, addressed a crowded press conference that Thursday afternoon in Dublin. He described the care which Savita had received as 'substandard' and suggested that had Savita been in his care in Britain, she would have been offered a termination on the Sunday, 21 October. She would have been advised to terminate the pregnancy after her waters broke at half past midnight on Monday the 22nd, to protect her from infection.

In the Irish context, where this was judged not to be possible because a foetal heartbeat was present, she should have been monitored closely, being vulnerable to infection.

The report stressed sepsis was difficult to diagnose in pregnancy 'due to the associated natural physiological changes [that come with being pregnant]'.

However, once her waters broke her condition required 'efficient assessment and monitoring', said the report.

'We established that the patient was monitored less frequently than required, that guidelines for the prompt and effective management of infection and sepsis were not adhered to. We also believe that legislative factors affected medical consideration in this case and that this resulted in a failure to offer all management options to the patient,' said the Professor.

Professor Arulkumaran's report states clearly that Savita was fighting an infection on the morning she arrived in hospital. Infection was causing the miscarriage, not foetal abnormality. This was important and should have been recognized as a clear probability by staff from the moment Savita was examined. 'Staff indicated that they were aware that infection was a common cause of second trimester pregnancy loss . . . they were aware that infection may have been an underlying cause of the patient's inevitable miscarriage at the time of her admission . . . Although the most common causes of second trimester loss are foetal abnormality, those presenting with a live foetus and bulging membranes are associated with infection in 77 per cent of cases,' said the report. 'The presence of infection should have been assumed and progression to sepsis closely monitored for.' But the clinicians' plan was to 'await events'.

The report is also critical of the fact that the Modified Early Obstetric Warning Score chart was not used at the time of Savita's death for pregnant patients in St Monica's ward, saying its absence 'contributed to these issues' (the failure to monitor adequately).

Once Savita's waters had broken, her risk of infection was further increased. 'The spontaneous rupture of the membranes at 00.30 on the 22nd of October . . . significantly increased the possibility of infection in the uterus with the progression of time. It meant that the chance of foetal death, either by miscarriage or by increasing infection, was certain, and the risk of maternal infection was also increasing . . . A decision not to terminate the pregnancy, for whatever reason, increases the need for clinical vigilance since the probability of worsening maternal condition is increased,' said the report. Twenty-four hours after her waters broke – at 00.30 on Tuesday the 23rd – Savita's risk of infection had increased again. At this point, 'the need for intervention to empty the uterus is increased. The balance of risks between conservative management and intervention is therefore changed. This means that the clinical situation needs constant review.'

Throughout, the report balances the lack of legal permission – as the clinicians interpreted it – to terminate the pregnancy with the failure in such a context to monitor Savita vigilantly. There was an 'apparent over-emphasis on the need not to intervene until the foetal heart stopped together with an under-emphasis on the need to focus appropriate attention on monitoring for and managing the risk of infection and sepsis in the mother . . . The interviewees stated to the investigation team that this was because of their interpretation of the law related to pregnancy termination.'

By 2.45 p.m. on Tuesday the 23rd Savita's heart rate was elevated, at 100 bpm, and this 'should have prompted more frequent observations and consideration for laboratory investigations including white blood cell count and a blood test for C-reactive protein'.

At 7 p.m. on Tuesday her pulse was 114 bpm. 'This tachycardia represented a significant change. In this specific clinical context this significant change should have triggered a medical review with investigations based on this review.' In another jurisdiction the termination would almost certainly have been carried out at this point if it had not been done already.

At 8 p.m. on Tuesday Savita's pulse was 108 bpm. She had had an elevated pulse since 2.45 p.m. and at this point, again her condition 'should have indicated a need to suspect sepsis and investigate further'.

Her condition at 9 p.m., when she was feeling weak as well as having a pulse of 106 bpm, warranted a sepsis workup. 'Removal of the septic focus [the pregnancy] needed to be urgently considered.'

At 4.15 a.m. on Wednesday the 24th, Savita was having a rigor: she was shivering with chattering teeth and had a rising temperature. This 'warranted immediate medical review, investigation and management as outlined above', said the report, referring to the need for a sepsis workup and, again, urgent consideration being given to an abortion.

'The investigation team considers that during the hours between 04.15 to 06.30 on the 24th October the patient went from sepsis to a clinical suspicion of severe sepsis . . . The clinical evidence is that women with maternal infection can deteriorate rapidly to sepsis, severe sepsis and septic shock,' says the report.

At the 08.25 ward round on Wednesday the 24th, Savita's temperature was noted as 37.9 degrees and her pulse as 144 bpm. Her blood pressure was 98/54 at 7.50 a.m., significantly down on her admission blood pressure of 113/73 on Sunday the 21st. 'There was no noted clinical direction about this reduction in blood pressure or the episodes of tachycardia observed overnight recorded in the observation chart.'

The report lists the litany of failures with which many in Ireland were familiar by the time of its publication: lack of communication between staff, failure to follow up blood tests, lack of knowledge of blood and lactate test protocols, inadequate monitoring, and failure to consider a termination in time.

It notes the lack of clear guidelines in the hospital either from national or international sources for the management of inevitable second-trimester miscarriage, and speculates: 'The reason for the absence of such guidelines may be that the clinical practice in other jurisdictions would have led to an early termination of pregnancy in equivalent circumstances.'

Indeed, the report notes at page 71: 'International best practice includes expediting delivery [i.e. abortion] in this clinical situation of an inevitable miscarriage at 17 weeks with prolonged rupture of the membranes and infection in the uterus because of the risk to the mother if the pregnancy is allowed to continue.'

It was difficult to be sure, stressed Professor Arulkumaran, when an abortion could have been either-life saving or legal in the Irish context, as Savita's vital signs were not being properly monitored. It seemed also that doctors in Ireland were interpreting the legal situation individually in the absence of national clarity. In Savita's case the doctor was conservative in her interpretation, he suggested.

The report quotes Dr Astbury saying that the law in Ireland was such that, 'If there is a threat to the mother's life you can terminate. If there is a potential major hazard to the mother's life the law is not clear . . . There are no guidelines for inevitable miscarriages.' The difference between a 'major hazard' to Savita's life and a 'threat' is not explained.

Professor Arulkumaran commented at the press conference:

'Some might have done it [a termination] much earlier. Some might have done it even much earlier [than that]. So it seems to be a little bit individual variation even within Ireland. We don't want that to happen, individual variation, to a poor woman. So, as I have said, it is important for the medical community to meet with the legal community – the lawmakers, regulators and so on, to see how best we can resolve the situation . . . We have to get the whole entire community together and to work something out, so that the poor doctor who is looking after is not put into the same situation.'

He went further in the press conference than his team had in the report, saying that legislation to protect the health and not just the life of the mother might be necessary, to ensure no woman died again in the way that Savita had. 'There are certain conditions that a pregnant mother might have that can suddenly escalate from – for example in this particular situation – an infection where it is very localized . . . to the whole body [to sepsis and then severe sepsis]. If she goes into septic shock that means the blood pressure drops and, despite giving fluids, if the blood pressure doesn't come up the mortality rate is as much as 60 per cent. This can be in a very short period of time. Sometimes intervening at a later stage it is difficult to bring the patient back to normality and control.'

He went still further, saying a woman's health could be permanently damaged if a timely termination was refused in such circumstances.

'If you have infection, by the time it comes to sepsis and severe sepsis fallopian tubes might be injured, she might become sub-fertile, she might come later on [with an] ectopic pregnancy. Life–long, she might have pelvic inflammatory disease. So that is left really to the medical community and the legal system here to discuss. I mean, how much are you prepared to take before you start considering termination of pregnancy? We must have some definitive meaning as to when you think this should be done

. . . This is something that has to be discussed . . . At what point do we think it is going to give permanent injury to the woman? Or what point in time it might escalate to death.'

The response of the Pro-Life Campaign was to repeat that Savita's death had nothing to do with abortion. The group said the report clearly indicated that it was a series of medical short-comings that were at fault.

Its spokeswoman Dr Berry Kiely said the review 'highlights yet again that the key issues in the death of Ms Halappanavar were multiple failures to properly assess and monitor her condition.

'This confirms what the Pro-Life Campaign has always claimed, that the way some politicians and media fastened on Savita's tragic death as somehow bolstering their call for abortion legislation was misplaced and even opportunistic.

'Surely it is a moment for reflection on the rush to judgment in this tragic case?

'I hope the findings of the HSE and inquest reports will give some measure of comfort to Praveen Halappanavar and Savita's extended family and that all the lessons to be learned will be implemented,' she concluded.

The report is anonymized throughout. Even the title mentions no names: *Final Report of the Investigation of Incident 50278*. This was to try to ensure that staff felt free to contribute and speak openly. It attributes no blame and casts no staff in an un-sympathetic light.

The report does shine interesting light on some of the divergences in evidence at the inquest in April.

Of significance to Savita's family will be the differences between Dr Astbury's testimony at the inquest and what she told the HSE inquiry about her discussion with Savita and Praveen about a termination. Dr Astbury is identified in the HSE report as 'O&G Consultant 1'.

At the inquest in April Dr Astbury said that the only

discussion she had had with Savita about a possible abortion had taken place on Tuesday, 23 October. Her counsel and that of the HSE were insistent too this discussion took place not on Monday, when Praveen said it had, but on the Tuesday.

'There was no request for any [termination on Monday]?' the coroner, Dr McLoughlin, asked Dr Astbury at one point.

'No,' she answered.

The inquest also heard detailed evidence about Praveen not being in the hospital on the morning of Tuesday the 23rd as he was taking the Yalagis to Dublin airport.

In her statement to Professor Arulkumaran's inquiry, Dr Astbury is quoted saying that Praveen was present for the discussion about the termination, on Tuesday the 23rd, at 08.20 hours.

'O&G Consultant 1 [Dr Astbury] stated that the patient and her husband were very emotional and upset when told a miscarriage was inevitable. The consultant stated that the patient and her husband enquired about the possibility of using medication to induce miscarriage as they indicated they did not want a protracted waiting time when the outcome of miscarriage was inevitable.

'O&G Consultant 1 stated that the patient and her husband were advised of Irish law in relation to this.'

This discussion could not have taken place on Tuesday in the circumstances described: Praveen was at Dublin airport. If Praveen was present for the discussion, the discussion must have taken place on Monday the 21st – as Praveen had always said.

At the inquest, Praveen's evidence that he and Savita had been told on Sunday the 21st by Dr Andrew Gaolebale that the miscarriage would be over 'in a few hours' was keenly rejected by the hospital. Declan Buckley, SC for the hospital, told Praveen that Dr Gaolebale would say in evidence that the 'conversation didn't run along those lines', and that, in fact, 'He said to you it was not possible to predict timing and you have to wait and see.'

According to the HSE report, 'O&G SpR 1 [Dr Gaolebale] recalled at interview that the patient was actively having pain and that "it was probably a matter of hours before miscarriage".'

Ten days after the HSE published its report into their daughter's death Savita's parents gave their reaction. The report was, they said, a 'whitewash'. Speaking in their neat, quiet home in Belgaum, on Sunday morning, 23 June, Mr Yalagi said he had read sections of it online and news reports.

'It is only a clinical report. There is no responsibility in it. It is a whitewash for everyone. The Government is hiding behind the doctors and the hospital, and the doctors and hospital are hiding behind the law. It is not enough. There are lots of recommendations for what should have been done and what should be done in the future, but what about my Savita? Someone must take care and responsibility for my Savita.'

He knew about the failings and was satisfied these were all covered in the report, but again came back to the lack of culpability. 'Why is no one taking responsibility? In India, if a healthy person died like this in a hospital there would be responsibility. We have not got justice from this report. My daughter's life has been sacrificed and there needs to be justice for that. We want justice for that.'

A little over a week later Praveen issued proceedings against Galway University Hospital for medical negligence.

The HSE report and its failings from the family's point of view were the last straw. In an interview with Miriam O'Callaghan on RTE Radio the morning that news of his medical negligence proceedings broke in the *Irish Times*, Praveen said: 'Savita's father and the whole family are very angry. They want to take legal proceedings against the hospital. We want to get to the bottom of the truth. The HSE report is nowhere near it. I have to do it for Savita's parents. They want to know the truth and they deserve to know the truth.'

Among the questions they all want answers to are:

Why, when Dr Astbury was on her 08.20 ward round on Monday 22 October, did she not ask about the results of Savita's blood test taken on Sunday morning – particularly given the fact that Savita's waters had broken and she was vulnerable to infection?

Why were Savita's vital signs not monitored every four hours, as was hospital policy when a woman's waters break?

Why was the Modified Early Obstetric Warning Score system not used in St Monica's ward when it was in place in the other two obstetric wards?

Why was Dr Astbury not called directly on Tuesday evening and told about Savita's elevated pulse? Why wasn't a septic workup commenced at this point?

Why have two key midwives not given evidence? What do they have to tell?

Why was Dr Astbury not contacted directly and immediately when Savita had become so ill by 6.30 a.m. on Wednesday?

Why did Dr Ann Helps not read Savita's chart on Wednesday morning at the 8.25 a.m. ward round?

Why didn't she relay Dr Ikechukwu Uzockwu's diagnosis of probable chorioamnionitis to Dr Astbury at this point?

Why didn't she tell Dr Astbury about Savita's foul-smelling vaginal discharge?

Why did Dr Astbury not ask for the four-hourly vital signs observations on this ward round, particularly given how long it had now been since Savita's membranes had ruptured and the fact that she was clearly ill?

Why, when she accessed Savita's blood results on Wednesday at 11.20 a.m., did she not come running to the bedside of her extremely ill patient?

Why did a midwife who took care of Savita on Wednesday morning and who recorded her blood pressure falling continually through that period not tell anyone until the afternoon?

Dr Katherine Astbury described Savita's case as rare and unusual. Why didn't she reach out to her obstetric colleagues for advice before Wednesday afternoon?

Why did Dr Astbury decide she could not intervene with a termination until either Savita was *in extremis* or the foetal heart had stopped? Why didn't she consult with more senior colleagues about this before Wednesday?

Why, when Savita was brought out of theatre on Wednesday afternoon and taken to the High Dependency Unit, was Praveen told to return to wait on the ward and that Savita would be back in a few hours? Why was he deprived of this time with Savita during her last conscious hours?

Why was Savita allowed to die?

Who let her?

Epilogue

The Protection of Life During Pregnancy Bill was passed by the Dáil at 12.25 a.m. on Friday, 12 July 2013, by 127 votes to 31. There were three abstentions and four TDs were absent. There had been 165 amendments, two late-night sittings of the House and a High Court challenge on Thursday the 11th to try and prevent a vote being taken.

Fine Gael lost five TDs in the process. Alongside her parliamentary party colleagues Peter Mathews, Billy Timmins, Brian Walsh and Terence Flanagan, the Minister of State for European Affairs, Lucinda Creighton, defied the three-line whip to vote against the measure. All lost their party privileges and Creighton her ministerial position.

Along the way there had been calls for a free vote in the Dáil. But when this was put to the Fine Gael parliamentary meeting on 19 June it failed to find a seconder. There were threats and bullying of TDs. Minister for Health James Reilly received a written warning that his family home would be burnt down. Jerry Buttimer said he had been threatened with murder. Taoiseach Enda Kenny was told he was a 'murderer' and that he was going to have the death of 20 million babies on his soul. 'I'm getting medals, scapulars, plastic foetuses, letters written in blood, telephone calls all over the system and it's not confined to me,' he had told the Dáil on 12 June.

Anti-abortion activists were targeted too. Caroline Simons, legal advisor to the Pro-Life Campaign, said that three death threats had been received by the organization's offices in Baggot Street while the premises of Youth Defence were daubed with excrement in another attack.

Pressure from the Catholic Church against the legislation continued right up to its enactment at the end of July. On 10 June the Catholic Bishops accused the Government of 'misleading' the people on abortion. The country was at a 'defining' moment, they said from their summer meeting in Maynooth.

The following day, the Coadjutor Archbishop of Armagh and next primate of all Ireland, Eamon Martin, said the Government was using 'spin' when claiming that the legislation was 'about saving lives, that it is restrictive and that it represents no change'.

On Sunday, 26 May, and on each of the following nine Sundays, leaflets were distributed at Masses throughout the State, railing against the legislation.

In late June, the chairman of a south Dublin Catholic primary school, Eddie Shaw, a former spokesman for the retired Archbishop of Dublin Cardinal Desmond Connell, was forced to step down after he instructed teachers to put a leaflet advertising an anti-abortion rally into every child's schoolbag.

In early July, the Catholic primate of All Ireland, Cardinal Seán Brady, described the legislation as 'a legislative and political "Trojan horse" which heralds a much more liberal and aggressive abortion regime in Ireland', while Bishop of Meath Michael Smith asked of Fine Gael: 'Is party unity more important than a decision to enshrine the taking of the life of the innocent unborn child in our laws?'

On Sunday, 7 July, a senior Vatican prelate, Raymond Burke, was in Cork. In a striking challenge to the authority of secular governments everywhere, he said: 'We see before our eyes the evil fruits of a society which pretends to take the place of God in making its laws and in giving its judgements, of a society in which those in power decide what is right and just, according to their desires and convenience, even at the cost of perpetrating mortal harm upon their innocent and defenceless neighbours.'

On Tuesday, 9 July, as the Dáil was preparing for its marathon debate on the Bill, Bishop of Limerick Brendan Leahy told a congregation in St John's Cathedral in the city that 'on the eve of what is a defining moment for our country we cannot but focus on the life of the unborn'.

Throughout the three-day debate, hundreds of pro-choice and anti-abortion protestors gathered outside Leinster House. The anti-abortion protestors were in bigger numbers; many knelt, praying and carrying placards, having travelled from all over the island.

The vote was initially scheduled for 10 p.m. on Wednesday, then 1 a.m. on Thursday. The House rose at 5 a.m., resumed at 12.30 p.m. and finally voted in favour twelve hours later.

The enormity of the moment hit Labour Party TD Aodhán Ó Ríordáin moments afterwards.

'You know there were times over the years when I wished abortion had never been mentioned to me. It came up at every election, always used against you on the doorsteps. There had been abuse through the years, even worse over the last few months . . . But if you are serious about your politics and you believe something is right there are things you have to do – convince the mainstream of Irish politics of the validity of your position and then . . . convince other political parties of the justification of your stance. And then the late-night sittings, people outside the gates screaming and crying and praying and jubilant, and then finally, finally, finally, it's passed. In the dead of night 127 TDs pass the legislation. You do find yourself taking a moment. I did find myself in my office after and I did have to take a moment.'

There is no consensus on whether the Protection of Life

During Pregnancy Act would have saved Savita. Those who fought hardest to get it passed believe that it would. Health Minister James Reilly said that Savita's life would 'probably' have been saved. Justice Minister Alan Shatter took the same view, saying on Saturday, 6 July: 'I think if this legislation had been in force earlier, it may be the case that Savita Halappanavar would not have lost her life.'

With regard to Savita's specific circumstances, the truth is, we will never know. Sections 7 and 8 of the Act which address 'risk of loss of life from physical illness' and 'risk of loss of life from physical illness in emergency' certainly give doctors more solid ground on which to act and to abort a pregnancy where the woman's life is threatened. In Savita's case, however, by the time the threat to her life was real, from early on Wednesday, 24 October, she was already moving from severe sepsis to septic shock. Dr Boylan said in evidence at her inquest that by this stage a termination would not have saved her life.

The question is whether under this legislation a doctor could have formed an opinion that there was a risk to her life on Tuesday evening and terminated the pregnancy legally. We will never know whether an abortion at this point would have saved her life.

The arguments about better monitoring, better communication between staff, better record-keeping, better antibiotics are all for the Irish arena.

In another jurisdiction, none of the ifs and what-ifs would have arisen. Had she been in Britain, she would have been offered a termination on Sunday, 21 October; she would probably have been advised to have a termination on Monday, 22 October; she would have been strongly urged to do so by Tuesday the 23rd.

In the Irish context, one can argue whether Savita's death was down solely to bad care or lack of legal clarity, or both. In a Western, international context the issue is abortion and the fact that Savita was refused an abortion. It can be argued that, even with the new legislation, Ireland is not part of the international context. But even so, for those opposed to it the new law represented an enormous defeat.

'A huge loss for the pro-life side,' says David Quinn. 'I doubt if it will save a single woman's life. I have little doubt that it is going to lead to the death of a certain number more children. I think the "real and substantial threat" will be interpreted strictly at first and in time it will be less strictly.'

Breda O'Brien described herself as 'very sad' about the legislation. 'It is a defeat for the pro-life movement but more importantly, I don't think the legislation on suicide will help a single woman. There are so many worrying aspects – the much repeated mantra that "you cannot put a time limit on a right", which was used to justify the lack of term limits on abortion. A moment's thought would show that many constitutional rights are time-limited – the right to vote, for one. Why was a time limit not included? I am also concerned about the issue of conscientious objection, which is far weaker than most countries, including the UK.'

Caroline Simons, in the hours leading up to the Bill's successful passage through the Dáil, said to pro-choice activists outside Leinster House: 'You've won and I would have thought you'd make a dignified withdrawal today and let people who are very upset about this make a dignified stand for life,' she said.

Pro-choice campaigners see the legislation as a significant step, but not a victory. Campaigner Anthea McTeirnan says the legislation 'palpably will save women's lives'.

Campaigners on both sides see the legislation as part of a single continuing process. It will 'change things culturally and socially', says O'Brien. 'For the first time, due to the suicide clause, terminations will be carried out with the express intent of killing an unborn child.'

To Quinn, the change is fundamental. 'I do think eventually

they [pro-choice] will get everything they want. Everything, on everything, because we live in their age. There will be full abortion on demand within twenty years in Ireland. Some would like to see an English-style law here. This idea has not entered the Irish middle ground, yet . . . At the moment, the liberal or left viewpoint is very dominant, so I would expect the liberal left view to prevail eventually.'

Says McTeirnan: 'The very existence of this legislation will begin to change mindsets. It is a chink of light for Irish women, to have control over what they do with their bodies. That will happen. Ireland cannot be an island for ever.' Both she and Sinead Kennedy of Action on X say that pro-choice supporters must now move on to secure repeal of the 1983 Eighth Amendment to the Constitution.

Support for the view that abortion should be accessible to protect a woman's health, not just her life, came from senior medical experts including Professor Arulkumaran, Dr Peter Boylan and Dr Rhona Mahony, and, in the Oireachtas, from some members of Fine Gael, some members of Fianna Fáil, most members of Sinn Féin and all members of both the Labour Party and the United Left Alliance. There are nuances which will have to be teased out. How serious does the threat to a woman's health have to be before an abortion is allowable? Who should make this decision?

These will be aspects of the next stage of the Irish abortion debate. An indication of where public opinion might take the debate – should it have the appetite for such a discussion – could be found in opinion polls through late 2012 and the first half of 2013. One, published in the *Irish Times* on 13 June, just as the Dáil began debating the Bill, found that 89 per cent of Irish people supported the right to abortion where a woman's life was at risk. Some 81 per cent said it should be allowed in cases of rape or abuse, while 78 per cent were in favour in cases where a woman's health was at risk. Asked if abortion should be permitted where a woman deems it to be in her best interest, 46 per cent said no, 39 per cent said yes, and 15 per cent had no opinion. (Some commentators argued that the 15 per cent expressing no opinion were implicitly saying the matter was none of their business and should be left to the woman concerned.)

None of these options can be legislated for without repeal of the Eighth Amendment. But while the evidence of opinion polls might seem to show support for repeal, by the time the legislation had been passed it is doubtful that there was political energy left for another battle. This could be seen as a victory of sorts for the anti-choice side. So all-encompassing and effective, loud and at times frightening has been their campaign that few politicians would relish entering the abortion fray again. The Eighth Amendment, for now, seems safe.

Says Ó Ríordáin: 'For us to even legislate for what's already in the Constitution has taken a huge toll on the political system. Fine Gael has lost five TDs, two Senators. They are not going to relish the prospect of another conversation about this.'

Nonetheless, a campaign for Repeal of the Eighth was in the process of formation even as the Protection of Life During Pregnancy Act was entering the statute book. 'There is fight still in people,' says McTeirnan. 'There are lots of younger people involved now and older women back. It's not over. We will have proper reproductive rights here the same as in other countries.' Kennedy too believes there is a new appetite to talk openly about going further. 'I would love to have that discussion. I think most people would.'

Just as the Bill was being passed, the UK Department of Health published its annual abortion statistics, which showed that 3,982 women who had abortions in England or Wales in 2012 gave Irish addresses. The true figure is likely to be higher, given that many from Ireland do not give their Irish addresses for fear of being 'found out' – should correspondence from the abortion provider arrive at their homes, for example. At the same time, the number of Irish women and girls ordering medication to induce abortion over the internet seems to be increasing. It is illegal to import such medication. Under the terms of the new Act, anyone ordering 'abortion pills' faces up to fourteen years in prison.

The Protection of Life in Pregnancy Act 2013 may well herald significant cultural and social change. It may 'change the national mindset' and 'alter the ground rules', says Anthea McTeirnan, and even, in another formulation, usher in a 'culture of death', says the anti-abortion lobby. But it will make no difference to vast numbers of Irish women for whom abortion is an unwelcome necessity.

It will not stem the flow of women who travel every year to Britain and places further afield for abortions. Nor will it allow the hundreds of Irish women each year who decide to terminate their pregnancy because they cannot carry a wanted baby diagnosed with a fatal abnormality to term, to do so in their home country. It will not provide comfort to women and girls impregnated by a rapist or an abusive family member. It will not reassure the unknown but growing number of women importing medication to perform their own 'back-room' abortions that, should things go wrong, and should they seek help in an Irish hospital, they will not be prosecuted.

Nor, perhaps, will the new law save the next 'Savita'.

The debate triggered by her death was conducted on all sides in urgent, passionate, angry tones. Few exchanges started and ended without at least one voice raised. Only rarely did we hear the voices of those who would instinctively have known what Savita would have wanted.

Just over a month before the legislation was passed, Andanappa and Akhmedevi Yalagi spoke to me of Savita. I was greeted at their peaceful, pretty home in Belgaum, by a gentle, smiling man.

'Welcome, welcome to Savita's home,' says Mr Yalagi.

Breaking down several times while being interviewed, he apologizes.

'Every time I think of her I cannot help it. She was our only daughter. She was a very sweet daughter for us.'

Savita's older brothers, Sanjeev and Santosh, both live long distances from home. Santosh is in Bangalore, 600 kilometres away. Sanjeev is in the Netherlands. Neither they nor her parents can understand how their 'Bubba' could have gone into a modern Western hospital, healthy, fit and in her prime, and died.

Andanappa repeats several times that he and his wife were in Ireland when Savita was first in Galway University Hospital. They spoke to her from Dublin airport, he says. 'I was there. I was there in Dublin.'

'I was in Dublin on the 23rd,' he says several times. 'We were there and we got on a plane. I was speaking to her,' he tells me, looking down and shaking his head. 'I was with her in the hospital for two hours on Monday [the 22nd] and she was sitting up and she said, "Poppa it's OK. I am fine. This is an Irish hospital. It is a good hospital and they will take care of me."

'We were in Dublin the next day at the airport and she called about three or four times, always checking that we were OK. Even on the plane she was saying, "Turn off your phone now Poppa, I will talk to you when you are home." That was the last time I spoke to her.' They will always regret not calling her when they got to Bangalore, seventeen hours later, Wednesday morning Irish time. 'We were tired,' he sighs.

His wife, Akhmedevi, has been standing by the door while we speak. Conscious that she speaks little English, I ask her to come and tell us her memories of Savita. Ravi Uppar, a local journalist, translates. 'She was always a happy girl. When she was here, she was always with me, very funny and loved fun and mischief. Her friends were always coming to the house, having little parties. Even when she was away her friends still came to visit. Since she died, many come still. It is hard for everyone who loved her.'

When she moved to Ireland she bought her parents a laptop and showed them how to use Skype. 'Every day she stayed in contact,' smiles Andanappa. 'At nine o'clock in the evening, every day, she came on the Skype and she would tell us about her practices during the day. She was practising her dentist-work in Ireland.'

She would also show her mother what she had cooked that day, having done little cooking before she left India. 'When we were in Ireland she showed us what she had learnt to cook. Chapattis and dosa. She was good. I was impressed,' she nods.

'Her brothers are not so good at contacting us, maybe once a month. But Savita every day at nine o'clock. Now, we can't bear to see that laptop,' says Andanappa.

Akhmedevi gets up to make tea, and returns with hundreds of photographs of Savita. She sits down beside me and, despite the fact neither of us can speak the other's language, we go through them. She is able to tell me Savita's age in them. 'Three,' she says pointing to a black-and-white photograph in my hand, of a little girl with short, brown hair in a heavy-looking dress and charms about her ankles. 'Baby,' she says, showing me another black-and-white photograph, this one of an infant on her belly, looking at the camera and as if she'll crawl any day now.

In another, Savita is about seven, in a splendid red and gold costume, poised and focused on her dance position, with flowers holding a matching headdress in place. She stands in front of an old television at home, probably before she was taken to a dance or some similar event. In others she's older – at KLE college in her dentist's overalls; with her best friend Smita on a trip to Mumbai in April 2012 just after she had married Praveen; relaxed at home in jeans and a sweater; sitting at home with her dad beside her, on the same red leather couch we are sitting on now.

Her father joins us to look through the photographs too. 'She was a wonderful daughter,' he says. 'Yes, we miss her every day.

It is like a dream, you know. We still cannot believe it. It is just us in this house now. We cannot bear our future now.'

He tells how she had planned to meet them in London when they were on their way to visit her in Ireland, but as the London Olympics were on, getting a visa proved too difficult and so they decided to do London another time. 'No, we won't go to London,' he says. 'Not now, not without Savita.'

He tells how he and Savita's mother had planned to return to Ireland on 15 March 2013, two weeks before her baby would have been due. They had left clothes there and would return both for the birth of their grandchild and also to complete the Lingayat ritual, Garbhalinga Dharane, that they had started in October.

'We had this plan to go to Ireland again for the eight-month ceremony, but this happened [Savita's death]. We were helpless.'

He doesn't think they will visit Ireland again. 'It would be too painful,' he says.

He invites me to see Savita's bedroom and we pass the large kitchen and a small worship room on the way. 'This, this is where she studied and practised her dancing,' he says. It's all pink. Sparsely furnished, the double bed has a pink and white bedspread, the walls are pink and there are two pictures on the wall – a large photograph of Savita and a painting of one of the Lingayat deities, Shiva. 'He is our God,' explains Andanappa. 'Savita worshipped every day.'

Almost immediately he says that religion should play no role in medicine. He firmly believes it was the application of Catholic teaching to Irish law which saw Savita being refused a termination. Had Savita been granted an abortion when she had asked she would not have developed sepsis, severe sepsis and septic shock and died, he says. His daughter's health would not have been allowed to ebb away, and her life with it. Her death was needless.

He had spoken on numerous occasions of his and his wife's hope that any new legislation would prevent another woman dying in such circumstances as Savita. His daughter, he tells me, would rest in peace if such legislation were passed. There would be comfort too for them in that.

Immediately after the Bill passed the Dáil, Andanappa would be quoted widely as welcoming it. But in conversation with me he is more nuanced. From what he can gather of the proposed law, he says, it may not prevent another woman dying in the way his Savita had died. He has heard Professor Arulkumaran say the health and not just the life of the mother needs to be protected in order to prevent further deaths. The fact that the legislation doesn't go this far disappoints him and Savita's mother, he says.

'A woman's health is as important as a man's. A law that does not protect a woman's health will mean my Savita has been sacrificed for nothing. How can this be called a Christian law? God is merciful. He does not want women to die.

'How many Savitas do they want?' he asks.

Savita.

The name. Her face. Both became iconic. Both were appropriated and used, almost becoming nothing to do any more with the young woman from a small city in south-west India who loved Ireland and seems to have lived her life with joy, generosity and humanity.

We know in painful detail the circumstances of the last week of her life and we can only surmise the pain and fear she must have felt throughout it. Those circumstances came to be entangled in the reignition of a two-decade-old debate arising from the X case.

There were two strands to this debate: Savita's death and the constitutional imperative to legislate for abortion. They sometimes ran parallel. More often they became entwined.

So often it was unclear whether it was the 'suicide clause' which was under discussion or the level of the threat to the life of a woman which might justify an abortion.

But the heart of the matter surely rested within the room, in

St Monica's ward in Galway University Hospital where for three days Savita lay in great distress and pain, knowing that she had lost the pregnancy which she and Praveen had longed for and which had so delighted her parents, surrounded by medical staff with their own concerns and beliefs and uncertainties, her health ebbing away, having repeatedly asked for a termination.

The heart of the matter was: who had the right to decide whether an abortion should now be carried out?

Many in Ireland who would never have imagined themselves 'pro-abortion' took an instinctive view.

This was a decision for Savita to make. Her wishes should have been respected.

It was the woman's right to choose.

Acknowledgements

This book was written over nine weeks through May and June 2013. Almost everyone who helped me with it did so graciously and at short notice. To all who did, I am extremely grateful.

Those that did me the greatest honour in giving me their time and their emotional energy were Savita'a parents – her father Andanappa and her mother Akhmedevi, who welcomed me into Savita's home. They humbled me with their kindness, openness and trust.

Her widower Praveen told me first about Savita's story, and for his quiet trust I will always be grateful. He felt unable to contribute to this book but he gave his solicitor, Gerard O'Donnell of O'Donnell Waters solicitors, Galway, permission to speak to me and I am in his debt for that. Gerry has at all times been generous with his time, and patient with my persistent phone calls and questions, since first I spoke to him in November 2012.

Praveen's and Savita's friends in Galway were always helpful, while always being first loyal to Praveen and Savita. Dr Chalikonda Prasad and his wife, Devi, welcomed me to their family home in Spiddal and helped me contact Praveen in India when researching the story. Sunil and Mrdula Vaseali helped with photographs and with meeting Praveen. Also the great photographers in the *Irish Times* who were involved in this story – Brenda Fitzsimons, Eric Luke, Dara Mac Donaill and on the picture desk, Dave Sleator, Frank Millar and Bryan O'Brien.

Sarah McCarthy, John Walshe and Dette McLoughlin of Galway Pro Choice, who were the first outside Savita's circle in Galway to know about her death, also put their trust in me when I arrived in Galway in November 2012. They provided contact details for Dr Prasad and introduced me to him. Again, I am in their debt.

In the *Irish Times*, I must thank my news editor, Roddy O'Sullivan for encouraging me to pursue the story and for his guidance and care with it once it was written; my colleagues Muiris Houston, Paul Cullen, Eithne Donnellan, Hugh Linehan, David Cochrane, Irene Stevenson and my editor, Kevin O'Sullivan, for having the vision to ensure the story was given the prominence and journalistic fire-power it merited.

I had intended to include a chapter on the Irish women who travel in their thousands every year for terminations and interviewed several people for the chapter. In the end, due to time and the trajectory of the narrative, I didn't include that chapter. My biggest regret is that I could not include the stories of Amanda and James Mellet, Arlette Lyons and Ruth Bowie of the Terminations For Medical Reasons (TFMR) group. They were incredibly generous with their time. Their experiences are too important to ignore. Alas, the Protection of Life During Pregnancy Act 2013 does ignore them. They deserve better. I also met Ann Furedi, chief executive of the British Pregnancy Advisory Service and Mara Clarke, founder of the Abortion Support Network, in London, both of who gave me a lot of time and their insights.

Galway coroner, Dr Ciaran McLoughlin was good-humoured and munificent throughout Savita's inquest and again when he spoke to me over a number of hours in his surgery in Clifden, Co Galway.

In politics I must thank Labour Party TD Aodhán Ó Ríordáin who met and spoke to me on two occasions; also Jerry Buttimer TD, Clare Daly, TD, Caoimhghin O Caolain TD, former Minister Mary O'Rourke and Senator Ivana Bacik. Master of the National Maternity Hospital, Dr Rhona Mahony, and Clinical Director of the NMH, Dr Peter Boylan, both met me, while Master of the Rotunda maternity hospital, Dr Sam Coulter-Smith, spoke to me a number of times by phone. Dr Anthony McCarthy, perinatal psychiatrist at the NMH, generously met me at very short notice.

Journalistic colleagues and commentators helped me with their insights, including in Ireland Mary Minihan and Noel Whelan of the *Irish Times*, Gerry Howlin, columnist with the *Irish Examiner*, Marc Coleman of Newstalk radio, Alyson Henry, free-lance radio journalist and Vincent Browne, of TV3; in London, Loveena Tandon of India Today TV, Peter Taggart of CNN and Rahul Joglekar of New Delhi TV; and, in India, Edwin Suhir of the *Times of India* and his Belgaum-based colleague, Ravi Uppar, who went beyond the call of duty in helping me navigate Savita's hometown, as well as bringing me to meet her parents.

I approached several anti-abortion commentators for their per-spectives. Breda O'Brien spoke to me at length in person and by email, and gave me much to think about, as did David Quinn who was also extremely generous with his time. Fr Kevin Doran, parish priest in Donnybrook, Dublin, too was generous with his time and thoughts, and saw me at short notice. Pro-choice activists Sinead Kennedy, Anthea McTeirnan, Sinead Ahern and Stephanie Lord too were open and thought-provoking. I must thank Niall Behan, chief executive of the Irish Family Planning Association; Alison Begas, chief executive of the Well Woman Centres; Orla O'Connor, chief executive of the National Women's Council of Ireland and Geoff Lillis, social media expert, for their time.

I am eternally grateful to Mary Robinson for doing me the enormous honour of writing a foreword for my first book.

Thanks also to Faith O'Grady, the agent who took my proposal, saw merit in it and encouraged me to pursue publication, and Eoin McHugh and all at Transworld Ireland.

It is a book that may well not have happened if I had not been semi-harassed into writing it, by my colleague at the *Irish Times*, Conor Pope, and by Valerie Cox of RTÉ (Raidió Teilifís Éireann). The person who first urged me to write a detailed account of Savita's story was my wonderful friend, writer Antonia Hart. I must thank several other friends who encouraged and supported me all the way: Mary Lynch, Billy O Hanluain, Suzanne Connolly, Susan Cahill, Ali Curran and Annette Mooney.

My family: dad Eamonn McCann for his unstinting encouragement, wise suggestions and patient proof-reading; my brother Luke and sister Matty; my father's partner of almost 30 years, who has become the best 'step-mother' a girl could ask for, Goretti Horgan. Thank you *all*. And to the gorgeous lights of my life, Rosie (eleven) and Alfie (three), thank you both for doing without mum through most of your summer holidays.

I hope I've done you all justice.

Kitty Holland, September 2013

Picture Acknowledgements

All photos were kindly provided by the family and friends of Savita except for those taken by *Irish Times*' photographers as indicated. Every effort has been made to trace the copyright holders, but any who have been overlooked are invited to get in touch with the publishers. Page 5: Top: Cyril Byrne, *The Irish Times*; Middle: Dara MacDonaill, *The Irish Times*; Bottom: Eric Luke, *The Irish Times*. Page 6: all photographs: Eric Luke, *The Irish Times*. Page 7: Top: Brenda Fitzsimons, *The Irish Times*; Middle: Eric Luke, *The Irish Times*; Bottom: Eric Luke, *The Irish Times*.

Index

A, B and C v. *Ireland* case 62, 88, 127,
    144–5
Abortion Support Network (ASN) 237–8
Abortion Tears Her Life Apart campaign
    (2012) 63, 70
Action on X 63, 256
Ahern, Bertie 59, 140
Ahern, Sinéad 94–5, 97, 99
American Life League 126
Ancient Order of Hibernians 125
anti-abortion campaigners 42, 225
    X case 47, 49, 50, 53, 56, 57
    referendum campaign 60
    Youth Defence 69
    March for Savita 100–1
    reaction to Savita's death 102–33
    Health Committee hearing 155
    response to Dr Knowles's evidence
        209–10
    response to Dr Boylan's comments
        212–13, 220
    reaction to inquest 219–20
    Protection of Life During Pregnancy
        Bill 229, 230–1, 253
    Rally for Life (2013) 229–30
    receive threats 252
Anti-Amendment Campaign (AAC) 43–4,
    47, 51, 110
Aquinas, Thomas 120
Arulkumaran, Professor Sir Sabaratnam
    HSE investigation 15, 137, 138, 139,
        155, 170, 173
    publishes report 240–6, 247–8, 262
    accessibility of abortion 256

Astbury, Dr Katherine 10, 167
    evidence given to HSE inquiry 14–15, 18
    Savita's risk of infection 16
    reviews Savita 23–5, 189–91, 192–3, 206
    consent forms 26
    visits Savita in ICU 28
    Savita requests a termination 168–9,
        171–2, 173–4, 178–81, 210
    contacted by *Irish Times* 76, 77, 78–9
    gives evidence at inquest 178–81, 183,
        186, 189–97, 246–7
    HSE report 244, 246–7
    questions relating to 249–50
Australia, and the Irish legal situation 50

Bacik, Ivana 139, 148, 152
Bacterial Sepsis in Pregnancy (RCOG) 15,
    21
Bagalkot 1
Bannon, James 148
Barrett, Richard Boyd 86
Barrington, Eileen 167, 170–3, 178, 215
Basavanna, Lord 1
Basaveshwara 2
Bates, Dr John 25, 28, 193, 199, 200–1
BBC World Service 90, 92
Beesley, Arthur 238
Begas, Alison 88
Belgaum 3–4, 67–8
Binchy, William 53–4, 106
Bonnar, John 119–20
Bonner, Bernadette 49–50
Bord Altranais (Nursing Board of
    Ireland) 215

Boston Scientific 6
Boylan, Dr Peter
  Morning Ireland 116–17
  Primetime 117–18, 120–1
  gives evidence at inquest 164, 188, 197,
    198, 254, 210–13
  reactions to evidence 212–13, 220, 221–3
  Protection of Life During Pregnancy
    Bill 234
  accessibility of abortion 256
Brady, Maxine 48–9
Brady, Cardinal Séan 64, 229, 252
Brahmins 2
Brehona, Tom 132
Browne, Noel 40–1
Browne, Vincent 82, 94–5, 113, 148, 231
Bryan, Kate 127
Buckley, Declan 165, 167, 214–15, 247
  cross-examines Praveen 169–72
  cross-examines Mrdula Vaseali 175–6
Bunreacht na hÉireann (1937) 34–5, 38,
    42–55
Burke, Ann Maria 18–19, 174, 197, 206
  evidence given to HSE inquiry 20
  cross-examined at Savita's inquest
    177–8, 184–6
Burke, Gerry 159
Burke, Raymond 46, 252–3
Buttimer, Jerry 148
  Oireachtas hearing 155–6, 158–9, 160–3
  receives threats 251

C case 58–9, 62, 88, 112
Callagy, Dr Grace 66, 78, 80, 204, 205
Canavan, Tony 217
Cantwell, Jim 47
Carolyn 89–90
Carr, Patrick 129
Casey, Dr Patricia 220
Catholic Bishops Council for Marriage
    and the Family 160
  Protection of Life During Pregnancy
    Bill 229
Catholic Church
  in Ireland 35, 36–43
  Expert Group 64
  Savita's death 104, 105
  and child sex abuse 150
  resists call for legislation 152–3
  Oireachtas Health Committee hearings
    159–60
  role in defining Savita's care 197

  Protection of Life During Pregnancy
    Bill 239–40, 252
Catholic Comment Ireland 128
Catholic Emancipation Act (1829) 37
Catholic Press Office 47
Catholic World Report 131, 132
Chalikonda, Dr Devi 8, 30, 31
Children's Court, Dublin 58, 59
Choice Ireland 94
chorioamnionitis 21, 23, 188, 190, 207, 209
Clann na Poblachta 41
Clarke, Desmond 120
Clarke, Mara 237–8
Clarkson, Dr Kevin 31, 203
Clinton, Hillary 153
Cloyne Report (2011) 150
CNN 82, 84, 90
Coleman, Marc 86, 104, 110–11, 112
Coleman At Large 110–11, 112
Collins, Stephen 146
Company 45
Confidential Enquiry into Maternal
    Deaths (CEMD) 121, 184, 206, 221
Connell, Desmond 252
Connolly, Therese 32
Conroy, Deirdre 1
Constitution of Ireland (1937) 34–5, 38,
    42–55
  Article 31.1.1 35–6
  Article 34 42
  Article 34.4.6 226
  Article 40.3.3. 34, 44, 55, 60, 61, 117
  Article 41.1.2 35–6, 55
  Eighth Amendment (1983) 44, 95, 49,
    51, 53, 54–7, 256, 257
  Twelfth Amendment 57
  Thirteenth Amendment 57–8
  Fourteenth Amendment 57–8
Constitution of the Irish Free State
    (1922) 35
contraceptives, ban on importation of 41–3
Conway, Ciara 86, 143, 148, 225
Cosmopolitan 45
Costello, Mr Justice Declan 48, 52, 56
Coulter-Smith, Dr Sam 233–5, 158
Council for the Status of Women 53
Council of Europe 154
Cowen, Brian 58, 59
Creighton, Lucinda 148, 152, 227, 251
Crisis 131
Crisis Pregnancy Agency (CPA) 60
Crowley, Dr Philip 136–7

Cullen, Paul 76, 78, 79, 107, 240

D v. Ireland case 88
Daly, Clare 64, 85–6, 99, 143, 145, 224
Deasy, John 148
dentistry, in Ireland 9
Disseminated Intravascular Coagulation
  (DIC) 204
Ditum, Sarah 83
Diwali 8
Doherty, Regina 86, 148, 231–2
Donnellan, Eithne 78
Doran, Father Kevin 39, 104, 105, 239–40
Dowds, Robert 144
Dublin Declaration (2012) 118–19
Dublin Simon Community 132
Dukes, Alan 49, 50
Dunleavy, Miriam 20–1
  gives evidence to HSE inquiry 21
  gives evidence at Savita's inquest 185,
    186–8, 211
Dunne, Kate 99

Eames, Healy 235
Eastern Health Board (EHB) 58, 59
E. coli ESBL (extended spectrum beta-
  lactamase) 29, 204–5, 207
Eighth Amendment to the Irish
  Constitution (1983) 44, 95, 49, 51, 53,
  54–7, 256, 257
Electoral Act (1997) 133
Eternal Word Television Network
  (EWTN) 128, 129–30
European Community, and SPUC 45
European Convention on Human Rights
  45
European Council, and SPUC 45
European Court of Human Rights
  (ECHR) 62, 87, 127, 144
  A, B and C v Ireland 144–5
  and legislation 147, 149, 152, 154
European Court of Justice 45
Expert Group
  set up by Government 62, 63–4, 144
  publishes report 87, 145–9, 151–4, 161,
    231

Family and Life Ireland 59, 105, 106, 129
  anti-abortion rally 122, 124
Family Solidarity 49, 53
Farrell, Alan 230–1
Fennell, Nuala 49

Ferris, Anne 86, 148, 225, 226
Fianna Fáil 43–4, 50
  is criticized for inaction 143
  Sinn Féin's call for legislation 144
  accessibility of abortion 256
Fine Gael 43, 49
  Fine Gael-Labour coalition 44
  anti-abortion TDs within 86
  Sinn Féin's call for legislation 144, 145
  resistance to liberalization 148–50,
    151–2, 159
  stance on abortion 148–50, 151–2,
    224–5, 227
  Protection of Life During Pregnancy
    Bill 230–2, 251–3, 257
  accessibility of abortion 256
Finlay, Chief Justice Mr Thomas 53, 54
Finucane, Elaine 18, 20, 184–5
FitzGerald, Garret 43, 44
Flanagan, Charles 87, 148
Flanagan, Terence 251
Fleming, Dr Catherine 137
Fourteenth Amendment to the Irish
  Constitution 57–8
Fox News Network 84
  Huckabee 108, 116, 127
Freeman, Seamus 122
Friends of Savita 68–73
  research abortion laws 94

Gaffney, Dr Geraldine 25, 181–2, 192, 196
Gallagher, Cathy 20
  notices Savita is very weak 21
  Savita's inquest 185, 188
Galway 6, 7
Galway Clinic 30, 75
Galway Pro-Choice 64, 70–2, 74, 84–5, 108
Galway Roscommon University Hospitals
  Group (GRUHG) 77–8, 165, 217
Galway University Hospital 10–33,
  137–8, 167
Gandhi, Mahatma 2
Gaolebale, Dr Andrew 170, 182, 247
  examines Savita 14–15
  gives evidence to HSE inquiry 14–15
Garbhalinga Dharane 12–13, 261
Gately, Jacinta 31, 32
Geoffsshorts 125–6
Geoghegan, Justice Hugh 59
Gilligan, Patricia
  looks after Savita 23, 24, 25
  gives evidence at inquest 190–1, 192, 196

Gilmore, Eamon 151
Gleeson, Eugene
  inquest into Savita's death 167, 168,
    169, 176, 186, 187–8, 201, 213–15
  cross-examines Dr Astbury 179–81, 196
  cross-examines Dr Helps 190
  cross-examines Dr Knowles 205, 207–9
Gorman, Father Owen 129–30
Grace, Wendy 128
Great Famine (1845–52) 37–8
Green Paper (1999) 59–60
Grover, Anand 154
The Guardian 83

Halappanavar, Praveen
  character 7
  meets and marries Savita 6–8, 260
  Savita moves to Galway 7–8
  wedding anniversaries 8–9, 224
  takes Savita to Galway University
    Hospital 13
  Savita's membranes rupture 14–18
  enquires about a termination 16, 116,
    247
  Savita shows signs of sepsis 22–3, 243
  last conversation with Savita 26–7, 193
  tells Savita's parents about miscarriage
    29–30
  told of Savita's cardiac arrest 32
  response to Savita's death 65–7, 214,
    218
  returns Savita's body to Belgaum 67
  talks to Dr McLoughlin 74, 75, 80–1
  talks to *News at One* 84–5
  keeness for Savita's story to be told 88
  returns to Ireland 133–6
  lacks faith in HSE inquiry 137–42
  meets James Reilly 154–5
  inquest into Savita's death 164, 165–73,
    178, 213, 217–19
  view of medical staff 198
  issues proceedings against Galway
    University Hospital 248–9
Halappanavar, Savita (Savita Andanappa
  Yalagi)
  personality 8
  childhood 1, 3–4
  and Lingayatism 3
  moves to Belgaum 4
  desire to be a dentist 5–6, 9–10, 76
  school and college 5
  interest in dance 6, 8, 76

  meets and marries Praveen 6–7
  moves to Galway 7–8
  wedding anniversaries 8–9, 224, 260
  discovers she's pregnant 10
  Garbhalinga Dharane 11–13
  suffers lower back pain 13
  membranes rupture 13–18, 205–6
  condition deteriorates 15–16, 199–204,
    209
  enquires about a termination 16, 18–19,
    33, 68, 110–11, 168–9, 171–2,
    173–4, 178–80, 210–12, 218, 247
  complains of feeling cold 20–1, 187,
    189, 206, 243
  shows signs of sepsis 21–5, 186, 187–8,
    190, 202, 204, 207–9
  shows signs of chorioamnionitis 21, 23,
    188, 190, 193, 204, 207–8
  goes into septic shock 24–7, 193, 199,
    201, 245
  contracts E. coli ESBL 204–5, 207
  delivers Prasa 26, 193, 199
  transferred to HDU 26, 28–32
  dies 32, 65, 204
  post-mortem 66, 80, 204, 217
  body returned to Belgaum 67
  funeral 68–9
  media reaction to her death 82–5
  inquest into her death 166–224, 246–7
  HSE report 240–3
Hanafin, Des 50, 53, 105
Harney, Mary 57
Harris, Simon 86, 148
Harte, Dr Brian 137
Harte, Mickey 124
Haughey, Charles 43
Haveri 6
Health (Family Planning) Act (1979) 43
Health Information and Quality
  Authority (HIQA) 142–3
Health Safety Executive (HSE) 112
  Miss D case 61, 112
  investigates Savita's death 136–7, 164
  Praveen's lack of faith in inquiry
    137–42
  Dr Astbury's evidence 14–15, 18
  Dr Gaolebale's evidence 14–15
  Dr Uzockwu's evidence 21
  Ann Marie Burke's evidence 20
  Miriam Dunleavy's evidence 21
  report into Savita's death 185, 240–6,
    247–8

healthcare, the Church's involvement
    with 39–43
Helps, Dr Ann 23–4, 189–90, 249
Henry, Alyson 130–1
Higgins, Joe 86
Higgins, Michael D 140
High Court
    Mary McGee goes to 41–3
    and SPUC 44–5
Hinduism 1, 2, 8, 177, 178
    Diwali 8
Hodgers, Brendan 96
Hodgers, Gemma 96
Hodgers, Sheila 95–6
Hogan, Gerard SC 61
Holland, Kitty, reaction to *Irish Times*
    article 110, 111–12
Holland, Mary 47, 110
Horgan, Goretti 98
Horgan, Professor Mary 138
Hourihane, Anne Marie 47
Howlin, Brendan 146
Huckabee, Mike 108
Huckabee (Fox News Network) 108, 116,
    127–8
Hug, Chrystel, *The Politics of Sexual
    Morality in Ireland* 42
Human Life International 129
Hunt, Conor 99
Hurley, Sandra 96
Hussey, Sinead 124

Ike, Dr 189
The Independent 50
India
    Lingayatism 1–3
    coverage of Savita's story 90–1
    abortion in 91, 92
India Today 92, 100
Indian Independence Day 8
Indian Ministry of Human Resource
    Development 5
Indian National Congress (1924) 2
indiatimes.com 91
inquest into Savita's death 166–224, 246–7
Institute of Dental Sciences 4, 5–6
International Day for the
    Decriminalization of Abortion 64
International Planned Parenthood
    Federation 127–8
Iona Institute 105
    David Quinn 40, 103, 106, 129, 163, 227

Breda O'Brien 102, 162
Dr Patricia Casey 220
Ireland
    joins the EC 43
    maternal death rate 122
Ireland Stand Up 126
Irish Catholic Church 35, 36–43
    Expert Group 64
    Savita's death 104, 105
    and child sex abuse 150
    resists call for legislation 152–3
    Oireachtas Health Committee hearings
        159–60
    role in defining Savita's care 197
    Protection of Life During Pregnancy
        Bill 239–40, 252
Irish Catholic Doctors Association 118–19
Irish Choice Network 63–4
Irish Constitution (1937) see Constitution
    of Ireland
Irish Council for Civil Liberties 152–3
Irish Dental College 9
Irish Family Planning Association (IFPA)
    41, 127
Irish Historical Studies 37–8
Irish Institute of Obstetricians and
    Gynaecologists 230
Irish Medical Council 215, 220
    guidelines 114–15, 118, 166, 195, 196,
        220
Irish Standards in Public Office
    Commission (SiPO) 133
Irish Times 42, 45, 63
    X case 52, 53–4
    Miss C. case 58
    and the Expert Group 64, 146
    publishes Savita's story 75–80, 82–3, 107
    Sheila Hodgers' story 95
    accused of creating hysteria 106–7,
        108–9
    quotes Dr Michael O'Hare 122
    Patsy McGarry writes in 153
    attack on Dr Boylan 221–2
    Protection of Life During Pregnancy
        Bill 228, 230–1, 238–9
    HSE report 240
    Praveen launches medical negligence
        proceedings 248
    opinion polls 256–7
Irish Women Abortion Support Group 50
irishtimes.com 92
ishtalinga 1–2, 12

Ishtalinga Deeksha 2
Ishtalinga Dharane 2

Jezebel.com 84
Joglekar, Rahul 92
John Paul II, Pope 125
Jones, Bishop Christopher 160

Kale, Dr Alka 4, 5, 6
Kannada 1
Karnataka 1–5, 12, 91
Karnataka Lingayat Education (KLE) 4,
    5–6, 260
Kavanagh, Ray 47
Keady, Dr Deirbhile 193
Kelehan, Dr Peter 205
Kelleher, Billy 144
Kelly, Mark 152–3
Kennedy, Geraldine 160
Kennedy, Sinead
    Action on X 63, 256, 257
    response to Savita's story 95
    Sheila Hodgers story 96
    Protest Savita's Death (2012) 97
    March for Savita (2012) 99, 100
Kenny, Enda 160, 227
    Fine Gael's resistance to legislation 99,
        148–50, 151–2
    public inquiry 139, 140
    receives threats 251–2
Kenny, Shane 50
Keohane, Geraldine 137
Kerrisk, Mark 65
Kiely, Dr Berry 115, 117, 219, 246
Kiely, Niall 45
Kinirons, Dr Brian 26, 27, 200
Knight, India 83
Knowles, Dr Susan 164, 220
    gives evidence at inquest 198, 204, 205–9
Kumar, Anbu 91, 92

Labour Party 86
    Women's Committee 94
    call for legislation 143–4, 145, 147–8,
        151, 227
    Daly's Bill 225
    accessibility of abortion 256
Late Late Show 63, 115, 117
Laxmish 65, 70
Leahy, Brendan 253
Lee, Suzanne 98
Lenihan, Brian 60, 162

Liaugminas, Sheila Gribben 131
Libération 50
Life House Ireland 132
Life Institute 105
    Niamh Uí Bhriain 108
    releases press release 111
    Justine McCarthy 112
    anti-abortion rally (2012) 122
    funding 125–6
    and US anti-abortion lobby 130,
        132–3
    Dr Peter Boylan 212–13
    rejects Praveen's views 220
    Dr Coulter-Smith's testimony 235
lifesitenews.com 111–12, 126
Lillis, Geoff 125–6
Lingadharane 2
Lingayatism 1–3, 5, 7, 68, 261
    Garbhalinga Dharane 12–13
Live Action campaign 126, 127
Liveline 89
Lord, Miriam 123
Loughran, Dr James 41
Lucey, Dr Mary 53
Lynch, Kathleen 85

MacBride, Seán 41
McCaffrey, Mary 158–9
McCann, Eamonn 110
McCarthy, Dr Anthony 235–7
McCarthy, Justine 112
McCarthy, Justice Niall 55, 56, 57
McCarthy, Sarah 64, 108
    meets Friends of Savita 70–2
    meets Dette McLoughlin 74
    March for Savita 100
McCaughan, Cora 137
McCrystal, Patrick 129
McDonagh, Oliver 37–8
McDonald, Mary Lou 143
McDonnell, Des 49, 53
McDowell, Michael 46
McGarry, Patsy 153
McGee, Harry 54, 86, 231
McGee, Mary 41–3, 54
McGuinness, Justice Catherine 56, 162,
    226
    Protection of Life During Pregnancy
        Bill 238
McGuinness, Martin 143
McInerney, Sarah 227
McKechnie, Mr Justice Liam 61

McLoughlin, Dr Ciaran 141–2
  inquest into Savita's death 163–224,
    246–7
  makes recommendations to jury
    215–16, 217, 219–20
McLoughlin, Dette 72–8, 84
McQuaid, John Charles 35
McTeirnan, Anthea 255, 256, 257, 258
  March for Savita 97, 98, 100
Magdalene laundries 40, 237
Magee, Dr Aidan 25–6, 198–9, 200
Mahony, Dr Rhona 56, 143
  Dublin Declaration 118, 119
  at Oireachtas Health Committee
    hearings 156–8
  Protection of Life During Pregnancy
    Bill 233, 234, 235
  accessibility of abortion 256
Manly, David 124
Maratha Mandal Dental College 5
Marsh, Dr Brian 138
March for Choice (2012) 64
March for Savita (2012) 97–101, 123, 124
Martin, Eamon 229
Martin, Micheál 60, 139, 140
Mater Misericordiae University Hospital
    239–40
Mathews, Peter 251
media interest in Savita's story 82–5
Medical Treatment Bill (2012) 224
Mills, Simon 161
Minihan, Mary 152
Miss C. case 58–9, 62, 88, 112
Miss D case 88, 61–2, 112
Modified Early Obstetric Warning Score
    181–2, 194, 216, 242, 249
Moloney, Martina 163–4
Moran, Caitlin 83
Morning Ireland 82, 116–17
Morrison, John J. 137
Mother and Child Scheme 40
Mulherin, Michelle 224–5
Mullen, Ronan 126
Murphy, Kieran 118

Nash, Ged 145
National Health Service 40
National Novena in Defence of Life 106
National Union of Journalists (NUJ) 112
National Vigil for Life (2013) 124
National Women's Council 85, 88, 154
Naughton, Dr Paul 29, 31, 201–4

Neary, Michael 122
Netherlands, X case (1992) 50
New Delhi TV 92
New Statesman 83
The New York Times 83–4
News at One 49–50, 84
Newstalk 106 82
  Coleman At Large 110–11, 112
Nic an Bheath, Áine 32
Nic Mhathúna, Ide 129
Norway, maternal death rate in 122

O'Brien, Breda 102–5, 109–10, 161,
    162–3, 220, 255
O'Callaghan, Miriam 139, 248
O'Connor, Orla 85, 88
O'Donnell, Anne 47
O'Donnell, Gerard 'Gerry' 136–7, 140
  meets Praveen 66
  meets James Reilly 155
  preliminary hearing 165
  inquest into Savita's death 176, 217–18
O'Donnell, John 165, 167, 181–2
  cross-examines Dr Helps 189
Odone, Cristina 112
O'Donovan, Patrick 148
O'Dwyer, Eamon 118–19
Offences Against the Person Act (1861)
    42–3, 62, 118, 194
O'Flynn, David 9–10
O'Hare, Dr Michael 121–2
Oireachtas Committee on the
    Constitution 60
Oireachtas Health Committee 56, 256
  Professor Kieran Murphy 118
  hearings at 152, 154–8, 162, 166, 215,
    221, 226
  Protection of Life During Pregnancy
    Bill 232–3
O'Keeffe, David 136
Olatunbosun, Dr Olufoyeke
  examines Savita 14
  gives evidence at Savita's inquest 182–3
O'Mahony, John 87, 148
Open Door Counselling 44, 45
Oranmore Garda Station 142, 167
O'Reilly, Emily 96
O'Reilly, Kieran 122
O'Reilly, Leo 122
O'Rourke, Andy 107
O'Rourke, Mary 84, 87, 141
O'Rourke, Sean 84

O'Sullivan, Kevin 78, 107
O'Sullivan, Roddy 73, 76, 78, 107

Palin, Sarah 126
Parasiva 1
Penal Laws 37
People Before Profit 86
Phelan, Ann 225
Prasad, Dr Chalikonda
  Praveen after Savita's death 65–6, 67, 68
  meets Dette McLoughlin 74–5, 76
  investigates Savita death 69–70, 71, 72, 79
  Praveen returns to UK 136
Primetime 117, 119–20
principle of double effect 120
pro-choice campaigners
  referendum campaign 60
  Action on X 63
  March for Choice (2012) 64
  Savita's death 94–9, 108–9
  Health Committee hearing 155
  Protection of Life During Pregnancy
    Bill 253, 255–6
Pro-Life Action League 130
Pro-Life Amendment Campaign (PLAC)
  43–4
  case X 47, 50, 53–4
Pro-Life Campaign 105–6, 113, 115, 121
  anti-abortion rally 122
  social media followers 126
  on EWTN 128
  rejects Praveen's views 220
  Protection of Life During Pregnancy
    Bill 230–1
  response to HSE report 246
  advisors receive threats 252
Pro-Life Galway 100
pro-life rally (2013) 125
Progressive Democrats party 46
Protection of Human Life in Pregnancy
  Bill (2001) 60–1
Protection of Life During Pregnancy Bill
  (2013) 251–4, 227–38, 262
protests
  X case (1992) 48, 50, 51
  March for Choice (2012) 64
  Protest Savita's Death (2012) 96–7
  March for Savita (2012) 97–101, 123, 124
  National Novena in Defence of Life
    (2012) 106
  Vigil for Life (2013) 106, 124
  anti-abortion rally (2012) 122

Unite for Life (2013) 123
National Vigil for Life (2013) 124
pro-life rally (2013) 125
Rally for Life (2013) 229–30

Quinn, Dr Aoife 32
Quinn, David 40, 103–4, 105, 109, 126,
  129, 163
  founds Iona Institute 106
  Government publishes draft abortion
    legislation 227
  Protection of Life During Pregnancy
    Bill 255–6

Rabbitte, Pat 151
Rafftery, Veronica 32
Rally for Life (2013) 229–30
rape, and abortion 45–58, 224, 228, 237
Ratzinger, Cardinal Josef 150
Reilly, James 87, 140–1, 148, 151, 232
  meets Praveen 154–5
  ops for legislation plus guidelines 154
  receives threats 251
  Protection of Life During Pregnancy
    Bill 254
Repeal of the Eighth 257
Reynolds, Albert 45, 51–2, 53
Reynolds, Mary 57
Ríordáin, Aodhán Ó 87, 145–6, 148
  Daly's Bill 225
  taped conversations 226
  Protection of Life During Pregnancy
    Bill 253, 257
Robinson, Mary 44, 45, 51
Roe v. Wade case (1973) 43
Roman Catholicism 39
Rose, Lila 126, 128
Rossa, Proinsias De 47
Rossiter, Ann 98
Royal College of Obstetricians and
  Gynaecologists (RCOG) 15
RTE 50, 248
  News at One 49–50, 84
  Late Late Show 63, 115, 117
  Morning Ireland 82, 116–17
  Liveline 89
  Protest Savita's Death 96
  Primetime 117, 119–20

Sacred Heart Paris 39
St Patrick's Day parade (2011) 8
St Vincent's University Hospital 239

Sarma, Dr Susmita 192
savitatruth.com 107, 110
Schacht, Chris 50
Scheidler, Joseph 130–1
Schittl, Scott 132, 133
Schone, Jeurgen 32
Scully, Dr Michael 199
Scully, Peter 59
sepsis 16, 216, 220, 221, 241
  definition 15
  Savita shows signs of 21–5, 186, 187–8,
    190, 202, 204, 207–9
  Dr Uzochwu diagnoses 21–2, 23, 26,
    188, 199
  Savita goes into septic shock 24–7, 193,
    199, 201, 245
serum lactate tests 22, 188
Shatter, Alan 49, 254
Shaw, Eddie 252
Shettar, Jagadish 91
Shiva, Lord 1–2, 261
Simons, Caroline
  Pro-Life Amendment Campaign 106, 252
  Tonight 113–15, 116
  Late Late Show 117
  Unite for Life vigil (2013) 123
  on EWTN 128, 129
  Protection of Life During Pregnancy
    Bill 255
Sinn Féin
  calls for legislation 143, 144–5
  accessibility of abortion 256
Sinnott, Kathy 128–9
Sky News 83
Smith, Ailbhe 99
Smith, Michael 252
Smithwick Tribunal 139
Smyth, John 231
Socialist Party 86
Society for the Protection of the Unborn
    Child (SPUC) 44–5, 90
  case X 49, 53
Special Olympics (2010) 8
Staunton, Denis 78
suicide in pregnancy 225–6, 227, 228–9
  and Protection of Life During
    Pregnancy Bill 233–7, 255
The Sunday Business Post 130
The Sunday Independent 108, 226, 227
  Protection of Life During Pregnancy
    Bill 233
The Sunday Times 112, 226–7, 229

Supreme Court
  X case ruling (1992) 34, 51, 53–4, 56,
    85
  and ban on importation of
    contraceptives 41–3
  and SPUC 44
  suicide issue 162
Sweden, maternal death rate in 122

Tandon, Loveena 92, 100
The Telegraph 112
Thirteenth Amendment to the Irish
    Constitution 57–8
Thomas More Society 132
Time 84
The Times 50
The Times of India 92
Timmins, Billy 144, 251
Tonight 82, 113–14
Toronto Star 84
Trade Union TV 99
Travelling community, Miss C. case 58–9
Tubridy, Ryan 115–16
TV3, Tonight 82, 113–14
Twelfth Amendment to the Irish
    Constitution 57

Uddo, Chelsea 98–9
Uí Bhriain, Niamh (née Nic Mhathúna)
    59, 105, 108, 111, 112, 113, 121
  Huckabee interview 116, 127–8
  Morning Ireland interview 116–17
  anti-abortion rally (2012) 122–3, 124
  LifeSiteNews 126
  Chicago fundraiser 131–2
  interviewed by Crisis magazine 131
UK Department of Health 257–8
UN Population Fund 121
UNICEF 121
Union of Students in Ireland 48–9
Unite for Life 123
United Left Alliance 85–6, 145, 224
  accessibility of abortion 256
United States of America
  Roe v. Wade case (1973) 43
  view of X case 50
  Savita's story breaks in 83–4
  anti-abortion sympathisers in 125–7,
    130–1
Uzochwu, Dr Ikechukwu 20, 206
  diagnoses sepsis 21–2, 23, 26, 188, 199
  diagnoses chorioamnionitis 249

Uzochwu, Dr Ikechukwu
  Savita's inquest 185–6, 188–9, 191

Valera, Eamon de 35, 38
Vanita Vidyalaya, Belgaum 4
Vaseali, Mrdula 10, 76–7
  visits Savita in hospital 18–19, 169, 172,
    173–5
  told of Savita's condition 30
  cross-examined during inquest 174–6
Vaseali, Sunil 18, 19, 174
Vatican 150, 252
  reviews 1937 Irish Constitution 35
vigils
  National Vigil for Life (2013) 124
  Unite for Life (2012) 123
  Vigil for Life (2013) 124

Walker, Professor James 138
Walsh, Dr David 115
Walsh, Justice Brian 42, 54, 227, 232, 251
Walshe, John 71–2, 109
  meets Dette McLoughlin 74
War of Independence (1919–21) 37
The Washington Post 84
Waters, John 128
Well Woman Centre, Dublin 44, 45, 88
Whatcott, Bill 126
Whelan, Noel 87, 113, 138, 140, 160–1,
  163
Whelehan, Harry 46–8
women, and the Irish Catholic Church
  39–40
Women's Committee (Labour Party) 94
Workers Party 47
World Bank 121
World Health Organization 121

X case 45–58, 60–1, 88, 101
  20th anniversary of 62–3, 85, 86, 132
  Sinn Féin's calls for legislation 143,
    144–5
  Labour Party calls for legislation 145, 147

legislation 160, 161, 224, 226–7, 228
Supreme Court ruling 195, 225, 226,
  232

Yalagi, Akhmedevi (Savita's mother) 1, 3
  visits Galway 10–11, 12–13, 15–16
  Garbhalinga Dharane 13
  Savita's reluctance to tell parents of
    miscarriage 13–14, 15–16, 17–18
  Savita's death 91
  describes Savita 258–62
Yalagi, Andanappa (Savita's father) 1
  career 3
  moves to Belgaum 4–5
  Savita and Praveen 6, 7
  visits Galway 10–11, 12–13, 15–16
  Savita's reluctance to tell parents of
    miscarriage 13–14, 15–16, 17–18
  Savita death 91–2
  reaction to HSE report 248
  describes Savita 258–62
  Protection of Life During Pregnancy
    Bill 262
Yalagi, Sanjeev (Savita's brother) 3, 259,
  260
  told of Savita's miscarriage 29–30
Yalagi, Santosh (Savita's brother) 3, 259,
  260
  told of Savita's miscarriage 29–30
  Savita's death 68
Yalagi, Savita Andanappa see
  Halappanavar, Savita
Yeates, Padraig 95
Youth Defence 63, 69, 105, 108, 125–6,
  129
  Abortion Tears Her Life Apart 70
  anti-abortion rally (2012) 122
  social media followers 126
  and US anti-abortion lobby 130–1,
    132–3
  response to Dr Knowles' evidence
    209–10
  receives threats 252